Archetypal Forms in Teaching

Recent Titles in
Contributions to the Study of Education

ARCHETYPAL FORMS IN TEACHING

A Continuum

WILLIAM A. REINSMITH

Contributions to the Study of Education, Number 56

GREENWOOD PRESS
New York • Westport, Connecticut • London

Library of Congress Cataloging-in-Publication Data

Reinsmith, William A.
    Archetypal forms in teaching : a continuum / William A. Reinsmith.
      p.   cm.—(Contributions to the study of education, ISSN
  0196–707X ; no. 56)
    Includes bibliographical references and index.
    ISBN 0–313–28405–9
    1. Teaching.   I. Title. II. Series.
  LB1025.3.R45   1992
  371.1′02—dc20   91–44433

British Library Cataloguing in Publication Data is available.

Library of Congress Catalog Card Number: 91–44433
ISBN: 0–313–28405–9
ISSN: 0196–707X

First published in 1992

Greenwood Press, 88 Post Road West, Westport, CT 06881
An imprint of Greenwood Publishing Group, Inc.

Printed in the United States of America

The paper used in this book complies with the
Permanent Paper Standard issued by the National
Information Standards Organization (Z39.48–1984).

10 9 8 7 6 5 4 3 2 1

If he is indeed wise [the teacher] does not bid you
enter the house of this wisdom, but rather
leads you to the threshold of your own mind.

Kahil Gibran

Contents

Preface

This book is the result of a thinking process that began five years ago with the simple question: What is the nature of teaching? At the time, I had no idea that the search for a meaningful answer would become so complex and far reaching. In my naivete back then I was not aware that countless attempts had already been made to answer this seemingly innocent question.

In 1986 I took a short sabbatical, partly because I wanted to step back and assess my own growth as a teacher. By this time I had been in the classroom for over twenty years on both secondary and college levels. Heretofore, I had never asked myself what it was I did. Like the teachers described by Philip Jackson in *Life In Classrooms* I was too busy teaching to wonder about its "true meaning."

However, during the three years before my sabbatical I had noticed changes in my teaching for which I had no chart or road map. I also noticed the relationships with some of my students taking on a more profound dimension. This was especially true of those relationships extending longitudinally through the years. I found my curiosity aroused and a new sense of responsibility taking shape.

During the sabbatical I read widely and learned much about teaching theory. I learned, as have others who have studied pedagogy, that there are many facets to teaching, that teaching can be a number of different acts within varied settings and circumstances. I saw that teaching could be approached as a science and as a craft, but also that it could be apprehended as an art. I found there is no consensus model of the ideal teacher. In short, I found bits and pieces of the puzzle. Yet I was unable to attain a vision of the whole.

I remained dissatisfied with a number of the emphases and explanations offered by theorists—especially in regard to higher education. Often they

seemed to leave only the husk or external appearances of the teaching encounter. I continued to explore on my own, to sift and weigh what I found
in the light of my own personal teaching experience which has covered a
wide range of courses in the humanities. As I reflected, a larger view gradually
rose up before me. I worked with each part of that picture until the whole
became clear and distinct. What resulted were the insights and observations
that comprise this book.

But the perspective set out here, while having root in personal experience,
is not merely subjective. Constant allusions and references are made to the
insights of educators who have written on the subject over the years, some
of them theorists or philosophers of education. Others are simply teachers
who have documented their own reflections on the craft. I admit I have been
most deeply influenced by those who have portrayed teaching in its advanced
stages as a subtle and spiritual art. (I use the world "spiritual" in the sense
of a diminishment of ego—something which is at the heart of all inward
growth.)

This book, then, is intended to be one way of addressing what is, and will
probably always be, an open issue: the nature of teaching. I should point out
that those searching for a solution for the seemingly intractable economic
and political issues hounding (I might say interfering with) education today
will not find much here. My book treats teaching pure and simple. If these
pages shed greater light on what it is we actually do—or could do, given
appropiate environments in higher education—then the book will have its
own objective value beyond the meeting of one teacher's personal need.

I would like to give my thanks to a small number of people who were
especially helpful to me in preparing this book: the faculty and staff of the
Joseph W. England Library at my college who conducted numberless searches
and requisitions for me; Deborah Lynn Williams who read the chapters in
rough draft and offered valuable comments from a student's perspective;
James Appleby for his constant encouragement over the last two years; my
wife, Anne, for her quiet belief in the worth of this project and for her
wonderful patience with my volatile moods.

Finally, I pay tribute to that first, great mentor in the Western world, Socrates, whose spirit pervades this book. Inducer, Inquirer, Dialogist, Facilitator—he would not be, I hope, too critical of my attempt to chart the full
range of teaching practice.

Introduction: A Teaching Continuum

TEACHING AS PRESENCE AND ENCOUNTER

According to Webster's New Collegiate Dictionary, *teaching* comes from the Middle English "techen"—to show or instruct, and means first of all "to cause [someone] to know a subject." Indeed, this has always been the general understanding of the word for the average person. In reductive terms, the teacher is thought of as someone who "learns you" and when the teacher is finished teaching the student should know something. The causative factor appears to be obvious. Much of the literature on teaching theory and pedagogy in higher education is rooted in the matrix of definitions surrounding the central concept of teaching as instruction or transmission: "to provide instruction," "to impart the knowledge of," "to instruct by precept or example," "to supervise or guide [manage] studies". Words synonymous with teaching are: "instruct," "educate," "train," "discipline," "school."[1]

John Passmore points out that teaching is a deeply rooted word with a multitude of idiomatic applications and thus cannot be summed up in a definition which will give us the "essence" or the "real meaning" of teaching.[2] While this is certainly true it does not discount the fact that the definitions given above are commonly accepted and place the teacher in an exceedingly active role, leading the more naive to suppose that teachers create learning in the student.

In this book I will propose that teaching is both less and more than the matrix of definitions set out above. It is less in the sense that teaching or instruction can never be a causative factor in someone else's learning. At best, teaching is a process of creating different encounters by which students can learn and thus come to know (the word "know" having various levels of meaning). N. L. Gage's definition of teaching as "any activity on the part of one person intended to facilitate learning on the part of another" comes closer to the mark.[3] However, the activities of teaching are diverse and many-faceted, not only in their behavioral sense (which has been well documented), but also formally or archetypally, as we shall see. Thus, the range of teaching possibility is far greater than is indicated by Webster's matrix of definitions.

Teaching, as David Denton has stated, is a way of being in the world.[4] In this sense it is ontological, yet specialized and thus to be distinguished from the kinds of teaching anyone can do. More concretely, teaching is a way of being present to students which establishes, should they be receptive, a specific engagement. Out of such an engagement arises learning or what is called educational growth.

In higher education, when a teacher acts upon others, the others at least implicitly consent to that action, and by that consent open themselves to something called a teaching encounter. To attempt to teach an unwilling pupil—that is, a person who has not consented in some way to being acted upon, is to impose oneself, to abrogate that species of educational freedom unique to the encounter. Teaching then is nullified and deteriorates into something irrelevant or even harmful. Trying to teach when it is not agreed to can be a form of violence. More will be said on the topic of students and educational freedom in Chapter 3.

However, when I teach I do not so much act *upon* another as *move toward* and act *in concert with* another. Successful teaching (which issues in learning) connotes a partnership, even a communality, of a special kind. For the teacher addresses the learner, not in a mechanical way, but as a palpitating presence. And being present or available to one for the sake of creating a learning process is not like acting on an object. Rather, teaching involves a meeting of subjectivities who address and respond to each other in increasing fashion as I-Thou.[5]

A conventional issue could be raised here. Numerous observers have pointed out that one just doesn't teach somebody, but rather something to somebody, though that "something" isn't always stated. In fact, Passmore describes teaching as "a covert triadic relation."[6] The "something" has traditionally been called subject matter. This is to objectify needlessly. It is more fruitful to say that teaching encounters take place within a universe of discourse[7], an ongoing, ever changing conversation into which teacher and student enter. This term will be more illuminating for our purposes than "subject area" or even "field of knowledge," both of which suggest an abstract sphere removed from any knower. For knowledge inheres in human subjects. Within this humanized realm, then, teaching can involve any number of skills traditionally known as methods or techniques. Students will also grow in the use of various skills or abilities appropriate to their learning. But these come into play within the ambit of a particular teaching encounter and can be identified there—just as a particular encounter can be defined by the way in which the teacher is present to the learner. The notion of "encounter" is essential to teaching and prior to all empirical/behavioral considerations, in the same way that living human beings precede and control the instrumentology of their learning. A teaching encounter is not simply a group of skills or methods assembled in a particular way. It may engender these, but the "meeting" between teacher and student(s) has a form or being of its own.

We live in an age where we are witness to the increasing mechanization of society. One can see the effects in the field of education with phrases like "instructional strategies," "behavioral objectives," "learning management," holding forth as if we were all objects acting upon other objects. This book is meant as a corrective, an attempt to place the relational dimension back at the center of the teaching act. It is not that the relational aspects of teaching go unmentioned during discussions of teaching in the literature. But they rarely hold center stage. And the variety of human encounters possible in the classroom are either ignored or underdeveloped.

TEACHING AS A SERIES OF FORMS

It should be obvious by now that the terms "presence" and "encounter" will be central to the phenomenological approach being taken toward teaching in this book. Put simply, a teaching presence creates the possibility of encounter. Kenneth Eble, in his two books on college teaching, first opened up for me new territory beyond the instructional methods and techniques outlined in most of the literature. In *The Aims of College Teaching* (1983) he pointed out that the impression the teacher makes lasts longer than any information conveyed and endures beyond the skills that may be inculcated: "Reading over dozens of testimonies to their teachers from men and women of great accomplishment in all fields, I am struck by how often the details remembered are aspects of presence rather than of any specific knowledge."[8]

This notion of "presence" is quite fertile. Previously, in *The Craft of Teaching* (1976) Eble called teaching "a presence of mind and person and body in relation to another mind and person and body, a complex array of mental, spiritual and physical acts affecting others."[9] We have here the teacher as "embodiment" who addresses the student in a certain way depending on a number of variable physical conditions and emotional contexts, and can leave a lasting impression. Eble makes the further point: "The compound of how one appears and what one does, what one says results in the active presence that declares a teaching style."[10] Eble thinks the notion of "style" is central to teaching and given the manner in which he uses it I would agree. Nevertheless, the word connotes to many educators a certain idiosyncrasy—even a superficiality—and for this reason may fail to adequately delineate the compound of inner character and outer presence that constitute a teacher's embodiment. Whatever the case, I am grateful to Eble for providing an emphasis on teaching that is all too uncommon.

Eble goes no further in this approach to teaching and leaves things pretty much in the realm of the impressionistic. I suggest that a teacher's presence (or style), shaped somewhat by contextual conditions, not only is essential in creating, with the students response, a particular teaching encounter, but that encounter is of a less fleeting nature. In fact, we can say that a teacher who successfully sustains a teaching encounter works within or inhabits a *teaching form* with all the energies attendant to it. There is a certain constancy, even timelessness, to such a form which can be teased out of the daily stream of experience and which transcends, to an extent, the individual teacher present here at this moment. We can postulate in the form a kind of ideal purity which contains certain recognizable boundaries that are changeless. Thus, the form underlies the more disparate teaching acts, just as an essence is said to underlay more accidental or transient qualities.

To put this succinctly, when a teacher comes together with a student or students in a given way a teaching encounter is born. Within that encounter certain predictable (in the midst of other more sporadic) energies unfold which constitute or reflect a specific teaching form. Each teaching form is invested with a particular teaching presence or embodiment, making it possible for the learner to respond in a manner appropriate to that form. Obviously, the form is not as "real" or as complex as the daily vicissitudes of the classroom. But underlying this complexity are certain recognizable patterns which are perennial to teaching and for this reason hold a permanence that transcends an individual teacher. To say that the teacher works within a form is both to preserve the individuality of the teacher (without whom the form would not come into being) and at the same time to see or intuit beyond this to something more archetypal and enduring.

Teaching Presence creates *Appropriate Response*
Becomes *Teaching Encounter*
When sustained = *Teaching Form*

TEACHING FORMS ON A CONTINUUM

I maintain that in higher education there are seven archetypal forms inhabited by teachers. They can be subsumed under four general teaching *modes* which I will call Presentational, Initiatory, Dialogic, and Elicitive. To complete the picture, we can postulate an eighth form in which the teacher changes back into a learner, just as there is a fifth mode (Apophatic) which represents the conclusion or successful termination of teaching. All of this will be explained in due course.

In this book I will trace and describe each of the eight teaching forms and attempt to place them on what I call a Teaching Continuum, moving from teacher-centered at one end to student-centered at the other. In so doing, we can view the entire range of teaching possibility in higher education. For

I believe it is important to counteract the popular notion, even in educational circles, that teaching is limited largely to presentational, transmission-oriented, teacher-centered models. While this kind of teaching may be taking place in most classrooms today and on the increase, as Philip Jackson suggests,[11] it does not do justice to all the teaching encounters available on the university level.

I also suggest that as teachers mature in their craft they will gravitate toward more student-centered teaching. I follow Joseph Axelrod here at least in regard to the humanities teacher[12]—though I extend the claim and assert that such movement along the continuum applies to all teaching in the liberal arts.

ARTISTIC TEACHING AS STUDENT-CENTERED

Teaching has been viewed as a science, craft, and an art. Teaching is a science supposedly in the sense that its methods and techniques can be documented and assembled into a workable body of knowledge from which the classroom teacher can draw. Most of the concepts which have been used to deduce principles for a science of teaching are based on empirical studies of teachers in action—largely in elementary and secondary schools.[13]

Those who familiarize themselves with a knowledge base and become skilled in the application of methods and techniques are said to practice the craft of teaching. But craft is more than applying the rules of a science. Teaching is a highly humanistic endeavor since teachers obviously develop their craft through interaction with students. Every good, competent teacher is, to some degree, a craftsperson. John Granrose labels basic skills in teaching—choosing, preparing, speaking, listening, responding, testing, grading—"the details of one's craft."[14] A teacher learns the craft through a combination of knowledge, teaching experience, observation of others and reflection.

Teaching has also been viewed as an art. Gage calls it "an instrumental art with a scientific basis" to distinguish it from the fine arts.[15] As such it "departs from recipes, formulas, and algorithims" and "requires improvisation, spontaneity, the handling of a vast array of considerations of form, of style, pace, rhythm, and appropriateness . . ."[16] Indeed, this realm is somewhat mysterious (Granrose calls the advanced skills of artistic teaching "the greater mysteries") and transcends craft just as the true artist transcends the basic methods and skills of his medium. It is probably a case of higher creativity; artistic teaching becomes more intuitive, more effortless, more spontaneous. It is also more evanescent. According to Louis Rubin, "they [artistic teachers] differ from ordinary teachers in that they function with consummate skill."[17] Socrates is the earliest example of the artistic teacher in the West.

But there is more here. In higher education, the teacher's growth as an artist has also to do with his or her view of students' place in the teaching encounter. The highest kind of artful teaching is relational in an increasingly student-centered way. Few studies exist that deal with artistic teaching in this sense, particularly on a university level, but Joseph Axelrod's *The University Teacher As Artist* (1976) stands out. Axelrod holds the thesis that the only way for a university teacher to escape the bureaucratic labyrinth of today's academic life (which has only complexified over the last decade and a half) is to become an artist in the classroom, "to turn his mind toward unknown arts."[18] This can only take place within what the author calls "the evocative" teaching mode, a mode distinguished by a spirit of inquiry and discovery. In his portraits of evocative teachers, it is the fourth prototype, the teacher as student-centered, wherein one approaches the highest stage of growth in his or her art. According to Axelrod, to be an artist at teaching "requires a professor to have relationships with students that are of a different sort from those that students enter into with the professor who is a lecture-artist or [even] a teacher craftsman."[19]

Another more recent book, Ken Macrorie's *Twenty Teachers* (1984), portrays outstanding teachers on all school levels and very much in contrast to the professors who use the traditional, distancing lecture format found in colleges and universities.[20] Macrorie does not use the term "artists," but rather calls the teachers in his interviews "enablers": They are much less overtly forceful and authoritative, much more accessible. They are all by definition student-centered, engaging their students close up, holding high expectations; they are facilitating, encouraging, maiutic. The teachers described here do not demonstrate their own learning, but rather place the center of learning in the students themselves and are witness to their act of discovery. One of Macrorie's teacher/enablers, composition theorist James Britten, describes the process: "It's more what you give students for themselves than what you are doing that will change them."[21]

Philip Jackson, in *The Practice of Teaching* (1986), has given anecdotal accounts of teachers who have had effects on their students far beyond the mere imparting of instruction or "learning management." They belong to what he calls the transformative (as opposed to the mimetic) tradition of teaching and have the capacity to do more than transmit information or knowledge.[22] They change the lives of those they encounter in the classroom. As with others who have described artistic teaching, Jackson can share with the reader no ready formulas as to how these artist teachers accomplish their pedagogical feats.

I will propose in this book that as teaching moves through the forms on the continuum, it not only becomes more student-centered, but at the same time more artistic. This does not mean, as Axelrod has pointed out, that teachers in the earlier forms cannot become artist-lecturers, for example. But as long as they remain in this presentational mode they cannot reach the more intrinsically relational art of student-centered teaching. At the same time, as students involve themselves in encounters where they assume more responsibility for their own learning, the skills and abilities they acquire become more sophisticated and multi-leveled. Also, students who learn in a relational atmosphere find that changes take place in terms of personal meaning that are deeper and more lasting. All this will become clear in ensuing chapters.

A FURTHER BREAKDOWN

More needs to be said about the teaching continuum I am setting out. I use the word "continuum," according to Webster's second definition, in the sense of an ordered, progressive sequence on a line. The term "teaching continuum" has been used by others. N. L. Gage spoke of a continuum with the humanistic art of teaching at one end and those who seek to replace teachers by technology at the other.[23] Thomas F. Green presented a teaching continuum in "A Topology of the Teaching Concept" (1965) which expresses "gradations" within the family of activities covered by the concept of teaching. His purpose was to show the distinctions between instruction and other less rational forms of teaching such as conditioning, training, and indoctrinating.[24] My continuum is along a different line, but I will address the problem of indoctrination in Chapter 3.

While Joseph Axelrod (1976) never uses the word, in speaking of didactic and evocative modes of teaching he presents what amounts to a continuum of four prototypes within the evocative mode. These bear a general similarity to the teaching forms on the student-centered side of my continuum, but there are different emphases in the way a teacher progresses.[25]

Dennis Fox in "Personal Theories of Teaching" (1983) discusses what he called four basic theories of teaching that have emerged from British teachers over the years who were asked to respond to the question: "What do you mean by teaching?"[26] While again the word continuum is never used, Fox notes a progression in the responses, from teaching seen as transfer of learning (by the newer teachers) to teaching viewed as encouraging personal growth (by the more experienced and reflective teachers). This is similar to the movement toward student-centered teaching I set out on the continuum, as well as the change from mimetic to transformative discussed by Jackson.

Long ago, B. O. Smith stated in "A Concept of Teaching" (1960) that "We need studies of sorts of positions teachers assume, and what maneuvers and detailed actions they take under varying circumstances and with different sorts of materials."[27] The teaching continuum I will present here is less empirically founded and suggests, in its ideal aspects, a sequence rather than the hopscotch movement described by Smith as a teacher's response to classroom situations in everyday teaching. I will view teaching phenomenologically as a series of successive embodiments or encounters wherein particular relationships are established between teacher and learner(s). These encounters change and move gradually from peripheral engagement toward educational intimacy until at last the teaching presence comes to reside fully in the learner. Thus, both teacher and pupil are, in a sense, newly created through each stage of the encounter.

Conceptually, each one of these eight stages or teaching forms has an independent existence with its own rhythm and set of inner dynamics. It is these I will describe in the ensuing chapters, while bracketing out, so to speak, the clutter of the everyday world, in order to view the underlying features of each form more clearly. In the real world of teaching the forms are interconnected, often overlapping, entwined, or strewn within each other. However, even here one central form usually predominates depending on the particular stage of the teacher's growth and the pedagogical possibilities allowed by the environment.

We could borrow Howard Gardner's term "fictions" which he applies to his discussion of separate intelligences. He points out that we "reify" and set them completely apart to allow for a closer, clearer examination of a process though nature brooks no sharp discontinuities. But this is permissible as long as we remain aware of what we are doing.[28] Something similar holds true for the teaching forms set out in this book.

Thus, my continuum is idealized in the sense that such a seamless developmental sequence as presented here rarely takes place in an actual teaching career. It is also possible, even highly likely, that environmental factors may relegate a teacher to an earlier stage of the continuum for years or even a whole career. Nevertheless, I will defend the sequence as *an archetypal perception of teaching experience* and claim that a person is only teaching when inhabiting one of these forms.

Still, it would be incorrect to visualize the specific forms in the continuum as existing "out there" like Platonic archetypes. They only come to exist when teacher and student(s) share a particular encounter or engagement. Authentic teaching is thus participatory, an intersubjective experience—even at its faintest, as in the first form on the continuum. The teaching encounter originates in the teacher's specific presence—that is, a teacher becomes "present to" or available to a pupil in a particularized manner. The pupil can resist or be completely inattentive to the teacher's presence which means that an encounter will not take place. Any number of obstacles might prevent this.[29] But when an encounter does take place, teacher and student embody specific forms on the continuum with all their particularized energies.

One final assumption made is that teaching, if it is true encounter, implies learning. That is, if a teaching encounter is set up, we can also assume that some kind of learning is intended by the student. There is some dispute among educational theorists as to whether teaching and learning go hand in hand. But it would seem only common sense that teaching and at least the intent of learning go together.[30] Not only this, but that different kinds of learning will take place at different stages along the continuum. And the further along the line one goes the deeper and more personal the learning experience becomes. At the same time, the term "good" teaching can be used in both a relative sense (relative to the particular teaching mode) and an absolute sense as the teacher becomes fully student-centered, artful and creative.

The Teaching Continuum with its appropriate modes and the forms within these modes is set out fully in figure 1.1

FORMS 1 THROUGH 4: TEACHER-CENTERED

Presentational Mode

Form 1: Teacher as Disseminator/Transmitter. By its very name this teaching form assumes the greatest distance between the teacher and learner. There is hardly a teaching presence at all. The encounter is faint and only minimal skills are required of both teacher and student. Yet this form or pseudo-form of the teaching process may be the most common today in higher education and has been praised by some for its "objectivity." One sees here, in a sense, the non-presence of the teacher, or his or her eventual replacement by a machine or learning packet. Unfortunately, K. Patricia Cross (1986) has pointed out that research shows most college teachers are viewed as information disseminators.[31]

Form 2: Teacher as Lecturer/Dramatist. This is an advance on the first form in that the teacher initiates an *engagement* with students by recognizing the need to connect, albeit in a general way. Though we may be dealing here with a persona or artifice, the teacher comes across more vibrantly. Obviously, the performance factor is strong in this form and teachers may use any number of dramatic techniques to hold their audience. A good lecturer also communicates "meaning" rather than facts, which takes us a giant step away from the dissemination model. The lecturer/dramatist form also lends itself to technology in that students can watch and benefit from a lively presentation even at a distance on closed circuit television.

Teaching Forms 1 and 2 can be called *presentational* and assessment of student learning will be along conventional lines. In higher education today, apart from graduate seminars, small writing classes and labs, teaching is usually thought of in terms of these two forms.

Initiatory Mode

Form 3: Teacher as Inducer/Persuader. In this encounter the teacher engages individual students more directly, yet adroitly enough to slip through their learning defenses and suggest the possibility of new attitudes or approaches. Though this type of instruction is motivational, and can be done via lecture, something more than dramatization or eloquence on the part of the teacher is involved. The student is engaged in a subtler way and the teacher is more aware of the students realm of interest. Also, reciprocity

Figure 1.1
Teaching Continuum

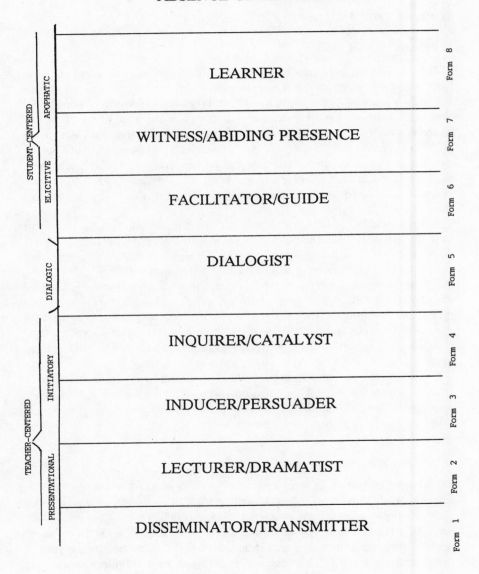

ABSENCE OF TEACHER

LEARNER — Form 8

WITNESS/ABIDING PRESENCE — Form 7

FACILITATOR/GUIDE — Form 6

DIALOGIST — Form 5

INQUIRER/CATALYST — Form 4

INDUCER/PERSUADER — Form 3

LECTURER/DRAMATIST — Form 2

DISSEMINATOR/TRANSMITTER — Form 1

STUDENT–CENTERED: APOPHATIC, ELICITIVE

DIALOGIC

TEACHER–CENTERED: INITIATORY, PRESENTATIONAL

begins to take place. In terms of interaction, truly persuasive teaching (which is neither indoctrination or manipulation), begins to take on the nature of a craft. It may be most effective with unmotivated students, appealing to their curiosity without violating their freedom.

Form 4: Teacher as Inquirer/Catalyst. In this presence the teacher engages students straight on. He has established enough of a bond with them to directly confront and question with only a minimum danger of withdrawal on their part. In doing so, he seeks to take them out of their familiar world, to help them recognize its limitations. A large swath can be taken in here— from questioning to assess intellectual comprehension to challenging students to question their basic beliefs and assumptions (transformative). This latter type of inquiry demands quite a bit of skill and assumes more than a superficial engagement with students.

Inquiry and catalyzation are most effective in smaller classes or learning groups since these allow opportunity for interaction. However, a compelling lecturer who has gained students' confidence can catalyze a large group to examine presuppositions or think about something in a new way. Whatever the format, inquiry arouses students' minds so that they are moved to take charge of their own learning.

Forms 3 and 4 could be called *initiatory* in that the teacher prepares or lays the groundwork for students' involvement in the central activities of learning. In truth, because so many institutions have inappropriate learning environments a teacher may not ever go beyond this mode. Assessment of learning here will usually be done by allowing students to express themselves in writing (essays, journal, papers.)

Dialogic Mode

Form 5: Teacher as Dialogist. The teacher's engagement with the learner now can be fully centered. The idea of learning as participatory takes precedence here. A discussion is viewed either as a dialogue between teacher and learners or as a conversation among equally involved and committed class members. Within the context created by the dialogic teacher, students develop a sense of community and personhood. While the teacher initiates from the outside and directs to some extent, she does not dominate the process as she does in previous roles. It is the most archetypal of learning contexts and all (non-lecturing) teaching involves it to some extent. In true dialogic teaching the scales are balanced between teacher and learner, and the former can be both teacher and learner. Though this teaching presence is more common with older students (especially in seminars or tutorials), many teachers are highly skilled at conversing with the young.

FORMS SIX THROUGH NINE: STUDENT-CENTERED

Elicitive Mode

Form 6: Teacher as Facilitator/Guide. The emphasis now shifts to the student as learner. The teacher's task here is more delicate—that of actively helping the student bring to fruition what already lies inside the mind. The guiding principle is Galileo's famous dictum: "You cannot teach a man anything; you can only help him to find it within himself." The mode is Socratic, in that the philosopher's overall method was to solicit first an admission of ignorance, then draw knowledge out of his interlocutor. It is the drawing out that involves the facilitative presence. A deep engagement exists here.

Facilitation as central to teaching has been recognized in modern times with the special emphasis on the child in education. No one employed it more fully than the Montessori schools. Here is Henry Perkinson's description:

The Montessori classroom is a free environment, a place where the student is free from a "judgmental" teacher, a place where the student is free to disclose his present knowledge. The teacher approaches the child in an invitational mode, encouraging him to talk, to act—to demonstrate his present skills and understandings.[32]

In higher education, the Facilitator/Guide teaching form is often most successful with older students. Where the teacher has to be judge as well as facilitator, the form is inhabited on a more superficial level, as we shall see.

Form 7: Teacher as Witness/Abiding Presence. Here the teacher's active role has diminished greatly. She becomes aware of the student in such a particularized way that she does no more than witness the learner's struggle to bring his knowledge to the threshold of articulation. Sylvia Ashton-Warner's concept of the teaching role expresses this beautifully: "For one thing, the drive is no longer the teacher's but the children's own. For another, the teacher is at last with the stream and not against it, the stream of the children's inexorable creativeness."[33]

A paradox begins to appear in this form. On the one hand, the teacher comes very close to identifying with the learner. Yet she remains apart in that students are given full existential freedom. For example, in this mode a teacher can be a witness in the sense of role model. Through the authenticity of the teacher's own search for knowledge and meaning, students see possibilities for their own growth—not in imitation of the teacher, but in terms of their own unique potential.

Forms 6 and 7 I will call *elicitive*. The bond between teacher and learner has become invisible and inward; the teacher is assisting students to learn, to grow—even by her silence. Since this kind of learning can take place only in smaller groups or on an individual basis, assessment of learning will be informal and conducted by the student. Group members in this context often teach each other. The deepest possibilities of self-knowledge exist in this mode.

Apophatic Mode

Form 8: Teacher as Learner. Here the teacher gives up the effort to effect the student's learning any further. The teacher reaches a point where once again he realizes that he knows nothing and must now learn along with, or even from, students. Again deep roots exist here in the Socratic notion of ignorance. Teachers who come to this realization do so usually toward the end of their career or at the end of an extended pedagogic encounter when they are given an unusually clear vision of the nature of education. Carl Rogers has offered us the most extreme example of this role: "When I look back at the results of my past teaching, the real results seem the same—either damage was done—or nothing significant occurred...As a consequence, I realize that I am only interested in being a learner."[34]

The role of abandoning the pretention to teach can be viewed as a prelude to a kind of final stage wherein teacher and learner fuse. In this situation the teaching function has been completely internalized by the learner, and one realizes what may have been true all along: One is one's own teacher, at least in matters of consequence. Teachers outside the learner are now dispensable—even counterproductive. But their various presences have led to this stage.

This last phase of teaching, or non-teaching, could be called *apophatic* in the sense that the teacher blows out the flame of his influence, or more accurately, that the flame is fully inside the student. It is a sign that the teacher has extinguished and given over the teaching self in an act of pedagogical love.

This brief breakdown of teaching forms and modes is marked not only by more individualization of learning as one moves along the continuum, but by an increasingly rich encounter between teacher and learner(s), what I call a gradual interiorization of a teaching presence until in the last mode the distance between the two is collapsed. At this point the learner is fully released to work on his or her own. This echoes Heidegger's definition of teaching as a "letting learn." "To be a teacher is, above all, to let others learn."[35]

I will spend the remaining chapters expanding on the specific teaching presences or forms contained within the continuum set out above. Obviously, there are numerous vantage points from which to view teaching. However, the perspective I am taking—that of phenomenological presence and engagement—establishes the relation between teacher and learner as central to teaching. In doing so it contains insights that other approaches may not allow.

Also, I am proposing a more comprehensive view of the teaching act than is usually the case, one that consciously joins together particular teaching forms (with their implications for learning). If this book has any originality it lies not in inventing these forms—they have been in existence for centuries—but in bringing them together on a continuum that not only broadens, but deepens the engagement between teacher and learner as both move toward educational liberation.

As we explicate these specific forms in the following chapters a number of practical questions may come up in readers' minds connected to the everyday world of teaching. For example, the reader may want to know if progress (or regress) actually takes place along a teaching continuum, and if so, how is it achieved. She may ask whether movement to more student-centered forms is a realistic option for teachers who seem to have personalities adapted to presentational or initiatory modes. Another question is whether the forms and their sequence along the continuum are equally relevant to all disciplines within higher education. Finally, something will need to be said about the research on student learning styles and approaches to study in higher education. I have chosen to postpone any detailed discussion of these issues until the concluding chapter so that the teaching forms themselves can be set out along the continuum in as clear a light as possible. This does not mean, however, that I have entirely neglected "real world" problems of teaching in the ensuing chapters. Not only are many examples of teachers working within a particular form taken from actual accounts of classroom teaching, but I constantly allude to the obstacles and restraints within higher education that militate against more student-centered encounters. I will also say something about the level and quality of student learning that can take place within a given encounter, as well as specific skills and abilities necessary for the teacher to be effective within a specific form.

That being said, the reader must still understand that the main focus of this book is not empirical. Neither is it meant as another in the long line of prescriptive manuals on effective teaching. It is rather a description of the possibilities or archetypes of teaching within a relational perspective. And while I trust that the idealized developmental forms set out in these pages will appear in a clear light, the vision of any one of them will be holistic rather than piecemeal. Meticulous breakdowns or extremely specific matchups between teacher-learner, skills and attitudes will not be found here.

NOTES

1. *Webster's New Collegiate Dictionary* (Springfield, Massachusetts: G. & C. Merriam Company, 1973).

2. John Passmore, *The Philosophy of Teaching* (London: Gerald Duckworth & Co. Ltd., 1980), p. 20.

3. N. L. Gage, *The Scientific Basis of the Art of Teaching* (New York: Teachers College Press, 1978), p. 14.

4. David Denton, "That Mode of Being Called Teaching," in *Existentialism and Phenomenology in Education: Collected Essays*, ed. David E. Denton (New York: Teachers College Press, 1974), p. 103.

5. Martin Buber, *I and Thou* (New York: Charles Scribner's Sons, 1958).

6. Passmore, *The Philosophy of Teaching*, p. 23.

7. The phrase is taken from the title of James Moffett's book, *Teaching the Universe of Discourse* (Boston: Houghton Mifflin Company, 1968) which sketches a pedagogical theory of discourse for the teaching of English.

8. Kenneth E. Eble, *The Aims of College Teaching* (San Francisco: Jossey-Bass Publishers, 1983), p. 4.

9. Eble, *The Craft of Teaching* (San Francisco: Jossey-Bass Publishers, 1976), p. 8.

10. Ibid., p. 11.

11. Philip W. Jackson, *The Practice of Teaching* (New York: Teachers College Press, 1986), p. 131.

12. Joseph Axelrod, *The University Teacher as Artist: Toward an Aesthetics of Teaching with Emphasis on the Humanities* (San Francisco: Jossey-Bass Publishers, 1976).

13. Michael J. Dunkin and Jennifer Barnes, "Research on Teaching in Higher Education" in *Handbook of Research on Teaching*, 3rd ed., ed. Merlin C. Wittrock (New York: Macmillan Publishing Co., 1986), p. 774.

14. John T. Granrose, "Conscious Teaching: Helping Graduate Assistants Develop Teaching Styles" in *New Directions For Teaching and Learning: Improving Teaching Styles*, ed. J. L. Bess (San Francisco: Jossey-Bass Publishers, 1980), p. 24.

15. N. L. Gage, "What Do We Know About Teaching Effectiveness?" *Phi Delta Kappan* 64 (October 1984): 88.

16. Ibid., p. 87.

17. Louis J. Rubin, *Artistry in Teaching* (New York: Delacorte Press, 1985), p. 15.

18. Axelrod, *The University Teacher As Artist*, p. 1.

19. Ibid., pp. 229–230.

20. Ken Macrorie, *Twenty Teachers* (New York: Oxford University Press, 1984).

21. Ibid., p. 177.

22. Philip W. Jackson, *The Practice of Teaching*, pp. 120–138.

23. Gage, *The Scientific Basis of the Art of Teaching*, p. 15.

24. Thomas F. Green, "A Topology of the Teaching Concept," in *Concepts of Teaching: Philosophical Essays*, ed. C. J. B. MacMillan and T. W. Nelson (Chicago: Rand McNally, 1968), pp. 71–78.

25. Axelrod, *The University Teacher as Artist*, pp. 7–41.

26. Dennis Fox, "Personal Theories of Teaching," *Studies in Higher Education* 8, no. 2 (1983): pp. 151–163. Most recently, Thomas Sherman and his associates in *The Journal of Higher Education* presented a developmental description of teaching excellence composed of four stages of increasing complexity. But the emphasis is not on the relationship between teacher and student. See Thomas M. Sherman et al., "The Quest for Excellence in University Teaching," *Journal of Higher Education*, 48, no.1 (January/February 1987): 66–82.

27. B. Othanel Smith, "A Concept of Teaching," in *Concepts of Teaching: Philosophical Essays*, p. 51.

28. Howard Gardner, *Frames of Mind: The Theory of Multiple Intelligences* (New York: Basic Books, Inc., 1985), p. 70.

29. Gabriel Marcel, the French phenomenologist, speaks of the ways in which a

person can resist encounter or "be unavailable." He uses terms such as "encumbrance" (surrounded by one's own self), "crispation" (a shriveling of the self), "susceptibility" (heightening of self-consciousness). These and other states of unavailability keep the self from reaching out for engagement. See Joseph McCown's study of Marcel, *Availability: Gabriel Marcel and the Phenomenology of Human Openness* (Missoula, Montana: Scholars Press, 1978.)

30. T. E. Moore points out that "teaching necessarily involves the intention that someone should learn as a result of what one does." See T. E. Moore, *Philosophy of Education: An Introduction* (London: Routledge and Kegan Paul, 1982), p. 67.

31. K. Patricia Cross, "A Proposal To Improve Teaching Or What 'Taking Teaching Seriously' Should Mean," *AAHE Bulletin*, 39, no. 1 (1986).

32. Henry J. Perkinson, *Learning From Our Mistakes: A Reinterpretation of Twentieth Century Educational Thinking* (Westport, Conn.: Greenwood Press, 1984), p. 10.

33. Sylvia Ashton-Warner, *Teacher* (New York: Simon and Schuster, 1963), pp. 92–93.

34. Carl R. Rogers, *Freedom to Learn* (Columbus, Ohio: Charles E. Merill Publishing Company, 1969), p. 153.

35. Ignatio L. Gotz, "Heidegger and the Art of Teaching," *Educational Theory*, 33, no. 1 (1983): 8.

Part One

Presentational Mode

The two forms in this teaching mode have the nature of set pieces wherein the teacher, wholly outside, addresses students in an impersonal or generalized manner. Both formats are designed for a one-way flow of energy. They are firmly within the transmission metaphor of learning or what Jackson calls the "mimetic." This, however, does not mean the student is a pure receptacle and many educators today doubt whether such a completely passive condition on the part of the receiver is possible.

Still, the first form in the Presentational Mode does seem to be structured that way. There may be some activation of the student's mind, but it is more of a reactive nature and on a quite superficial level of learning. There is not the kind of response we come to see in the later modes, nor is there any reciprocity since the two protagonists in the teaching forms do not meet as individuals. The personal contact, the specific awareness of each other that we will observe later on is not a key element here, even in the Lecturer/Dramatist Form. Even less is there possibility of educational intimacy.

Although the Presentational Mode is completely teacher-centered, in the more dynamic stages of the Lecturer/Dramatist Form there is an intent on the part of the teacher to become aware of students as a living group of learners.

The Presentational Mode may be the most common one in higher education today. Wagner Thielens, in a 1987 study of a random half of American universities, found lecturing to be the mode of instruction of 89 percent of the physical scientists and mathematicians, 81 percent of the social scientists, and 61 percent of the humanities faculty.[1] Because of their commonality and the comparative simplicity of the interactions involved the two forms within this mode come closer to being realized in their pure state in the everyday classroom or lecture hall than the succeeding forms on the continuum.

NOTE

1. Wagner Thielens, "The Disciplines and Undergraduate Lecturing." (Paper presented at the Annual Meeting of the American Educational Research Association, Washington, D.C. April, 1987.)

Chapter 1

Teacher As Disseminator/ Transmitter

> Man becomes predictable as soon as he becomes a machine.
> Aubrey Menon

The word "disseminate" originally meant "to spread abroad as though sowing seed, to disperse widely." Today the word has been narrowed down somewhat in certain circles and means "to hand or give out." In education the word is often linked up with factual information in the way of reports, articles, lists, mimeographed notes and the like. The word "transmit" literally means "to send across from one party to another" or "to forward." In this, the first dictionary definition, one has the idea of a relay wherein someone passes on rather than originates a message. Such, in fact, has been the purpose of teaching in the "mimetic" tradition which gives central place to the transmission of factual and procedural knowledge from one person (teacher) to another (student) through essentially an imitative process.[1] In its broadest sense it is an ancient tradition of teaching/learning, for peoples often passed on their skills, myths, and cultural heritage in this manner.

The word "transmit" also has an impersonal tinge to it in that the message is emphasized more than the sender or receiver. Religions pass on sacred doctrines which are to be kept inviolable; political ideologies are revered and stored in the mind almost verbatim. That such a process is rarely successful is another matter. History is full of controversies that ensue when one group accuses another of altering the fundamental tenets of an original doctrine. Two examples that come to mind are the doctrinal controversies surrounding tenets of the early Christian faith and the endless arguing over the "proper" interpretation of the United States Constitution.

One sees in both "disseminate" and "transmit" a certain inertness and objectification—even a purity—as if the information or text is to be kept separate from the soiled humanity of those writing or reading it. Such an approach resembles the New Criticism in the field of literary theory where the work is viewed as an artifact set apart in its integrity, eschewing both subjective interpretation or biographical addenda.[2]

The teacher in the pure Dissemination/Transmission Form becomes completely submerged in what today is called "information delivery." On the college level, the task is often that of presenting facts of a technical sort, along with brief explication, to students who passively take notes in a large lecture hall and who will be expected to reproduce, sometimes verbatim, what has been handed to them. The teaching presence is faintest at this pole and the disseminator usually makes use of overhead transparencies, flow charts, and other technologies, though not in any creative way. These simply add to the information flow. The teacher may also distribute reams of notes—and in some cases read from them as he would (and often does) from a text. A few years ago at the professional school where I teach, the senior editors, making a clear judgement on their education, designed the yearbook to look like a large sheaf of classroom notes and titled it "The Last Handout." It was the most popular yearbook in decades.

In the Dissemination/Transmission Form the personality and uniqueness of the teacher remain hidden except for eccentric quirks of speech or delivery which are more noticeable in the absence of the instructor's attempt to impart meaning to the material. The terms used to describe these lectures connote the idea of lifelessness ("dull," "boring," "deadly"), although students may agree on the importance of the material. Occasionally, one hears the telling remark: "I saw Dr. Smith in his office yesterday. He's different from the way he is in class. He's human! He actually smiled!"

The disseminator form of teaching implies the memorize-regurgitation model of learning which means that learning will take place only on a most superficial level—what Marton and others have called "surface level processing."[3] The student, like the instructor, responds in a mechanical manner, and the model of the student mind, even in recitation, is that of information processor similar to a computer. A lockstep attitude sets in whereby the student rote learns for the purpose of reproduction and does not come to see beyond the constituent (and often isolated) elements of a subject or to reflect on what is being absorbed.[4] Time is often the chief factor here; large amounts of material need to be taken in or crammed for weekly or bi-monthly exams. For example, at a college with a heavy technical curriculum, pharmacy students may be required to take a huge twenty credit course in Pharmacotherapeutics in the space of one year. Since each "block" of material (renal, vascular, circulatory, etc.) must be covered in two weeks for the bi-weekly exam both instructor and students can become locked into a dissemination/regurgitation cycle.[5]

Even unexperienced instructors (who often begin their careers in this manner) sense that the Disseminator Form is the most foreign to the act of teaching. They are so subordinated to the flow of information that a pre-recorded tape would do just as well. College professors who limit their teaching to recital of facts encased in technical jargon or who read at length from manuals or textbooks would seem wholly dispensable since they allow no real opportunity for encounter. Thus, dissemination/transmission is the most reductive form of teaching in that both teacher and student become machine-like and are set apart from one another atomistically like isolated monads. Strict dissemination allows for only the most linear and one-dimensional kind of instruction. Philip Jackson has described its limitations well: "Under the control of a machine (or of a teacher who behaves like one) the unsystematic and often alogical quality of spontaneous interaction is all but eliminated and the opportunistic quality of the teaching process is thereby diminished."[6]

It might be argued that the scenario set out above is extreme and only in rare cases does the college instructor mechanically impart information in such a way. However, in talking with college students one gets the impression that teachers who function in this first mode are quite common today, and according to K. Patricia Cross, the research shows that most college teachers regard themselves as information disseminators. She points out that many are victims of their own past:

There is some danger that students in our classrooms are drowning in information now. Many of their bone-weary teachers teach as they were taught. There is nothing in their preparation and training to break the cycle of teaching as telling. All too often information flows from the notes of the professor into the notebooks of students without passing through the minds of either.[7]

There are other reasons than habit for this practice: College teachers often feel they must adapt to the perceived quality of today's students which they have been told is quite low. There is also a need to supply concrete evidence for student learning and this can be done most easily through testing which involves students reproducing what they have learned. Connected with these reasons are the time pressures on faculty which may necessitate requiring straightforward oral or written presentations.[8] Above all, college teachers may be victims themselves of what Naisbitt calls "the information society," feeling they are locked in to this method because students come to college already socialized by their prior schooling to absorb and regurgitate information.[9] If we are to believe the studies and commission reports of the 1980s very little is happening at any level of schooling to expose students to more sophisticated learning skills. Perhaps these claims are overstated.

This author recalls two teachers from high school—one a priest, the other a coach teaching health studies—who spent every class period in the same manner. We sat with the open text in our hands while it was read aloud word for word. No explanation or expansion of the material, no intellectual inter-change, ever took place. What struck us most of all was the sheer deadness of the situation. In each case, for the duration of that period at least, the teacher was a non-person who was simply putting in time. No impact was ever made on us either by the material or the teacher. For exams, paragraphs from specific chapters were assigned and we regurgitated them verbatim. We never saw any larger meaning beyond the literalness of what we had to memorize. It is hard to believe that anyone could enjoy "teaching" in this context. One wonders how big a role such depersonalization plays in teacher burnout? Or why on an elementary or secondary level it is necessary at all? For without some kind of authentic teaching encounter one functions in a classroom or lecture hall without meaning.

REPLACEMENT OF TEACHER BY MACHINE OR TEXT

It is appropriate here to raise the question of whether the teacher as Disseminator/Transmitter could be replaced by a teaching machine or simply a text. If one is talking about pure dissemination the answer must certainly be yes. For as we have noted, it is hard to distinguish between teacher and machine since both are impersonal and completely mechanical. But as the teacher begins to move away from the sheer relaying of information or the one-dimensional transmission of "knowledge" the question becomes more problematic since a teaching presence begins to emerge. Teaching machines to date exhibit a rigidity and kind of linear logical masculinization that could never replace the human engagement which a teacher working beyond the dissemination model fosters. Even teachers working essentially within the form, but who occasionally lift from the information to expand or explicate may be giving students something that computers can't supply. However, in a sheer question and answer recitation where no discussion or real inquiry takes place a teaching machine can easily be employed which carries out the same function.

Computers, as Robert Taylor has pointed out, have three general roles in schooling: that of tutor, tool, and tutee. As tutor their value lies in presenting drill work on subjects where rote learning is necessary or in taking the learner through a domain of knowledge, asking appropriate questions at each stage before proceeding to more complex subjects. Here the teacher is probably replaceable.[10] As tool the computer enables students to work more efficiently in the medium of their choice—for example, a word processor for writing. One sees here as an extension of the student's own capability; thus, the processor assists him in active learning. As tutee the computer allows the student to design a program to exhibit certain relationships within a field. Along with getting a feel for such relationships the student learns program-ming.[11]

One does not have to go as far as Seymour Papert who believes that the "computer presence" will enable us to totally modify the environment outside the classroom to see that CAI (Computer-Assisted Instruction) can have a definite place in instruction and certain kinds of learning.[12] It is when we get into the higher realms of skill acquisition that complexities of learning arise which make the human teacher irreplaceable. For example, once a question is asked by the student which engenders discussion rather than straightforward informational answers dynamics are employed that can only be poorly simulated by any kind of teaching machine, even those designed to function interactively. According to Robert Sardello, extended use of teaching machines or programmed instruction have already shown themselves to be dismal failures "precisely because they turn the learner into a mechanism, who responds with frustration and boredom."[13]

Here we have the same condition as portrayed in the Dissemination/Transmission Form. Those who believe computers can take on more human dimensions and set for students complex learning tasks have yet to prove this can be done. Even someone as optimistic as Derek Bok expresses reservations about what more fanatic devotees believe are the computer's infinite possibilities as a teaching instrument.[14] The chief drawback is simply the inability of the computer to substitute for the personal contact the live teacher provides. Nothing replaces the relationship with a real teacher, in what Robert Menges calls "the tutorial conversation" which often takes place after the student works with the computer.[15] Perhaps more has to be learned about how information flows, not only from teacher to student but from the student and class back to the teacher before we can think about designing machines to perform complex communication tasks, if indeed they can ever be so designed.

Also, the dangers inherent in providing teaching or learning models based on computers which function purely in functional, operational, and instrumental terms have been pointed out by a number of critics. The central question, according to Douglas Sloan is not whether one is for or against computers in education, but to define the human and educational criteria that can make a truly human use of the computer possible.[16]

One of the most important questions in teaching is the relation of teacher to the textbook. As we have shown on the college level, in pure dissemination where the teacher does not add or interpret, the student is just as well off— perhaps better off—alone with the text. Even on the elementary and secondary levels situations occur where the teacher completely subordinates herself and her students to the recitation model in viewing the text as absolutely authoritative. Elizabeth Bernhardt shows us how the triangle works:

Texts are perceived as holding truths or facts. Their function is to bring these truths or facts to students so that they may absorb them, and student responsibility is to then tell the teacher, generally in response to questions either oral or written, what these truths or facts are; that is, to reproduce the text.[17]

The text has become the central presence in the above example. This practice in grade schools is probably much rarer today than it used to be in our country—even in private schools where religious teachings are transmitted. Once the teacher begins to expand on the text or interact with the students in more than a mechanical way she moves beyond the Dissemination/Transmission Form and, as we saw with the computer, the text is not sufficient. Over a century ago John Henry Newman explained why the text can never replace the vital presence of a human teacher when he pointed out that no book can convey "the special spirit and delicate peculiarities of its subject with that rapidity and certainty which attend on the sympathy of mind with mind, through the eyes, the look, the accent, and the manner, in casual expressions thrown off at the moment, and the unstudied turns of familiar conversation."[18]

The many ways in which the teacher's presence blends with the use of a text will be addressed in succeeding chapters. We will simply say here that any employment of the textbook beyond mere mechanical reading or recitation brings the teacher alive and out of the Dissemination/Transmission Form.

MIMETIC TEACHING

Before concluding this brief chapter, something needs to be said about the transmission of knowledge advocated by the mimetic tradition in education. Though I may seem to have suggested it here, it would be an oversimplification to view the teacher in this tradition as a pure disseminator. Admittedly, the intent is to present or hand on a body of knowledge to students. But in real classrooms such a passing down usually involves other teaching forms. For example, the instructor may lecture and model a type of learning; she often uses persuasive power to gain student interest, or she may assess students' grasp of the material by creating discussion and asking leading questions. The teacher may explore ways to help students go beyond memorizing and use other thinking skills to work their way through a particular body of knowledge. Nevertheless, it is true that these and other forms of teaching are subservient to the view that knowledge can be transferred from the teacher's mind or textbook to the student. In this sense, the Lockian metaphor of student as vessel or receptacle into which the teacher pours knowledge holds true.[19] During this century we have seen how chillingly effective this metaphor is when the purpose of instruction is indoctrination or the spread of propaganda. Minds can be bound up, sometimes forever, in ideology and "authorized" versions of reality. The classroom teacher's use of a text in this manner is described well again by Bernhardt:

Students learn to how to fulfill teacher expectations in classrooms: They answer questions accurately and reproduce textual information. They learn over time that they are to protect certain "truths" handed down by the text through the teacher. Thus, unless the teacher specifically requests their interpretations, volunteering them would be perceived as disrespectful of textual authority and an interruption of planned instruction.[20]

The more activated the student's mind the less the metaphor of a vessel or receptacle is useful. And the less straightforward learning becomes. Many educational theorists today question whether a one-dimensional transfer of knowledge (as opposed to information or statements) from teacher to learner is really possible at all. Whatever the case, as we will see in some detail, the mind begins to come alive once the student responds to a more authentic teaching presence.

NOTES

1. Jackson, *The Practice of Teaching*, pp. 117–120.

2. See Rene Wellek and Austin Warren's definition: "The work of art, then, appears as an object of knowledge 'sui generis' which has a special ontological status." *Theory of Literature* (New York: Harcourt, Brace & World, Inc., 1942), p. 156.

3. Marton's research is discussed along with that of others in Noel J. Entwistle, *Styles of Learning and Teaching: An Integrated Outline of Educational Psychology For Students, Teachers and Lecturers* (London: David Fulton Publishers, 1988), pp. 75–116. For a briefer account see George Brown, "Studies of Student Learning: Implications For Medical Teaching," *Medical Teacher* 5, no. 2 (1983): 52–55.

4. Learning for reproduction is one of three possible student approaches or orientations to studying outlined by John Biggs. The other two are learning for achievement and for personal meaning. Cf. Noel W. Entwistle, *Styles of Learning and Teaching*, p. 102. More will be said about these in Chapter 6.

5. This is the situation at my college for students in their fourth year. However, they also have weekly labs where more interpersonal encounters take place—usually with lab assistants.

6. Philip Jackson, *The Teacher and the Machine*. Horace Mann Lecture. (Pittsburgh: University of Pittsburgh Press, 1968), p. 10.

7. Cross, "A Proposal to Improve Teaching or What 'Taking Teaching Seriously' Should Mean" p. 9. See also, Richard C. Richardson, Jr., Elizabeth C. Fisk, Morris A. Okun, *Literacy in the Open Access College* (San Francisco: Jossey-Bass Publishers, 1983), pp. 42–62.

8. Cross, pp. 9–10.

9. John Naisbitt, *Megatrends: Ten New Directions Transforming Our Lives* (New York: Warner Books, Inc., 1982).

10. Joseph Axelrod says this kind of drill should take place in the Lab Center so the faculty member can be free to work on a higher level in the classroom. He is speaking in this context of the basic information and elementary skills that apply to humanistic studies. See *The University Teacher as Artist*, p. 213.

11. Robert Taylor, ed., *The Computer in the School: Tutor, Tool, Tutee* (New York: Teachers College Press, 1980).

12. Seymour Papert, *Mindstorms: Children, Computers, and Powerful Ideas* (New York: Basic Books, Inc., 1980).

13. Robert D. Sardello, "The Technological Threat to Education," in *The Computer in Education: A Critical Perspective*, ed. Douglas Sloan (New York: Teachers College Press, 1984), pp. 93–94.

14. Derek Bok,. "Looking into Education's High-Tech Future," *Harvard Magazine* (May-June 1985): 29–38.

15. Robert J. Menges, "Instructional Methods," in *The Modern American College*, ed. Arthur Chickering (San Francisco: Jossey-Bass Publishers , 1981), p. 575.

16. Douglas Sloan, ed., *The Computer in Education: A Critical Perspective*. See especially, Douglas Sloan, "Introduction: On Raising Critical Questions About the Computer in Education," pp. 1–9; Herbert L. Dreyfus and Stewart E. Dreyfus, "Putting Computers in their Proper Place: Analysis vs. Intuition in the Classroom," pp. 40–63; Robert J. Sardello, "The Technological Threat to Education," pp. 93–101.

17. Elizabeth Buchter Bernhardt, "The Text as Participant in Instruction," *Theory Into Practice* 26, no. 1 (Winter, 1987): 32.

18. Quoted in Jacques Barzun, *Teacher in America* (New York: Doubleday & Company, Inc., 1944), pp. 42–43.

19. Philip Jackson stresses how rare it is to witness either mimetic or transformative teaching in isolation. But he points out that it is not at all uncommon for one or the other of the two traditions to predominate in various teaching situations. Also, certain subjects or whole curricular programs seem more closely associated with one or the other traditions. Cf. *The Practice of Teaching*, pp. 130–132.

20. Bernhardt, "The Text as Participant in Instruction," p. 36.

Chapter 2

Teacher As Lecturer/ Dramatist

The best general advice to the teacher who would lecture well is still, "Don't lecture."

Kenneth Eble

The dictionary meaning of the word "lecture" is that of a discourse delivered on any subject—especially a formal discourse intended for instruction. It is derived from the words "lectura" and "legere" meaning "to read." Its historical origins are contemporaneous with the rise of the theatre in Greece where both developed in what John McLeish calls "the context of the classical Greek democratic process."[1] The training of the citizen in oratory was a major component of the educational curriculum and the delivery of the teacher was expected to conform to the standards of a stage presentation or Senate oration:

The living personality and the trained artistry of the teacher constituted the medium by which materials of human interest were presented to a highly receptive, but at the same time perceptive, critical and thoughtful audience. The lecture was a carefully prepared, probably rehearsed, but seemingly improvised performance."[2]

Both the attractions and the limitations of the lecture format are contained in this historical definition.

In the Middle Ages the function of the lecture had altered to a formal reading of, or commentary on, a book of which the lecturer had the lone copy. Students would often copy down the "reading" word for word and commit it to memory so they could be reproduced when the lecturer required it. This is not to say that discussion and disputations did not take place in the Middle Ages, as anyone familiar with the university life of those centuries knows, but the passing down of sacred text or words of lecture was of central importance to auditors.

In modern times, with the demise of public readings and the relative infrequency of general oratory, the lecture is alive in the university setting where it exists today as the most commonly employed teaching method. Paulson long ago outlined the threefold purpose of the lecture in higher education: To provide a survey of a whole field of knowledge through the medium of a living personality; to relate this body of knowledge to the primary aims of human life; to arouse an active interest, leading to an independent comprehension of the subject on the part of the listener.[3] Wilbert McKeachie adds that the popularity of the lecture method in higher education probably derives from a conception of the instructor's primary goal as being the transmission of knowledge and its effectiveness in summarizing content in a form understandable to a particular group of students.[4] Thus, in contrast to the goals of dissemination, those of the lecture have a decidedly humane cast.

There are, for general purposes, two kinds of lecture in higher education today: The traditional, "straight-on" discourse whereby the speaker attempts to transfer concepts, interpretations, or judgements to the students' receptive minds; and the participatory lecture in which the teacher interrupts the flow to answer questions or allow other activities which keep the student involved. Even in the traditional lecture the students cannot be completely passive if a positive effect is to be engendered. For we note that in ancient Athens the audience not only was assumed to be receptive, but to be perceptive and critical.

It is in the Lector/Dramatist Form of instruction where the teacher attempts an engagement with his listeners. This image of a "living personality" constitutes for the first time a real teaching presence which places the instructor in a different teaching form than that of Disseminator/Transmitter, though both forms remain presentational. The instructor recognizes a need to connect and if the student audience is receptive, an encounter takes place, even though generalized and at a distance.

THE ENTHUSIASTIC LECTURER

For example, on a college level, the teacher through an intense involvement with her materials or her love of learning desires to share what she knows with her audience. Thus, she not only organizes her materials, but takes care to modulate her delivery, make the proper emphases, highlight central concepts. Most of the rather extensive literature on the craft of lecturing concerns itself with offering tips and advice on how to present subject materials in an organized and articulate manner—in short, what amount to the basic skills of public speaking.[5] This intense enthusiasm for a subject creates in a competent lecture presentation a kind of vibrant presence which the students notice and imbibe. Dubrow and Wilkenson point out that a surprising number of students will regularly report that what they value most in a lecture is enthusiasm. In the words of one undergraduate: "I always wonder what makes a professor devote his life to scholarship—watching a lecturer really get turned on by his material helps me understand."[6] Another word for enthusiasm is "teacher expressiveness" which includes such terms as rapport, charisma, dynamism—terms often used by students to describe favorite lecturers.[7] Often such a teaching presence can come through sheerly on love or command of learning. Many of the teachers in Joseph Epstein's *Masters* emit this quality and it remains in the memory of their students, often despite lecturing skills that leave something to be desired.[8] "Integrity of instruction" is the term often used when love of learning is combined with technical competence in presenting material.

THE STUDENT-ORIENTED LECTURER

The presence of the teacher to students through her materials, no matter how vibrant, is still somewhat distant in that she doesn't directly establish a relationship with them. However, when the lecturer seeks *primarily* to adapt materials to her listeners a richer encounter can take place. The speaker, then, seeks not only to understand and present, but to achieve a maximum effect on the audience—i.e. communicate meaning at her auditor's level. The teacher's concern for the students here has increased and they will benefit even in terms of measurable learning.

For example, lecturers who are primarily aware of their audience will create and sustain eye contact, knowing how to take in the class as a whole, then move from left to right, momentarily resting on one part of the group and then another. Even more than this, they will have the ability to read student expressions, to gather a genuine sense of whether a point has been grasped. This means they will allow for intervals in which students can gather in an idea, digest what has been said, ask questions, or briefly consider a model that has been graphically presented.

The student-oriented lecturer will endeavor to find points in his presentation that connect with the wider concerns of the students' world; he may sprinkle the lecture periodically with anecdotes and examples, order to mix exposition or argument with brief narrative since the latter can often drive a point home effectively. He will be especially attuned to the alternating rhythms of student attention spans, building to climactic points or insights within twenty minute intervals, while at the same time recognizing the value of some redundancy. She will in the same manner get in tune with the rhythms of a semester, the organic confluence of events and activities that make up general student life at the college. Thus, the lecturer will have moved out of the artificial, egoistic mentality (all too common among teachers in higher education) which assumes that students who enter the lecture hall have only her subject on their mind to a more realistic attitude in which she understands that the students live within a constant stream of consciousness tracing a myriad of concerns, daydreams, and anxieties. Howard R. Pollio has summed up this point well in discussing phenomenological research on the complex human beings we call students:

Within the context of teaching, this means that students come into our lecture halls not as disembodied minds eagerly waiting to be filled with knowledge but as human beings having a full and rich complement of experiences against which our lectures must compete for focal awareness. The structure of human experience in the lecture hall and elsewhere, is always one in which some event stands out against some background within some context.[9]

As time progresses student-oriented lecturers will learn to distinguish among levels of students, between those who are learning oriented and grade oriented. Most of all they will try to identify levels of anxiety in students, both as a general group and, to the extent possible, as individuals, and do their best to ease the tension. Of course, the larger the class, the more difficult it becomes to notice individuals.

LECTURER AS DRAMATIST

The effect of an encounter with teachers who are in full command of their material while at the same time acutely aware of their audience can be indelible. However, the richest kind of teaching in the Lector/Dramatist Form lies in the creation of a persona through a studied performance. The instructor, in looking for ways to "get home" to a student audience is now willing to create or experiment with a dramatis personae which can bridge the gap between his vision and their experience. When successful, the teacher inhabits the full range of the Presentational Mode. The element of theater inserts itself here. Jacques Barzun has called the lecture room "the place where drama may properly become theater."[10] The teacher needs to project since he is still working in a context where more intimate encounters are not possible. Often, however, in carrying out such a projection the teacher creates a visible and distinct model of knowledge or a presence which can bring to life corresponding images from within the student. Even a quick thirty second role play can bring the response: "I see it now" or "My god, that's me, or a new facet of me, I'm seeing!" This is what Vivian Hodgson calls the "intrinsic experience of relevance" where the student sees the meaning of what is presented in relation to her own world.[11] Often the dramatic representation of a scientific model can give the student a similar experience in that it relates to his existing framework of thinking. I recall watching a young teacher at an inner city college humorously illustrate Newton's three laws of motion by using students in the class to create brief scenarios wherein a student in front of the room stayed inert, was pushed into motion by another and finally involved in an action/reaction. In the last of these the teacher put on a black cap, came around the desk and simulated an attempted mugging of the student only to be repulsed and thrown backward.

The teacher as dramatis personae in a lecture context inescapably employs a degree of narrative form involving psychodrama and suspense—whether it involves a sustained role play, a humanized modeling of a scientific theory or concept, or simulated interaction with others. The effects of such a performance can be exciting, often stunning, moving students cognitively to what Alice Hornung calls "a new point of consciousness, the generation of an intellectual high that can last a long time."[12] At the same time, the student is engaged on an emotional and imaginative level which makes the experience richer and more life-like. This means that learning is likely to affect one's values.

I remember vividly an example of a modern drama class wherein the professor, in one of the introductory lectures, tried valiantly to get across to the students the idea that hidden within each of us lies a stranger who represents a polar opposite to the self we present to others in our everyday lives—and it is that opposite self that the actor often conjures. The students received this news lukewarmly. The following class, in a darkened lecture hall, an unkempt charwoman made her way unannounced to the stage with brush and bucket, and submissively began scrubbing the floor. After a few minutes she looked up, riveted the audience with her gaze, and started to spew out her seething rage for revenge in a chilling performance of Brecht's "Pirate Jenney" from *The Three Penny Opera*. When she finished the woman slowly removed wig and outer clothing to reveal yesterday's professor who whispered to a hushed audience: "Do you see now what I mean by 'the stranger'?"

A lecturer who is an accomplished actor can create a special kind of presence equivalent to a professional performance. John Rassaias of Dartmouth exemplified such an ability in his numerous impersonations of historical characters during his French language classes.[13] One also thinks of Steve Allen's brilliant "Meeting of the Minds" programs for educational television in which historical characters from disparate times meet and discuss the great ideas of the Western world. Students, of course, remember this kind of histrionics and the word spreads around the campus. Rassais himself has made the parallel between teaching and acting: "The mission of both is to reach the audience. If you don't make that relationship, the lesson is just mental acrobatics."[14] Travers has explained how the use of theatre techniques (in particular Stanislovski's theory of personality) is fundamental to creating a role or personality for the classroom—though he is quick to point out that teaching is not acting.[15] Thus, in those moments when they create a dramatic projection lecturer-artists reach their epitome.

A difficulty might be raised here. It often appears that a particular teaching

style or personality can leave its mark on students far more than the intellectual content or meaning of what was expressed. To some this would seem
to substitute personality, even idiosyncrasy, for substance and vague re-
membrance for precision. Viewed in this manner, such a teaching presence
can actually be detrimental to learning. If what remains are only accidental
qualities such as particular quirks or mannerisms, or even sensation for its
own sake, then such a critique is valid. But if one thinks of style or personality
in the sense of the phenomenological impression a teacher makes, then we
have the kind of presence which is something different altogether. We mentioned in the introductory chapter how Kenneth Eble stated that in reading
over dozens of testimonies to great teachers he was struck by how often the
details remembered were aspects of *presence* rather than any specific knowledge.[16] Though it sounds outlandish to the empirical temper, the probability
exists that what happens to a student through a phenomenological encounter
with a teacher may be more lasting and important than achieving the usual
learning objectives or thinking skills highlighted in Bloom's *Taxonomy*. When
a student tells a teacher fifteen years later, "I don't remember much of what
you said, but I'll never forget you or the impact of that class," the teacher
should not feel depressed. Something has taken place here aside from the
transmission of facts, concepts or even a knowledge system. The teacher,
even in a Presentational Mode, has created a dynamic presence which has
left a lasting, though unmeasurable, effect—something to do with character.
She may also have created in the student a motivation for learning which
makes new skills and abilities more readily attainable.[17]

Thus, it seems that even in the Lector/Dramatist Form teachers can communicate something beyond the intended material either by the obvious
devotion to learning evidenced in their presentation or in the dramatis personae effected by their performance. It should be clear that the more aware
instructors become of their student audience, the more they put themselves
in their place as listeners, the greater will be their effectiveness within this
teaching form. For the engagement and concern are now more intentional.
As we have seen, this is most noticeable when the teacher goes to the extent
of creating a dramatis persona in order to reach the students.

On the elementary and secondary levels the Lecturer/Dramatist Form is
less common, although the story-telling and various other presentational
efforts of an imaginative teacher can be the most memorable experiences of
early school. Even a teacher who reads well—as did the great public performers in times past—creates in the student a feeling and imagination which
are the most precious gifts of a teacher's didactic presence.

LIMITATIONS OF LECTURER/DRAMATIST FORM

We have seen that a teaching encounter in the second form of our continuum can be anything from communicating material in a straightforward man-

ner, with explication and commentary, to the full articulation of a dramatis personae wherein concepts, problems, or events are projected in a dynamic, living way. Still, there are inherent limits to this form that ordinarily restrict the teacher's encounter with students.

On an empirical level, traditional criticisms of the lecture method have a long history beginning in the Middle Ages. These criticisms are identical to the ones we constantly hear in our own time concerning poor lectures in the college classroom: "dreary commentary," "droning on," "a reading off" to passive listeners who take notes mechanically and reproduce rather than actively think.[18] One can argue persuasively for the importance, perhaps the indispensability, of the well placed introductory lecture or the overview lecture expounding general themes. Cashin points out that lectures can cover material not otherwise available, including original research, or recent developments available only from papers or articles not yet included in textbooks.[19] But it is impossible to argue convincingly that a system built on the lecture method is educating students in an effective manner since only a few lecturers will be artists, or even craftpersons, and class after class of large lecture with the taking of notes can be mind-numbing. Dubrow and Wilkenson show how in such a system the lecture method disintegrates into three kinds of poor presentation: the industrious, but boring lecturer who buries students in facts delivered in a monotone; the energetic but condescending lecturer who abuses rhetoric and alienates students; the friendly, well-meaning, but disorganized lecturer who rambles and leaves half of the material to cover in the last three lectures.[20]

In terms of measurable learning skills, research during the last twenty years has proven that traditional lecturing is ineffective when attempting to inculcate more than superficial knowledge or global impressions.[21] While it is true that "teacher expressiveness" in a good lecture results in better recall and that lecture has been proven superior to discussion in transmitting certain kinds of knowledge, when it comes to learning objectives that involve the employment of higher thinking skills—analysis, application, evaluation—the traditional lecture method should be abandoned. Robert Menges points out that to attain complex cognitive outcomes, such as classifying concepts, generating examples, and originating cognitive strategies, the learner must be actively engaged with subject matter and in large groups such involvement is quite difficult to engender.[22] Even the retention rate of students is poor compared to that produced by other instructional methods since attention spans are limited to fifteen or twenty minutes while most lectures in higher education drone on for fifty minutes to an hour.[23] A student-oriented lecturer can, however, assist her class in learning the one basic skill that almost always attends the conventional lecture: the taking of notes. Many students don't know how to combine intelligent note-taking with the listening skills necessary to get the most out of a lecture presentation. The teacher can be of great service here, particularly early in the semester by taking the time to show them how to coordinate the two as well as helping them adjust to the pace of material being presented.[24]

The worst thing about lecturing as underpinning for an educational system is that it leads to metaphors of learning which are shallow and depersonalized. Teaching is "pouring" knowledge into empty "vessels"; learning becomes "storage" and is "dispensed" by experts who are in Marshall Gregory's words "morally neutral conduits of information."[25] We have already used these terms in discussing the Dissemination/Transmission Teaching Form, and it is hard to completely disassociate them from lectures. Also, assessment and grading in large lecture classes are usually conventional and restricted to testing memory outcomes and basic cognitive skills on the part of the student. The more complex cognitive abilities simply can't be assessed in such a context, nor can non-cognitive aspects of learning be brought to the fore. Added to this, testing procedures that prove efficient for the teacher may be resented by the student as impersonal.[26]

Yet lecturing persists in our universities despite students' preference for other learning environments. The two main advantages of the straight-on lecture presentation, and perhaps the reasons why it persists, are that it is the only practical teaching method when dealing with large student audiences, and as Paulson and others have pointed out, it is an effective learning tool for the professor. This would be especially true for professors who uses the lecture hour to summarize their own research.[27]

LIMITATIONS IN REGARD TO TEACHING ENCOUNTER

From the standpoint of a teacher's phenomenological presence, an even greater limitation exists in the Lecturer/Dramatist Form. We have seen that as lecturer/dramatist the teacher moves a good distance from disseminator/ transmitter. The form allows the first authentic teaching presence in that a generalized encounter can take place. We have also shown that a dynamic dramatis personae can leave an impression on a student that is lasting, that in some cases—often unknown to the speaker—an image inside the student is called up which initiates an internal dialogue.[28] The well-delivered lecture which deals with meaning rather than merely facts can assist comprehension as well as stir feelings and imagination. But a teaching encounter in this form can go no further than this. The reasons are inherent in the very form itself.

First, the teaching presence is a general and unfocused one. Individualization, that personal touching which creates a relationship or reciprocity (meeting) between teacher and pupil, cannot take place in a large audience. Second, the lecture/dramatist mode is quite teacher-centered. The instructor is still very much the active force no matter how much he stimulates or enthuses even in situations where time is allowed for questions. The communication, as Menges has observed, flows primarily from teacher to learner and most student talk is in response to the teacher's questions. As we saw, the lecture is often a learning tool for the teacher. Edward Glassman in "The Teacher As Leader" puts it well: "I realized that when I lectured I was the one who learned most. I was the one whose thinking skills were enhanced and whose creativity was stimulated. I played the active learning role."[29]

This even applies to the richest aspect of the form where a dramatis/personae is created. Not only is the role initiated by the teacher, but the highest creativity and vision are his. And there is the attendant danger that in such a performance the teacher's ego-needs may take precedence over the desire to have the student learn. The presentation then becomes a show with the teacher "doing his or her thing" and the lecture a tool for aggrandizement in the eyes of students. The presentation, while spectacular, is vitiated and will not affect the student in any permanent way. Those who warn against the cult of personality usurping the teaching presence would be justified here.[30]

Finally, the very nature of a presentational form involves artifice, something mediated between teacher and student, a lecturing persona. Thus, we have, to use a term from scholastic philosophy, "actio a distans." There is no allowance for the specific interactions that are possible when the teacher is more directly present and where more complex learning skills can be developed and demonstrated. Neither is a sufficient context for student inquiry or discovery provided. Engagement is limited. Noel Entwistle has described this disadvantage at some length:

The whole lecture situation seems to be designed to increase psychological distance. The lecturer, typically, arrives after the students; walks to the front; retreats behind a long bench and then behind a reading desk; opens his notes; waits for latecomers—then begins. He is the focus of attention, but the physical situation and the formality of the lecture delivery must create an artificial atmosphere for communication. The lecturer, unless he tries to break down psychological distance, *will* confront the students, *will* intimidate, and so will also, unknowingly, affect the student's readiness to learn and his attitude to studying.[31]

Also, the "self" or personality which has been developed for lecture or performance purposes—what Charles Rivers Jr. calls the performing artist's "instrument,"—is not the more authentic self which begins to come through in forms of teaching further along on the continuum.[32] The lecturing self is authentic only in so far as it is appropriate to the demands of the form.

Participatory types of lecture, which are being advocated more and more today in higher education are certainly effective in increasing student involvement. For example, having students help germinate ideas for a lecture, or using the feedback lecture where after twenty minutes students are broken down into small groups and given discussion questions, involve them much more in the teaching/learning process and to some extent reduce the distance between teacher and learner.[33] But participatory lectures, in so far as they remain lecture/presentations (viz. feedback lecture format) don't essentially change the teaching presence, and should participation reach a point where the interaction between instructor and pupil is fairly constant the mode of encounter is then altered and we no longer have the Lecturer/Dramatist Form; individualized interaction has begun to take place. "Lectures" involving lengthy debates and extensive student role playing or problem solving are also no longer lectures because the activities which were meant to be subsidiary have now assumed a dominant role. The whole experience is more student centered. And, as we will see shortly, even when the teacher uses the lecture method to urge or persuade students another form of encounter may be taking shape.

The teacher may be a brilliant lecturer, even an artist at the form, but as Joseph Axelrod has demonstrated, teachers who are growing in relationship to their students will eventually find the Lecturer/Dramatist Form unsatisfactory and too remote—even artificial and contrived.[34] They will search for a more authentic teaching encounter which will necessitate a movement forward on the continuum.

USE OF AUDIO-VISUAL AND TEXTBOOK

A word needs to be said here about presentations which combine the lecture format with the use of audio-visual materials. The teacher who integrates these well obviously increases her effectiveness in the Presentational Mode. It is this skillful integration that distinguishes their employment from the one dimensional way they are used in the Dissemination/Transmission Form of instruction. Putting on this type of demonstration requires a high degree of coordination. Such presentations can stimulate along with being informative. It is even possible, as Peter Frederick has pointed out, to enhance the emotional involvement of the student as does the dramatis personae of the teacher's performance.[35] Lectures of this sort usually leave more of an impression than the straight-on, wholly spoken type. Brown and Bakhtar have labeled this kind of teacher who expertly combines the wide use of oral and visual techniques as the "exemplary lecturer" in contradistinction to merely "oral" or "visual" lecturers.[36] Unless teachers are charismatic speakers they should by all means learn to integrate audio-visual materials into their lecture presentations. However, the teaching presence remains the same: distant, teacher-centered, and focused on the generality of students.

In regard to "canned" lectures, those given in an empty studio for large nameless audiences or individuals who will watch at different times and places, these represent a regress of the teaching form back toward dissemination/transmission. The main reason is depersonalization. Brian Simpson has put it well:

An effective lecturer is aware of and responsive to the reactions of his students; this is not possible for someone lecturing in the vacuum of a studio. Also, an important motivator for students is the atmosphere created in the room by the lecturer. The same kind of atmosphere is not created by a televised talking head.[37]

Simpson points out that the only situation in which television has an important edge over alternative media is where a remote audience is shown something it could not otherwise see such as the behavior of wildlife in a distant country, the inside of a nuclear reactor, or a lecture by a uniquely brilliant lecturer.[38]

The place of the textbook in the lecture context depends on the type of connections the teacher wants to set up. If the text is meant to be the main instructional tool in the course then lectures can be used in the following ways: to introduce and advertise the text; to highlight aspects or main points of the text; to explicate particularly difficult passages or chapters in the text; to cover things not in the text; to critique the text.

If the text is meant to be subservient to the lectures then it should be used primarily as a reference tool (problems, quotes, scenes, illustrations, graphs, etc.) As McKeachie points out, the effectiveness of the lecturer over the text is that he or she provides a living model of scholarship or problem-solving, and in certain areas can make the text come more alive through an intelligent or heartfelt reading.[39] Put briefly, in the Lecturer/Dramatist Form the textbook should augment the teacher's presence, not replace it.

NOTES

1. John McLeish, *The Lecture Method. Cambridge Monographs on Teaching Methods*, No. 1. (Cambridge, England: Cambridge Institute of Education, 1968), p. 1.

2. Ibid., p. 1.

3. Quoted in McLeish, *The Lecture Method*, p. 2.

4. Wilbert J. McKeachie, *Teaching Tips: A Guidebook for the Beginning College Teacher* (Lexington, Mass.: D. C. Heath & Company, 1978), pp. 25–26.

5. To mention just a few of these studies: William E. Cashin, "Idea Paper No. 14: Improving Lectures," *Center for Faculty Evaluation and Development* (Manhattan, Kansas: Kansas State University, September 1985); Heather Dubrow and James Wilkinson, "The Theory and Practice of Lectures," in *The Art and Craft of Teaching*, ed. Margaret Morganroth Gullete (Cambridge, Mass.: Harvard University Press, 1982); Kenneth E. Eble, *The Craft of Teaching: A Guide to Mastering the Professor's Art* (San Francisco: Jossey-Bass Publishers, 1979), pp. 42–53; Joseph Lowman, *Mastering the Techniques of Good Teaching* (San Francisco: Jossey-Bass Publishers, 1984), pp. 96–118; Wilbert J. McKeachie, *Teaching Tips: A Guidebook for the Beginning College Teacher*, pp. 22–34. Two older works which have helpful chapters on lecturing are Jacques Barzun, *Teacher in America* and Gilbert Highet, *The Art of Teaching* (New York: Vintage Books, 1954).

6. Dubrow and Wilkinson, "The Theory and Practice of Lectures" p. 32.

7. Raymond P. Perry, "Instructor Expressiveness: Implications for Improving

Teaching," in *New Directions For Teaching and Learning: Using Research to Improve Teaching*, eds. J. C. Donald and A. M. Sullivan. (San Francisco: Jossey-Bass Publishers, 1985), pp. 35–49. See also Howard R. Pollio, "What Students Think and Do in College Lecture Classes," in *Teaching-Learning Issues*, no. 53 (Spring, 1984) University of Tennessee: Learning Research Center, p. 16.

8. Joseph Epstein, *Masters: Portraits of Great Teachers* (New York: Basic Books, Inc., 1981).

9. Pollio, "What Students Think About and Do in College Lecture Classes," p. 11.

10. Barzun, *Teacher in America*, p. 38.

11. Vivian Hodgson, "Learning From Lectures," in *The Experience of Learning*, ed. Ferrence Marton, Dai Hounsell and Noel Entwistle (Edinburgh: Scottish Academic Press, 1984) pp. 99–101.

12. Alice Hornung, "Teaching As Performance," *The Journal of General Education* 31, no. 3 (Fall, 1979): p. 193.

13. Terry Kirkpatric, "Dartmouth Professor Cries and Bleeds the Languages," *The Sunday Bulletin*, 16 April 1978.

14. Ibid., p. 10.

15. Robert M. W. Travers, "Training the Teacher as Performing Artist," *Contemporary Education* 51, no. 1 (Fall, 1979): 14–18.

16. Eble, *The Aims of College Teaching*, p. 4.

17. Such an impact on a particular student would probably take this particular act of teaching over into the Initiatory Mode.

18. McLeish, *The Lecture Method*, p. 32.

19. Cashin, "Idea Paper No. 14: Improving Lectures," p. 1.

20. Dubrow and Wilkinson, "The Theory and Practice of Lectures," pp. 25–26.

21. Cashin, "Idea Paper No. 14: Improving Lectures"; Michael J. Dunkin "Research on Teaching in Higher Education," in *Handbook of Research on Teaching*, ed. Merlin & Wittrock (New York: MacMillan Publishing Co., 1986), p. 756.

22. Menges, "Instructional Methods," p. 570.

23. McLeisch, "The Lecture Method," p. 5; Also, D. A. Bligh, *What's the Use of Lectures?* (Harmondsworth, Middlesex, England: Penguin, 1972), p. 70.

24. See McKeachie, *Teaching Tips*, pp. 74–76.

25. Marshall Gregory, "If Education is a Feast, Why Do We Restrict the Menu?: A Critique of Pedagogical Metaphors," *College Teaching* 35, no. 3 (Summer, 1987): p. 103.

26. Menges, "Instructional Methods," p. 570.

27. McLeisch, "The Lecture Method," p. 32; See also Cashin, "Improving Lectures," pp. 1–2. Beard and Hartley mention that teachers of science consider that lecturing is the best method to open up difficult topics which students cannot understand unaided. (Ruth M. Beard and James Hartley, *Teaching and Learning in Higher Education*, New York: Harper & Row Publishers, 1984 p. 154.) An advantage closely allied with this is when the professor uses the lecture as a model of the researcher or scientific discipline's thinking process. See Zdenek Valenta's interesting essay, "To See a Chemist Thinking," in *Teaching in the Universities: No One Way*, ed. Edward F. Sheffield (Montreal: McGill-Queen's University Press, 1974), pp. 54–60.

28. David Bergman, "In Defense of Lecturing," *Association of Departments of English Bulletin* 76 (Winter 1983), pp. 49–50.

29. Glassman, "The Teacher As Leader," in *New Directions For Teaching and Learning: Improving Teaching Styles*, p. 9.

30. For example, see Margaret Buchmann, "Role Over Person: Morality and Authenticity in Teaching," *Teachers College Record* 87, no. 4 (Summer 1986): 529–543. Also, Carl Perternite, "Teaching Philosophy and Methods: A Developmental Perspective," in *New Directions for Teaching and Learning: Revitalizing Teaching Through Faculty Development*, ed. Kenneth E. Eble (San Francisco: Jossey-Bass Publishers, 1983), p. 65.

31. Noel Entwistle, *Styles of Learning and Teaching*, pp. 267–268.

32. Charles Rivers, Jr., "The Teacher As Performing Artist," *Contemporary Education* 51, no. 1 (Fall, 1979): 9.

33. Peter J. Frederick, "The Lively Lecture—8 Variations," *College Teaching* 34, no. 2 (Spring, 1986): 43–50. Wilbert J. McKeachie, "Lecturing" in *Teaching Tips: A Guidebook For the Beginning College Teacher*, pp. 22–23; Dean Osterman, *The Feedback Lecture: The Process and Components*, a text used by Osterman, Oregon State University, 1980. Also, H. Douglas Johnson, "How To Give Up Lecturing For Fun and Profit," *American Journal of Pharmaceutical Education* 38 (May 1973): pp. 85–88.

34. Axelrod, *The University Teacher As Artist*.

35. Frederick, "The Lively Lecture—8 Variations."

36. See Beard and Hartley, *Teaching and Learning in Higher Education*, p. 157.

37. Brian Simpson, "Heading For the Ha Ha," in *The Computer in Education: A Critical Perspective*, p. 88.

38. Ibid., p. 88.

39. McKeachie, *Teaching Tips: A Guidebook For the Beginning College Teacher*, p. 26.

Part Two

Initiatory Mode

We have seen that even the most effective employment of the Lecturer/ Dramatist Form leaves the teacher removed and somewhat detached from the more intimate and creative forms of teaching. As Joseph Axelrod has pointed out: "To be an artist at teaching ... requires a professor to have relationships with students that are of a different sort from those that students enter into with the professor who is a lecturer-artist or a teacher-craftsman"[1]— these latter two being experts at didactic, i.e. teacher-centered modes of teaching.

To achieve this the teacher must shift into a new mode on the continuum, a mode we will call Initiatory. It is here that the professor creates the stimulative and catalytic forces which introduce students directly into the learning process. Within the two teaching forms set out here relational encounters are established which include some reciprocity; the student is both attracted and confronted in a more individualized manner than was possible in the Presentational Mode.

For their part, students in freely responding to the invitation of the teacher begin to see learning in a new light, one which motivates them to become a more active participants in the educational process. This change, along with the bond of trust created allows the teacher to challenge the students to leave the familiar and move on to new ground. As the questioning process grows students are awakened both to their previous ignorance as well as to the possibilities of new educational growth.

Though the teacher is still the dominant force in these two forms, she has moved the student sufficiently (on both cognitive and affective levels) so that a fundamental change in awareness takes place, one which will result in a more active engagement with subject matter and learning materials. It is also the Initiatory Mode that serves as the gateway to an educational intimacy wherein teacher and students will, in the words of R. S. Peters, "participate in the shared experience of exploring a common world."[2]

In some ways this is the most risk laden of the teaching modes. If the teacher fails here to engage the student, access to more student-centered forms of teaching and learning is delayed. When he or she succeeds the real purpose of teaching—that of helping students take control of their own learning—comes into view.

NOTES

1. Axelrod, *The University Teacher As Artist*, pp. 229–230.
2. R. S. Peters, "Education As Initiation," in *Philosophical Analysis and Education*, ed. Reginald D. Archambault (London: Routledge & Kegan Paul, 1965), p. 105.

Chapter 3

Teacher As Inducer/Persuader

The real task of a professor is to enable the learner to enjoy
learning.

Mihaly Czikszentmihalyi

With the Initiatory Mode the teaching presence becomes more authentic and
personal. Whereas before the speaker or lecturer was embodied through a
series of representations or artifacts, the teacher now seeks to engage the
student directly and at closer quarters. In the first of the two forms within
the Initiatory Mode, the teaching presence shifts to one of beckoning or
invitation. The Inducer/Persuader Form is often called "motivational" or
"stimulative." But such terms do not express its full possibilities. The teacher's
intent now is to gain access to the student or students, to induce them to
open themselves. Some personalization will be a natural consequence.

Until now the pupil has stood on the portico to the house of learning; she
is now called—or better, invited—by the teacher to enter. Before this, the
student could remain at a distance, enjoying a certain solitude even as he
sampled, or was drawn, by certain images and models presented by the
lecturer/dramatist. As Cashin points out, lectures present a minimum threat
to students in that they are not required to involve themselves actively.[1] But
now the student is not as easily able to avoid direct contact with a teaching
presence. Through the teacher's inducement the student is asked to commit
himself in a more individualized and ongoing way.

The concern for learning desired here is more than simple acquiring of
information or concepts. If the student responds to the teaching presence a
change in consciousness will be forthcoming. She will begin to care about
learning through a personal encounter. She will, in fact, assume a new position

in reference to the teacher, one which if carried over into the next form, involves a reciprocity or firm engagement. Joseph Schwab, in "Eros and Education" has described how this encounter begins even in the first meeting of a new class as the teacher's gaze wanders to each of the anonymous faces he sees before him, faces unpredictable as to promise and performance. In this "wandering inspection" the students may signal their readiness to be regarded as persons. If this happens a start has been made:

> The teacher thus answers the awareness he feels in the student; he examines more closely the person who has signaled interest in him. In reciprocity, this new inspection is no longer felt by the student as mere curious awareness, but as awareness of himself as a person. More, the student feels his own movement from item to individuality, from anonymity to personality. And he is grateful.[2]

The teacher acquires the skills that come from this initial concern: She makes it a priority to learn her students names within the first few class meetings. She associates name with face and then (in her mind) with unique physical characteristics. After a few classes she is able to dispense with the rollsheet. As time goes on she further individualizes—for example during brief encounters on the way to and from class or around the campus.[3] Early in the semester, perhaps the first day of class, she allows the students to get acquainted with each other by putting them in small groups and allowing them to chat for a brief time.

In the classroom the teacher moves out to them, expanding the physical boundaries, seeking to overcome the obstacles to engagement set up by podiums, huge desks in the front of the room, lecture notes and other paraphernelia. (In fact, as much as he can he jettisons notes entirely, learning to keep a few main points on a prompt sheet to which he can refer.) He takes a relaxed and informal stance, coming closer to the class, allowing students to "feel" his presence. He moves around in the room, never staying in one place, giving his students numerous vantage points from which to become aware of him. All the teacher's mannerisms—eye movements, gestures, body postures—create an aliveness which is contagious and puts the students at a certain ease. The diminishing of anxiety and tension is crucial for the teacher to work effectively within the Inducer/Persuader Form.

Though the teacher in the Inducer/Persuader Form will try to have some general information about his students before the class meets, it is only through initiating classroom interaction that the awareness can become bilateral. The teacher gets to know his students in the full flow of classroom communication. He must become skilled at coordinating name with face, background information with the real person emerging in front of him, new revelations and impressions so that he can in a brief time individualize students without stereotyping them.[4]

These initial class meetings where the above activities take place are what

DeVito calls the "contact" relational stage in teaching where student and teacher communicate, nonverbally at first, and then, verbally; where personal appearance, facial expression, vocal tone, and manner of speaking operate simultaneously for both the students and the teacher. DeVito believes these first impressions are crucial for both parties since "confirmatory information is received more easily and retained longer than contradictory information."[5]

EMPHASIS ON THE STUDENT'S WORLD

The energies of the teacher in this regard move her out of the Presentational Mode—though it is true that some of the above skills can be employed in the service of lecture. But the two pillars of public speaking—eloquence and dramatization—are not central here. Students are engaged in a softer, subtler way as the teacher becomes more aware of their realm of interest. In fact, to achieve her purpose, the teacher must not only let the students keep that realm for a time, but must enter actively into it.

The teacher begins to cultivate in students a habit of trusting in their own natural powers. To do this he must first acknowledge the validity of their world. By so doing he acknowledges the inner worth of the students themselves. But more is involved here than just an occasional classroom example from "real life." The teacher must ease onto the students' wavelength as a ground for communication and show genuine interest. This is most readily achieved through listening.

To illustrate: A young woman approaches the professor on the topic of a paper due for an Introduction to Philosophy course, one in which she has been asked to sort out her values and life-goals, using some basic philosophical reasoning. She shows him a preliminary rough draft in which she describes her interests in astrology and deterministic theory, but in language that is a mixture of obfuscation and indirection scattered with surrealistic imagery. (She has never been in a philosophy class before.) This is not quite what the teacher had intended; he sees that the thinking process is blocked. But he is accepting of the student and decides to chat with her to see what develops. A conversation ensues in which the girl gradually loses her shyness. He learns much about her world view, her dreams and fears, the untimely loss of a father, the refuge taken in arcane arts and rock music, with the implication that the larger world presents a threat to her identity. As the teacher begins to grasp the context in which the student lives he also sees possibilities for gradually leading her to experiment with new thoughts and more articulate ways of communicating with her audience. After a while, he pushes, but gently: "What would you think about trying . . . ?" while reassuring her: "You wouldn't have to give up your way of seeing things, but you'd have different parts of your mind working in tandem."

In this example, the teacher has become aware of the student's unique subjectivity. The "de-objectification" which began with the move out of the

Presentational Mode continues now to the point where the pupil comes into focus as a person—though at this point the relationship is still uneven with the teacher being the active force. But through listening the professor has opened himself to viewing the student in her world and prepares to invite her to move beyond it. The student, in turn, feels a new kind of teaching presence, one which accepts her on her own ground. She may now risk an openness where change and experimentation with a different mode of thought could occur. In the case of extremely insecure or fearful students much more patience and individualized attention will be required before they will feel at ease enough to talk about themselves. The teacher may need special skills here.[6] Though the teacher in the Inducer/Persuader Form seeks to dissolve barriers natural to the Presentational Mode she must allow all her students that space of privacy and be circumspect in drawing them out. Many students, like the girl above, will readily proffer information about their lives in a conference, thus giving teacher and student a baseline on which to work. Others may be unsure—even awed (even though at first superficially attracted)—about entering into this new dimension with a teacher. Hence, a teaching presence is necessary which is soft and sympathetic, which allows trust to build slowly, which encourages and generally nudges the student toward educational growth.

In dealing with learning materials, the inductive teacher follows pretty much the pattern of instruction described by Whitehead as "the stage of romance" where "the subject matter has the vividness of novelty" and education proceeds through stirring the "ferment in the mind."[7] Memorization, even drill, if necessary, should be undertaken within a larger context, so that the student does not lose the interesting perspective which the teacher has created. Through the persuasive power of the teacher an imaginative new world can take shape before the student's eyes—be it the Middle Ages, an atomic structure, or the activity of a cancer cell. At the same time the instructor must not lose touch with the world of the student which he has entered. From a cognitive standpoint, David Ausubel has stressed this emphatically:

Subject matter content . . . is always, and can only be, learned in relation to a previously learned background of relevant concepts, principles in a particular learner, and information that makes possible the emergence of new meaning and enhances their organization and retention.[8]

A very definite "courting" process takes place here with reciprocity as the endpoint. The act of combining worlds—the familiar with the new—is the key to realizing the Inducer/Persuader Form. According to James Buswell, the teacher "will anticipate with ever-increasing facility just how his particular area of knowledge is most meaningful, just how it must be translated into the students's interests . . . "[9] What the teacher actually tries to do is to juxtapose worlds in such a way that the students can recreate theirs, incorporating the new possibilities. What makes this kind of process different from what the teacher does in the Lecturer/Dramatist Form is the reciprocity: Not only is the teacher affecting the student in a more individualized way, but the student is responding cognitively and emotionally.

It is therefore crucial that the teacher involve the student emotionally in learning. Teachers often fail to recognize how vital such involvement is. Reason and a life of the mind build on the foundation of feeling. Douglas Sloan has pointed out that a primary educational concern revolves around what the Scottish philosopher, John MacMurray, calls "emotional rationality" wherein feelings themselves, when properly developed and educated, work as our most penetrating and indispensable organs of cognition. It is only through a deep, feeling-awareness that we can come to know the qualitative dimension of life—in nature, in other persons, in ourselves. It is in this larger matrix of qualitative reality that all reason, including the logical and calculative, ultimately finds its ground.[10]

To achieve this, the teaching presence must be warm and caring, vital, engaging—a drawing in. The teacher with both verbal and non-verbal cues, creates a total ambit which the student enters. Even the sciences can be taught within this wider perspective. Alvin White, quoting Sui, speaks of the intuitive suggestiveness of mathematics where "Without extra courses or time [the teacher] can soak the mentality of the apprentice with suggestiveness. He can develop in the student an awareness of the ineffable sensing and feeling beyond the formulas and equations."[11]

Thus, teaching is more than mind to mind; it is in a most fundamental sense emotional and multi-dimensional, involving the whole person. Affective learning not only enhances the popularity of the subject matter in the student's eyes, but is the avenue to lifelong learning.[12] Teachers can be quite successful here if they can tap not only into students' previous academic knowledge, but also the life experiences the students brings to class, as we saw in the interview with the young woman.

Through all these energies something profound is taking place: The teacher is initiating the student into the whole enterprise of thinking and learning, preparing the foundation for a shift to a new way of seeing, one in which intellect, feeling, and imagination cohere. This shift, of course, parallels—perhaps is made possible by—developmental growth in the student which, of course, will not be at the same level for every member of a class. As the semester goes on it will be especially important for the teacher to recognize, not only the uniqueness of students' personalities, but also differences in levels of cognitive and emotional development. If he is dealing mostly with young students—say freshmen—he will ease them in their move from seeing the teacher as someone who has absolute answers to a kind of enchanter who invites them to enter the adventure of learning.[13]

RESPECTING STUDENTS' FREEDOM

Yet the relationship in the Inducer/Persuader Form is delicate. For as students' emotional and conceptual world is affirmed they become more vulnerable to the teacher's influence. In those who are more insecure deep, perhaps neurotic, needs may assert themselves which place the student too readily in the hands of an authority figure. This is an area where the teacher, fully aware of the form in which she is working, shows discernment and restraint. She continues to respect the student's inner freedom, even though the student may temporarily wish to abandon it. The act of inducing can never be replaced by seduction; persuasive urging can never give over to the indecent rhetoric of indoctrination. Just as in the Presentational Mode, unanswered judgements and ego-centric histrionics can corrode an authentic teaching form, so in the Initiatory Mode, invitation can be replaced by manipulation and, as we shall see in the following chapter, catalyzation by a relentless browbeating.

Seduction, in its literal definition, is a leading aside or astray. It is a betrayal of the teaching charge wherein respect for another's mystery or integrity is vitiated by manipulation for the teacher's own ends. The delicate handling of a specific teaching form becomes distorted into an abuse of power. What makes a teaching encounter authentic is the willingness of both parties to exchange in the assurance that actions will be free. The teacher shows much patience with his students, as well as a wariness in regard to his own agendas. The student is allowed to breathe freely; entering a student's world does not mean violating it. At the same time, the students must be given time to assess the teacher, to open slowly to that emotional-cognitive world the teacher not only represents, but now embodies in his person. The hand is extended—nothing can be forced.

Indoctrination, subversion, conditioning, and similar terms have a long history in the field of education and time and again have been used as false substitutes for authentic instruction. They represent, perhaps, the chief danger to teaching. A few theorists—Thomas Green in particular—have refused to exclude terms like indoctrination and conditioning from what he calls "the whole family of activities called teaching." But he leaves little doubt that such activities lie on the periphery and that instruction is centrally concerned with activities that display intelligence such as explaining, arguing, reasoning—in short the pursuit of truth.[14]

To indoctrinate someone is to impose and distort rather than invite, encourage, and inspire which are the chief teaching acts of the Inducer/Persuader Form. An encounter can never be fruitful where one of the parties seeks to subdue or manipulate the other. As the ground of discourse is rational understanding, acceptance, and emotional honesty, those who believe that a certain amount of seduction is natural to teaching either confuse the term with its distant cousin or else seek a short cut to learning which violates the student's integrity and will lead to negative results in the end.

In contrast, the soft suasion of the teacher is based on a respect for the student's mind along with its potential for growth. Thus, for example, in a freshman writing class the teacher will begin by asking pupils to describe elements of their world in their own way while she gradually urges them to speak more honestly and forthrightly. She will also be trying to know them as individuals through their writing and will search for various ways to allow that individuality to come out.[15] Slowly, the group takes on its own identity, one within which the separate individualities are highlighted rather than repressed. As this process ensues the students are subtly called to move gradually out of themselves on to new terrain—or better, to see themselves functioning on such terrain. Here the two forms of the Initiatory Mode can overlap. The student is both invited and challenged, yet within the ambit of an emerging identity as part of and apart from the group.

So too, in assigning reading materials, the teacher must avoid dogmatism and allow for personalized interpretations. Students will view the same scene or events from the vantage points of their own personality, belief systems, cultural backgrounds. These factors will make any reading a unique inter-action between student and text. This does not mean, however, that there can be no common sharing; acknowledged diversity creates its own kind of underlying unity, flexible and all-inclusive. Norman Holland stresses in *Five Readers Reading* that though the value-system of each individual personality is unique and distinctive of that individual, "the unique quality of its inte-gration does not violate its capacity for shared meaning in the familial or communal aspects of its symbolic integration."[16]

In discussing literature—a play, short story—the teacher constantly begins with scenes which relate back to the student's world, perhaps a sub-culture many of them can share. For example, he might begin a discussion of Willy Lowman's plight in *Death of a Salesman* by handing out verses from a current rock song describing one man's loneliness and isolation.

Within such a familiar world the teacher can not only share new principles and concepts; he can slowly induce his students to entertain new applications, more profound feelings, greater ambiguities. This touches on the category of "valuing" in Bloom's Taxonomy of educational outcomes. The same thing can be done with materials relating to the sciences, though obviously em-pirical laws and foundational principles are the same for everyone. Certain terms, names of phyla or chemical compounds—the "grammar" of science—are indispensable to any genuine pursuit of the subject. But after this is accomplished there is much that can be left to open discussion and individual approaches, especially regarding practical or new applications of a chemical compound or a principle of physics that relates to the students' realm of interest. The teacher's creativity need not be limited here.[17]

As he gradually energizes students to assume new tasks and perspectives his teaching presence sinks into their consciousness and a bond of trust is formed. And since he has not violated their freedom the trust created is authentic. It will survive the hardships of the next (Inquirer/Catalyst) form. With this trust comes openness to learning and the possibility of inner growth.

This is a two-sided process, however, with the teacher also benefiting from the student's new attention and the establishment of reciprocity. The gratitude on the part of the teacher is not the self-assurance that comes from being recognized, but rather from being helpful. As Schwab describes it:

Rather, he is grateful for that reassurance which arises from notice of usefulness, of neededness. In a sense, he is grateful for the student's gratitude, for the sign that he has been useful. It is a parallel of Descartes's 'Cogito, ergo sum.' I have affected, therefore I am.[18]

Thus, we see how the student's response aids, not only in reaffirming, but even creating the effectiveness of the teacher within a particular form. As Inducer/Persuader the teacher is buoyed by the student's involvement and the educational bond between them that is starting to take shape. His confidence grows. In freeing them to learn, he also frees himself and becomes more authentic.

A DEEPER PROBLEM: JUSTIFICATION OF TEACHING

At this juncture a profound difficulty needs to be faced, one which takes us to the very heart of teaching. The difficulty may be best formulated as a question: By what right does a teacher come to teach? How does any kind of teaching justify itself? A surface response can be offered easily enough. If the purpose of teaching is the handing on of society's cultural heritage or what Michael Oakescott calls "the heritage of human achievements" (Dilthe's "Geistige Welt") then the teacher or sage is the agent of civilization and has a general mandate from society at large. However, this is an extremely broad definition and would seem to include more than the professional teacher; it encompasses parents, relations, and various other authority figures within the community.[19]

A somewhat more restrictive purpose for teaching may be that found in transmitting the ideal of liberal education which centers around the rational tradition of the West, nicely summed up by Robert Pirsig as the "Church of Reason." Here, according to Pirsig, the teacher gives witness to this tradition and has a mandate to go on teaching even in the face of opposition or condemnation by a particular society or institution.[20] Thus, Socrates claimed to be performing a service to the state even in the face of his condemnation by the state. He said his mission from the gods overrode the command to cease doing what he did.[21]

A third way of attempting to resolve the difficulty is to say that some people are born to teach, almost as if there were a genetic disposition towards the activity. Being born to teach, of course, implies that people exist who need to be taught and seems to close the circle. Donald Vandenberg has pointed out that it is the nature of the child to require help, to need teaching.[22] Looked at in this manner the audience will always be there for the teacher.

However, these answers do not completely address the problem, especially in terms of college teaching. Teaching needs to be approached in another manner, one more relevant to our age and to young adults. In modern times, in Western societies at least, we have come to hold as the highest good a person's right to autonomy, a right accentuated today in Western law and in medical ethics. To put it Kantian terms, we must never treat persons other than as ends in themselves. Existentialism and phenomenology have internalized this position by viewing the individual as a unique subjectivity who creates out of his own freedom the life he will live. From this ontological freedom come the innumerable every day decisions made in regard to other subjectivities. This includes permissions granted to act upon the self. Some years ago, Paul Komisar called teaching an activity that is by its very nature "intrusive"—"a service masquerading as a gift," "a contrivance urged on teachers by conventional educational wisdom."[23] A. S. Neill has so emphasized the natural freedom of the child that he finds it nonsensical to impose "subjects" on students before they have indicated a desire to be taught.[24] If this be true then such an intrusion represents a violation of a person's autonomy. Teaching is not an "automatic" or neutral activity; it is invasive, intrusive. This is especially true in teaching contexts where one seeks to alter attitudes and existing frames of mind.

Thus, the "right" to teach exists only in regard to those individuals who have requested or agree to such a service. Just as—to follow Komisar's analogy—we would not allow someone to fix our car or tend to our body unless we had first contracted such a service through verbal agreements (excepting genuine emergency where the agreement is implicit), so we would not allow a teacher to attend to our mind unless such attendance has been previously agreed upon. All of this reinforces the need to respect the integrity and freedom of the student we encounter in higher education. By what right do we teach at all? Society's mandate? Genetic disposition? A teaching appointment? These are not enough. A teacher functions, in the end, by permission of the student, at least in regard to those changes which will touch him most deeply. Teaching requires, in Komisar's words, "a mutual confidence between teacher and pupil; each must have trust in the general credibility and veracity of the other."[25]

The obvious implication of this bond is not ordinarily noted in educational circles: If that trust dies the teaching contract can be broken. And if the trust was never attained the contract doesn't exist at all. (Students break it silently in the real world of the classroom, just as it is often made there in the silence of the heart.) This is a crucial issue in education and it needs to be in the forefront of a teacher's mind because most students within a school system do not ordinarily view themselves as autonomous individuals, at least in the true educational sense. Rather, they see themselves as survivors or achievers doing what they must to reach certain pragmatic ends (degree, job, money). They often allow their teachers to be inflicted on them, which most will agree is an intrusion of the first order. It is therefore the teacher who must be acutely aware of this problem, for it is in the Inducer/Persuader Form where the bond of trust is being created. The Initiatory Mode should represent a genuine initiation rather than a hoodwinking process, a snow job, or trial by force. Peter Elbow puts it well when he says that "students only learn to choose and motivate themselves in spaces cleared by freedom."[26] Those spaces must be created by the teacher.

The practical application of these insights can be disturbing. What should a teacher do in a university undergraduate setting when she sees that the bond of mutual confidence between her and a student is dissolving or has never been created? What does she do when she sees this happening between her and her entire class? Needless to say, this occurs far more often than we like to admit.

In fact, more attention should be given to setting up this contract in the first place. If we take a Kantian view of the person or a phenomenological perspective on autonomy it is obviously not enough to assume that mutual agreement exists by the fact that a student enters a classroom at the beginning of the semester. True, students have tacitly consented to submit themselves to "teaching" when they enrolled at the college and attend a particular class. If the course is one that students have elected or freely chosen then the acceptance of the teacher's service—even a desire for a particular teacher's service—can be more readily assumed. However, often even elective courses are not "freely" chosen. The course may be a required elective or the student may need credits in the discipline for graduation and this course is the only one available.[27]

But it remains the teacher's pedagogic responsibility to be sensitive to the issue and to engage students only if they indicate an openness to a teaching presence. This alertness becomes even more important in those contexts where deep attitudinal change is one of the objectives, as opposed to courses where learning of concepts and information recall is paramount. (The issue of teaching for change will be discussed more fully in the next chapter.) The teacher may even have to apprise her students of the true nature of the relationship by reminding them that they should not automatically assume she has the right to teach them. Existentialist educators have been aware of the necessity for quite some time. For example, Maxine Greene, in *The Teacher As Stranger* observes the teaching energy that holds true for both forms in the Initiatory Mode:

He [the teacher] will not impose values or virtues on students; he will pose questions, do what he can to move them toward increasing awareness, deepening conviction. Granting them dignity, freedom and autonomy (unless they are little children), he becomes a catalyst in the process of their self identification, their learning how to learn....[28]

For example, if the teacher senses that a bond between him and a particular class is dissolving he needs to discuss this problem with the class without being picayune or maudlin. In an atmosphere of openness they need together to identify problems that have cropped up: Has the teacher ignored the needs and interests of the class in the pursuit of his own agenda (syllabus)? Have certain individuals been allowed to dominate in the discussions or recitations at the expense of the rest? Have the class members become distracted by activities outside the course? Of course, it occasionally happens that the interfering factors cannot easily be brought out into the open. Delicacy, tact are in order here and the teacher may intuitively sense that further discussion will not be useful, that it may be best to pull back and allow for breathing room. In practical terms, this may mean leaving the students alone or setting up contexts where they can work in groups or study on their own. Whatever the case, the teacher's sensitivity is the key to both creating direct encounter while at the same time respecting students' autonomy. These matters are of great import here because it is in the Initiatory Mode of teaching where students' freedom can be most easily violated.

Tableau: A student sits in the back corner of a Freshman Composition class. It is a month and a half into the semester; he has been absent three times, rarely participates in class activities and hands some assignments in late. After a fourth absence, the teacher decides to address the problem privately with the student:

Ins.: Greg, I think we might have a problem.

Stu.: Really?

Ins.: Well, you've missed four times now and to tell the truth you don't seem very interested in the course.

Stu.: On no! I like the class.

Ins.: What about the absences?

Stu.: Well—as I mentioned when I saw you at the Mall—my car broke down on the way to school this morning. The other two times I was sick. One I overslept.

Ins.: Even so, you don't participate much when you are there. And a couple of assignments have been late. Are you bored or preoccupied?

Stu.: No! I just don't say much in class. That's the way I am. I'm sorry about the assignments.

Ins.: If you want you could switch to a different section. I mean—if there is a personality conflict with me or others in the class...

Stu.: Oh no! I like this class.

Ins.: Okay, fine! When I discussed my philosophy on absences at the beginning of
the semester did you agree with my reasoning?

Stu.: Yes—I won't miss anymore.

One of two possibilities exists here: The teacher has either misread the
student's behavior or (more likely) the student does not wish to express his
true feelings to the instructor. In either case, until the student indicates a
desire for more engagement he should be left alone as much as possible,
even if it means letting him go through the motions without getting involved.
This is not to say that the teacher should ignore the student—he is aware of
him now in a new way—but neither should he "push" the relationship. He
may quietly look for new ways to create encounter. But he should allow the
student his distance so long as he understands and adheres to certain ground-
rules (such as absentee policy) which were established and agreed on at the
beginning of the semester for the common good.[29] Beyond these preliminary
agreements the student has apparently chosen not to involve himself in any
bond with the teacher or the other class members. This is his prerogative.
No more can be done for now. The teacher must be scrupulously fair and
non-judgmental while the student is left in his freedom.

When group work is in progress the situation can be more difficult. To
what degree is an individual student allowed to refuse to participate? The
teacher has to work out an arrangement so that the others are not penalized
for the student's refusal. On the other hand, it may be wisest at times to allow
the students in any given group to resolve the situation on their own.

Though it is the main activity of the Inducer/Persuader teaching form not
only to interest the student in educational growth, but to provide for this by
creating that fundamental bond in which students agree to engage themselves
with the teacher, there is no bond of trust unless freely entered into.

INTRINSIC MOTIVATION TO LEARN

A vital goal for the teacher as Inducer/Persuader is that of setting the stage
for the student to become intrinsically motivated to learn. The teacher in this
form documents the mind's innate curiosity and creates contexts wherein
this curiosity can be demonstrated. The importance of stimulating this curiosity through a teaching presence cannot be overestimated since the teacher
is trying to impress upon the student a whole new way of thinking about
education. The sad truth is that students in most schools today do not become
intrinsically motivated to learn. In point of fact, the idea is never even
broached in many college classrooms, either directly or indirectly. Yet, it is
a prime function of the teacher as persuader to bring this possibility home
to students so that they can apply it to their own study habits. And it is best
done in ways that are pleasing and attractive. The grimness of educational

settings and of teachers through the centuries have been so thoroughly documented that it almost seems—as it surely has to countless numbers of
students—the word "learning" connotes lifeless drudgery. One thinks of
Einstein's hatred of the gymnasium and his subsequent statement about
schools that work with methods of fear, force, and artificial authority: "Such
treatment destroys the healthy feelings, the integrity, and self-confidence of
the pupils. All that it produces is a servile helot."[30]

Thus, the teacher needs primarily to approach learning as an enjoyable
activity. Mihaly Czikszentmihalyi, in his work on flow analysis declares the
creation of enjoyment as the fundamental purpose in teaching. Obviously,
the acquiring of information is important, but the real task of the professor
is to enable the learner to enjoy learning: "Education works when the student
becomes intrinsically motivated to acquire the information or the goals to
be transmitted; at that point, the major part of the teacher's task is accomplished."[31]

The most immediate and effective way of helping students to enjoy learning
is to make the teaching presence itself a joyful one. Both Czikszentmihalyi
and Kenneth Eble and have discussed this topic at length. Eble, in *The Aims
of College Teaching*, seeks to overturn the debilitating habit (a long standing
one) many teachers have of thinking that little is learned if there was shared
pleasure in a teaching lesson:

If we cannot as teachers perceive in shared joy some incitement to learning, some
evidence, circumstantial to be sure, that learning is going on, then we rob ourselves
of the joy that should be in our work, a circumstantial evidence in itself, of a shared
love of subject and others and ourselves.[32]

We have seen how in the lecture form the teacher's enthusiasm for her
materials can be a positive model for the students. Now, in more directly
inducing students to view learning as pleasurable the teacher accents the
educational process itself as much as her own involvement in the subject
matter. Here, as Czikszentmihalyi points out, there will be changes in the
students attitude and performance directly attributable to teacher's actions.
When a teaching encounter creates intense interaction the students are immersed in a flow which absorbs their total concentration, ruling out boredom
or distraction. Class activities take on a life of their own; the work becomes
enjoyable and rewarding. If the teacher has interspersed clearly structured
activities with the novel and unexpected, students find themselves moving
through class time with ease and surprise. This can even be true even of
classes in undesirable time slots. The following student comment from a
Composition class makes this clear:

If anyone had told me I could enjoy an English class at six in the evening after a full
day of school I would have called them crazy. Yet after three weeks I have yet to doze

off. In fact, the time seems to breeze by. Our professor seems up to one of the toughest jobs of any teacher—keeping 22 students awake for an hour and fifteen minutes after dinner.[33]

Czikszentmihalyi claims that a decisive structural factor in the student's enjoyment of learning is to create a balance of skills and challenges. These must be kept continually in tandem: "When challenges overwhelm skills, we feel anxious; when skills outweigh challenges, we feel bored. Flow occurs when we come close to matching the two."[34] The balance is constantly changing and the teacher who is tuned in to her students, both as an ensemble and as individuals, knows when to conclude an activity, how to shift course and head in a new direction. All of this depends on the teacher's ability, not only to create enjoyable learning experiences, but to assess feedback. The feedback need not always be explicit, quite often it is subtle. But she must have a distinct sense of whether the class is with her or not. Often it may take a number of weeks for teacher and students to be perfectly at ease with one another, for students to be more responsive, for things to gel. Creating and sustaining an encounter in the Inducer/Persuader Form has its own inherent rhythm and the teacher waits until that moment is reached in the course when everything comes together: students, structured activities, teacher. Such fusion can be more difficult to achieve in colleges with brief semesters because this kind of bonding cannot be forced. It comes when it comes. When it does the teacher is grateful; should it not come she feels at a loss. A self-consciousness returns indicating that the flow of enjoyable learning has either been interrupted or never created at all.[35]

For the professor, teaching in this manner has its own intrinsic rewards. He can discuss learning openly with the students while providing numerous examples. He can even share why he became a teacher or continues to teach. A teacher who is alive and creative and obviously enthusiastic about his craft, by that very fact, will initiate students into the joys of learning. The teacher here is not so much seeking to pass on something as he is helping create a new reality—a way of seeing chemistry or the writing process for the first time. Even reluctant students may find themselves coming alive in the presence of the teacher's self-disclosure.

For example, a teacher hands out to students a copy of the very rough draft of an essay he is working on for review. It is messy, almost unreadable, with arrows every which way and innumerable crossing outs. The students are surprised to learn that the teacher goes through the same writing stages as they do, that he, too, starts out with such scribbling. He then explains to the students (or even brings in later drafts) to show how the writing takes shape, how paragraphs are rearranged, sentences restructured, new words substituted. The teacher becomes more enthused about writing as he describes for the students how the essay starts to flow and reveal a form, how it begins to say what he wants it to. He assures them that the same things can happen to their piece of prose as they tinker with it and attempt to create form. He will stress that, in fact, this is how the thinking process itself works: a potpourri of ideas—many of them half-baked—tumbling into the mind for review.[36]

The teacher is persuading his students to see writing as an open-ended process rather than some fait accompli that takes place within their brain. He has shared his world with them, just as they have with him. And now their worlds don't seem so far apart. His enthusiasm is contagious. "Writing isn't so cut and dried," they begin to think. "He goes through exactly what we do. All kinds of trial and error. Maybe that's what learning is. This can be enjoyable—unpredictable." The change in attitude begins.

With such self-disclosure the teacher has also to a degree made himself vulnerable, brought himself down off the mountain. Students see that he is human just like they are; he struggles and learns in the same manner as they do. It is through this kind of connecting that the teacher strengthens the bond of trust.

PLAYFULNESS AND HUMOR IN TEACHING

What Dale Baughman calls the first commandment of teaching, "Thou shalt be interesting," is most relevant to making learning enjoyable.[37] We need no empirical evidence to prove that interested students learn better than uninterested ones. And from a foundation of creating interest, the teacher moves to build a learning community. In this task he has no greater ally than the integrated employment of humor. In fact, the whole notion of play is fundamental to any kind of learning, play which is relaxed, creative, spontaneous, and quite at home in the classroom. This is true not only for the early elementary grades, but all the way up the ladder. Alvin White describes how creative thinking can be fostered by the mathematics teacher in the college classroom:

If mathematics is approached in the spirit of playfulness, there are many possibilities for invention. Symbolic formulas can be translated into ordinary language and vice versa. Symbolic formulas can be turned upside down. Parts of formulas or procedures can be omitted, and the class can be challenged to reconstruct them. Procedures, concepts, and ideas from earlier times can be compared with current ones. In what way are they similar or different? Is the germ of the current concept evident in the earlier one?[38]

Playfulness is also extremely important for creating the foundation on which learning in the classroom rests: the reciprocity we have previously discussed. Jean Civikly cites "play" theorists who argue that affection and good will (qualities of play) motivate the humor, which in turn develops increased trust and interpersonal bonding.[39] When a teacher has achieved this in a classroom she has opened the way to maximum effectiveness in the Inducer/Persuader Form. Positive humor relaxes the students defenses—to the point where the teacher can make a point, reveal an insight, allow a new idea to flood into what was before guarded territory. The break-up in laughter is often a perfect prelude for the drawing of an extremely serious moral. Teachers who employ humor well, react to it well, and make it a vital part of their teaching presence probably have a most persuasive tool for inducing learning.

Research has shown that although it may not improve learning directly, the effective use of humor fosters a classroom climate conducive to learning. Major benefits include stimulating interest, establishing rapport, and maintaining attention. Thus, its use in the inductive form of teaching. Humor may be vital when students are unmotivated, although its effectiveness is questionable when high motivation (intentional learning) is already present. In these cases, direct humor, at least, may be distracting.[40]

It has been demonstrated, for example, that using humorous aids in science activities contributes to positive feelings about science and problem solving abilities in the student.[41] It has also been shown that relevant humor—especially when rehearsed (as in a test)—can greatly aid information acquisition and perhaps retention.[42] Students will long remember a humorous question on an exam as well as its answer. (Testing, in general, in the Inducer/Persuader Form, should be playful and imaginative, showing some originality.) Finally, everyone knows that humor breaks monotony and revives vigilance. In this sense, it facilitates learning.

On the college level, the use of *unrelated* humor can be detrimental to learning. Teachers using it, other than to break monotony, are perceived as being funny and may become well liked. But it does not necessarily help in involving students in learning and can, in certain instances, lower the student's respect for the professor.[43] However, *wit*, in the sense of integrated and related humor, especially if it is relevant to the particular group the teacher has gotten to know, appears to be a highly valued trait in college professors. Wit is the most intelligent use of humor, and shared wit in a classroom increases mental alertness, although until recently, at least, this quality seemed more valued in men teachers than in women.[44]

So we see that humor, when playful and used in the interests of establishing or maintaining the bond of trust in the classroom, is invaluable. It helps teacher and student become genuinely fond of each other. (I might add that humor emanating from the other side of the desk can achieve the same purpose.) At the same time, it knits up the emotional and cognitive in ways that keep academic exercises rich and holistic. However, humor is a two edged sword and caveats are in order. Without establishment of a relational base, teacher humor is perceived as more defense-arousing than supportive and may be more detrimental than using no humor at all.[45] Humor can be misused by the instructor to foment power. The putdown, sarcasm, the sexist comment work directly against what the teacher is trying to achieve in the Inducer/Persuader Form. Playful wit can quite easily drift into satirical remarks which inhibit reciprocity. Even irony—which undoubtedly has a place in teaching—can be misunderstood. Thus, the teacher has to be wise in the employment of such a powerful tool. Above all, the teacher must not appear to strain. While prepared humor, in the sense of planned placement, can be effective, effective teachers maintain a naturalness and use the kind of humor that fits their personality. Spontaneity—since it is creative and playful—is priceless. Through it a teaching presence flows into the students' being.

Teachers lacking a sense of humor are not only at a disadvantage, but can be a bane to learning or growth if they are morose or completely lack playfulness. At the very least, they will have great difficulty inhabiting the Inducer/Persuader Form. The history of education has provided far too many accounts of such teachers.

PERSONAL DISPOSITION OF TEACHER

Even beyond a sense of humor is the disposition of the teacher. To succeed in the Initiatory Mode teachers will know more than their subject, more even than something about the student's world. There must be a largeness of spirit, a certain deep aliveness that relates in diverse ways to the world. Gilbert Highet has described this necessary quality and I quote him at some length:

Teachers in schools and colleges must see more, think more, and understand more than the average man and woman of the society in which they live. This does not only mean that they must have a better command of language and know special subjects, such as Spanish literature and marine biology, which are closed to others. It means that they must know more about the world, have wider interests, keep a more active enthusiasm for the problems of the mind and the inexhaustible pleasures of art, have a keener taste even for some of the superficial enjoyments of life—yes, and spend the whole of their career widening the horizons of their spirit.[46]

Thus, teachers must be interesting human beings with varied pursuits and those interests come into play through the genial all-embracing disposition they project through their teaching presence. It is a disposition open not only to witticism, but to the serendipity quality of life itself. Play or laughter come from within and cannot be just surface techniques. It is this all-embracing attitude that "hooks" students into learning. Quite often, great teachers have attracted students just by the breadth and expanse of their characters

Unfortunately, the various and sundry pressures of academia quite often crush or inhibit this natural flow of the teacher's disposition. Temperaments like this are not always found among those whose first priority is research rather than teaching.[47] Yet such a universalist temperament is indispensable for an effective teaching presence in the Inducer/Persuader Form and for initiating students into the romance of learning which is the essential function of that form.

It remains only to point out that the element of play—even fun—in promoting learning should never create the impression that there is no hard work involved. While the teacher persuades students to consider learning as enjoyable (probably a new perspective for most of them) and thus moves them to want to learn for other than extrinsic reasons, they will know soon enough once they are "hooked" how much it costs to enter deeply into a genuine learning process. But there has already been too much of a dichotomy created between work and play in the modern world. It must be remembered, as Huizinga has reminded us, that man is not peripherally, but fundamentally, Homo Ludens.[48] One can love one's work despite the costs. And it is the creative play element in work that keeps it from becoming drudgery. Enthusiasm for learning, for intellectual and aesthetic sensibility, for growth of the deeper self can exact an exorbitant price. But precious few who have paid that price ever have any regrets. They are more alive, even though life has become more complex. And they often remember most vividly the teacher who has led them to this level of vitality.

SUMMARY

Thus, the teacher as Inducer/Persuader encounters students directly for the first time, and in doing so, initiates them into a new kind of flow. At the same time, while respecting their freedom to learn, the teacher leaves an impression of unique particularity and of possibilities yet untried in them. The students, in their turn, feel valued as learners; they sense a largeness of dimension and the beginning of a subtle change of direction in their energies. Reciprocity is created; commitment is broached. Those energies and that new commitment will be tested by the second teaching form of the Initiatory Mode.

INDUCER/PERSUADER

Characteristics of Teacher
- recognizes student as individual
- aware of and interested in students' world
- respects student's autonomy
- acknowledges student's unique subjectivity
- affirms student's innate powers
- aware of whole person, not just the mind
- accepts diversity and levels of development within class
- sensitive to communication breakdown

- joyfully incites to learning
- personally enjoys teaching
- playful in approach to teaching/learning
- spontaneous and informal
- appreciates being useful
- cultivates largeness and breadth of spirit

General Aptitudes

- finds ways to learn about students
- creates positive first impressions
- expands boundaries of classroom, through appropriate facial expression, gestures, body movements
- sets atmosphere for reciprocity
- moves onto students' wave length
- inspires students to believe in their abilities
- tactfully broaches and discusses communication problems
- accents previous knowledge and experience of students
- creates exercises and assignments which help students connect with their previous knowledge and experience
- uses assignments and activities which create novelty and fascination in regard to subject matter
- cultivates spontaneity and playfulness in classroom
- creates assignments which interweave cognitive and affective levels
- initiates students into "flow" activities involving relaxed concentration
- learns to sustain student interest by creating contrasting activities and assignments
- creates activities and assignments which balance use of skills with new challenges
- uses appropriate humor to induce learning; avoids misuse of humor
- shares own thinking and learning process with students
- becomes attuned to rhythms of academic semester

Student Aptitudes

- responds positively to teacher
- appreciates teacher's concern and respect
- learns to trust in teacher
- personally relates to teacher
- gains confidence in self and abilities
- is more attentive and receptive
- becomes activated and finds satisfaction in responding
- learns the value of relaxed concentration through "flow" activity

- sees learning as enjoyable and playful rather than boring or anxiety-ridden
- sees that learning is more than memory and reproduction
- begins to view habitual world in new ways
- connects previous knowledge and experience with new world of subject matter
- sees broader aspects of subject
- reads/studies out of interest and for understanding
- begins to make personal investment in learning
- appreciates humor in classroom
- becomes more aware of other class members
- begins move toward intrinsic motivation in learning

NOTES

1. Cashin, "Idea Paper No. 14: Improving Lectures," p. 2.

2. Joseph Schwab, "Eros and Education: A Discussion of One Asset of Discussion," in *Science, Curriculum, and Liberal Education: Selected Essays*, ed. Jan Westbury and Neil J. Wilkof (Chicago: University of Chicago Press, 1978), pp. 110–111.

3. See "The Classroom Territory," in *The Teaching Professor*, ed. Maryellen Weimer, 4, no. 2 (February 1990): 3.

4. One common way to learn about students early on is to pass out index cards the first day and ask information that is not on a roll sheet such as previous schools they attended, places they have lived, why they enrolled in this course (if the choice was theirs), outside interests they have. The teacher can refer back to these from time to time as she gets to know the student and a fuller picture emerges.

5. Joseph A. DeVito, "Teaching as Relational Development," in *New Directions For Teaching and Learning: Communicating in College Classrooms*; ed. Jean M. Civikly (San Francisco: Jossey-Bass Publishers, 1986), p. 54.

6. This is not to say that the teacher should assume the role of counselor or psychologist. There may be a fine line here at times, but as a rule that line should not be crossed unless the teacher has some background training in these areas.

7. Alfred North Whitehead, *The Aims of Education* (New York: Mentor Books, 1949), p. 28.

8. David P. Ausubel, *Educational Psychology: A Cognitive View*, 2nd edition (New York: Holt, Rinehart & Winston, 1978), pp. 208–09.

9. Quoted in Sister Marie Brinkman, S.C.L., "On Teaching and Learning," *Teachers College Record* 75, no. 3 (February 1974), p. 376.

10. Sloan, *The Computer in Education: A Critical Perspective*, p. 4. See also Joseph Katz and Mildred Henry, *Turning Professors into Teachers: A New Approach to Faculty Development and Student Learning* (New York: Macmillan Publishing Company, 1988), pp. 22–24.

11. Alvin M. White, "Teaching Mathematics as Though Students Mattered," in *Teaching as though Students Mattered: New Directions For Teaching and Learning*, ed. Joseph Katz (San Francisco: Jossey-Bass Publishers, 1985), p. 40.

12. Janis F. Anderson, "Instructor Nonverbal Communication: Listening to Our

Silent Messages," in *New Directions for Learning: Communicating in College Classrooms* ed. Jean M. Civikly (San Francisco: Jossey-Bass Publishers, 1986) p. 48.

13. Most educators are familiar with William Perry's research on student cognitive development wherein the student moves from viewing issues in bi-polar terms (dualism) through various stages culminating in an ultimate stage of "contextual relativistic reasoning." I believe these stages would roughly parallel a maturing process in the student wherein a gradual movement takes place from teacher-centered, passive learning to a more active student-centered involvement. The teaching forms of the Initiatory Mode would be crucial in helping students begin that movement. For a summary and discussion of Perry's scheme and its implications for liberal education, see Patricia Bizzell, "William Perry and Liberal Education" in *College English*, 46 (5) (Sept., 1984): 447–57.

14. Green, "A Topology of the Teaching Concept," pp. 28–62.

15. A number of writing teachers/theorists have suggested ways to help to help students focus on their own experiences in writing. For example, see Ken Macrorie, *Telling Writing* (Rochelle Park, New Jersey: Hayden Book Company, Inc., 1970); also, Peter Elbow, *Writing Without Teachers* (New York: Oxford University Press, 1973).

16. Norman N. Holland, *Five Readers Reading* (New Haven: Yale University Press, 1975), p. 241.

17. For a pertinent discussion of such possibilities in the social sciences see Jaroslav Havelka, "From the Known to the Unknown," in *Teaching in the University: No One Way*, pp. 138–174. In the natural sciences see Peter G. Markow, "Teaching Chemistry Like the Foreign Language It Is," in *Journal of Chemical Education* 65, no.4 (April, 1988): 346–47. Also, Robert Pool, "Freshman Chemistry Was Never Like This" *Science*, 248 (April 1990): pp. 157–158.

18. Schwab, "Eros in Education," p. 111.

19. Michael Oakescott, "Learning and Teaching" in *The Concept of Education*, ed. R. S. Peters (New York: Humanities Press, 1967), pp. 157–158. For a refutation of the idea that anybody can teach see Passmore, *The Philosophy of Teaching*, pp. 23–24.

20. Robert Pirsig, *Zen and the Art of Motorcycle Maintenance* (New York: Bantam Books, 1974), pp. 142–47.

21. Plato, "The Apology," in *The Dialogues of Plato*, vol. I, ed. & trans. B. Jowett (Oxford: The Clarendon Press, 1953), pp. 329–66.

22. Donald Vandenberg, "Phenomenology and Educational Research," in *Existentialism and Phenomenology in Education: Collected Essays*, p. 198. It is also problematic because it implies that teaching skill cannot be learned. Maryellen Weimer describes this as one of the three obstacles to teaching development. See Maryellen Weimer, *Improving College Teaching: Strategies for Developing Instructional Effectiveness* (San Francisco: Jossey-Bass Publishers, 1990), pp. 5–7.

23. B. Paul Komisar, "Is Teaching Phoney?" *Teachers College Record*, 70, no. 5 (February, 1969): 407–11.

24. A. S. Neill, *Summerhill: A Radical Approach to Child Rearing* (New York: Hart Publishing Company, 1960), pp. 4–5. Jon Wagner also asks how a profession can develop integrity of practice if even its most expert performers play only to captive audiences. Teachers keep "trying to trick students into assuming responsibility for their part of a bargain they never struck themselves." See Jon Wagner, "Chefs and Teachers: A Hypothetical Exchange about Real Problems of Strengthening the Teaching Profession," *Teachers College Record*, 89, 2 (Winter 1987): 244.

25. Komisar, "Is Teaching Phoney?," p. 410–11. See also Wayne Booth, *The Vocation of a Teacher: Rhetorical Occasions 1967–1988* (Chicago: University of Chicago Press, 1988), p. 253.

26. Peter Elbow, *Embracing Contraries: Explorations in Learning and Teaching* (New York: Oxford University Press, 1986), p. 77.

27. In the case of children or minors the freedom issue shifts to the parents. But even here, as A. S. Neill has pointed out, subjects, even schooling itself, cannot be forced on children.

28. Maxine Greene, *Teacher As Stranger: Educational Philosophy For the Modern Age* (Belmont, California Wadsworth Publishing Company, 1973), p. 286. Other educators with an existentialist/phenomenological bent consider it the highest priority to free the student from the teacher. We will observe this in detail when treating the more student-centered teaching forms on the continuum. See Van Cleve Morris, *Existentialism In Education: What It Means*, (New York: Harper & Row Publishers, 1966); William A. Adams, *The Experience of Teaching and Learning: A Phenomenology of Education*.

29. One possible way of addressing the problem of freedom is obviously contract grading wherein teacher and learner agree right at the beginning of a course. We will discuss contract grading in Chapter 6.

30. Ronald W. Clark, *Einstein: The Life and Times* (New York: Avon Books, 1971), p. 31.

31. Mihaly Czikszentmihalyi, "Intrinsic Motivation and Effective Teaching: A Flow Analysis," in *New Directions for Teaching and Learning: Motivating Professors To Teach Effectively* ed. J. L. Bess (San Francisco: Jossey-Bass Publishers, 1982), p. 18.

32. Eble, *The Aims of College Teaching*, p. 50.

33. Anonymous freshman paper, Freshman Composition class, Fall, 1990, Philadelphia College of Pharmacy and Science.

34. Czikszentmihalyi, "Intrinsic Motivation and Effective Teaching," p. 22.

35. See Linc Fisch, "Getting a Class to Gel" *The Teaching Professor*, 4, no. 2 (February 1990): pp. 1 and 2. Czikszentmihalyi gives a number of ways that classroom structure can inhibit flow activity and thus enjoyment in teaching, including largeness of class size, students with widely different levels of preparation, structural adversary relationships between teacher and students (as in required courses). See "Intrinsic Motivation and Effective Teaching," p. 24.

36. The simultaneity of the writing-thinking process, or better, the dialectical relationship between thought and language is described at length by Ann Berthoff in *Forming, Thinking, Writing: The Composing Imagination* (Rochelle Park, N. J.: Hayden Book Company, Inc., 1978).

37. M. Dale Baughman, "Teaching With Humor: A Performing Art," *Contemporary Education*, 51, no. 1 (Fall, 1979): 26.

38. White, "Teaching Mathematics as Though Students Mattered," p. 43. More recently John Paulos, in discussing mathematical illiteracy, indicts both teachers and textbooks for excluding the element of playfulness in their instruction, a playfulness that gives the subject its essential affinity with humor. See John Allen Paulos, *Innumeracy Mathematical Illiteracy and Its Consequences* (New York: Hill & Wang, 1989).

39. Jean M. Civikly, "Humor and the Enjoyment of College Teaching," *New Directions For Teaching and Learning: Communicating in College Classrooms*, pp. 61–70.

40. P. E. McGhee and J. H. Goldstein, eds. *Handbook of Humor Research—Vol. 2: Applied Studies* (New York: Springer-Verlog, 1983).

41. James H. Vandersee, "Humor As a Teaching Strategy," *The American Biology Teacher*, 44 no.4 (April, 1982): 212–18.

42. McGhee and Goldstein, eds., *Handbook of Humor Research*, p. 179.

43. Ibid., p. 186.

44. Ibid., p. 187.

45. A. L. Darling & J. M. Civikly, "The Effect of Teacher Humor on Classroom Climate," in *Improving University Teaching, Contributed Papers*, Tenth International Conference, vol. 3 (Maryland: College Park, 1984), pp. 798–805.

46. Highet, *The Art of Teaching*, p. 49.

47. Morris Kline makes this point bluntly in regard to mathematics professors whose primary interest is research. He claims they often choose research "partly because mathematics per se does not pose the complex problems that are involved in dealing with human beings." I suspect these sentiments could be applied to many professors in the sciences whole primary focus is research. See Morris Kline, *Why The Professor Can't Teach: Mathematics and the Dilemma of University Education* (New York: St. Martin's Press, 1977), p. 80.

48. Johan Huzinga, *Homo Ludens: A Study of the Play Element in Culture* (Boston: Beacon Press, 1950).

Chapter 4

Teacher As Inquirer/Catalyst

The educator is by his very nature a disturber of the peace.
                    John Anderson, speaking of Socrates

With the second teaching form of the Initiatory Mode, the professor, relying on the preliminary bond of trust now formed, moves into a more trenchant teaching presence, one which challenges the student to grow and learn in ways that before this could not have been attempted. As in the Inducer/ Persuader Form, the encounter is direct, but now more forceful. If anything, rapport must be greater because the teacher can only confront pupils in this manner where a relationship has been established. The scope of this teaching form ranges from a mild dose of subject inquiry at one end to the relentless questioning which catalyzes students to take up their own search at the other. The teacher will most likely succeed in this form if students have already taken some preliminary steps toward committing themselves to learning. Even within the form itself the teacher must often proceed by degrees. Should he begin with the sharper catalytic techniques the encounter may be cut short by student withdrawal.

The Inquirer/Catalyst Form is not only where the teacher challenges students to acquire new knowledge, but dares to confront students' ignorance, their unspoken assumptions and prejudices. Here doubt replaces belief, skeptical questioning usurps uncritical acceptance, and the student's mental world is revealed as inadequate. Unless the teacher proceeds adroitly she risks rejection. What she must do is create (or have already created) in the students enough fascination and curiosity about the new to balance the dissonance and discomfort they will feel in relinquishing the old. Barzun has put it well in discussing the inner dialogue between opposite feelings that goes on in the student's mind: "The whole secret of teaching—and it is no secret— consists in splitting the opposition, downing the conservatives by making an alliance with the radicals so that [the student's] curiosity and desire to grow up may be aroused to action.[1]

The Inquirer/Catalyst can risk confronting the student's complacency if the relationship has already moved beyond initial impressions and preliminary contact to a stage of involvement where, according to DeVito, there can take place "a testing of personalities and relational dispositions by both parties."[2] The motivation for testing is different, however, for student and for teacher. Joseph Schwab points out that soon after establishment of personal relations the student may engage in an active, personal testing of the teacher's judgement. This testing manifests itself in behaviors which are false or distracting from the business of the moment. They are designed to be provocative, to indirectly ascertain a teacher's instructional integrity and can range anywhere from the raising of irrelevant issues to disruptive classroom behavior. The student wants to see whether the teacher will remain secure in his authority or allow himself to be seduced.[3] An appropriate response is called for, one which according to Schwab "is not always easy, for it must take a form which does not reject the student along with his offer."[4] If the teacher copes successfully with the situation, if he stays on course without being diverted while at the same time affirming in the student what William Adams has called the "metaself"[5] the relationship, instead of being threatened, will be even stronger. In the student's mind the teacher will have passed the test; he is to be relied on. The trust will increase.[6]

The testing and inquiry on the teacher's part is provocative in a deeper sense. Building on an original trust, putting faith in the stability of their encounter from the previous form (Inducer/Persuader), the teacher now centers on challenging the student both to recognize his present state of ignorance and to try out new ways of thinking or valuing. All learning involves leaving something behind, even if that something be only the refusal to work at the solution for an apparently insoluble quadratic equation.

This process is called educating for change and it has ancient precedent. Such a form of teaching produces conflict and a considerable tension. For the teacher has now moved to an adversarial position in which he tests the mind, challenges students' beliefs, and even shocks them into reconsidering what they have long taken for granted. He has become an enemy to one half of the student's psyche. John Rassais, a teacher of languages at Dartmouth University, has put the matter in its harshest form: "Teaching should be like the fire of hell, burning away inhibition that blocks communication and prejudice that prevents sensitivity."[7] John Wilson, in "Two Types of Teaching" has put it in more moderate terms, yet he is just as unsparing:

The teacher's first job is to have this out (reduction to ignorance) and to demolish the inner complacency which we all have ... Proper education, like proper psychoanalysis, is *disturbing*. There is bound to be a transference of some kind between pupil and teacher, because if the teacher does his job properly emotions will be let loose.[8]

The process is most obvious in learning contexts which deal with common knowledge, social attitudes, personal values, and metaphysical or religious underpinnings. Very often the Inquirer/Catalyst helps students move from a dualistic to a relativistic stage in their education, one where they confront multiplicity, ambiguity, and pluralism—often for the first time.[9] But the form is also involved in the learning of new concepts and structures or even on the level of basic skills such as the handling of a new language. As we saw in the last chapter cognitive and affective realms are interconnected. Resistance to a change in attitude can also inhibit progress in learning course material.

THE RANGE OF INQUIRY

Teaching in the Inquiry/Catalyst Form begins with the asking of questions and centers around the very nature of questioning. The purpose is both to sound the student out and to provide a pattern of questioning which students can gradually internalize. The teaching presence itself becomes a model for this questioning—and later for the questing mind. In this chapter I will posit five general levels of question-asking, moving from the simplest and most one-dimensional to the more sophisticated and probative in terms of learning. We can observe in this sequence a gradual shifting from mimetic to transformative goals in education.

A) Simple Recitation Pattern. Students, having studied assigned materials, are now asked about those materials—what Kolcaba calls "response questions."[10] Inquiry at this level belongs more to previous teaching forms. So called "objective" testing often uses this superficial kind of questioning. The only inquiry taking place in the question is the severely limited one of asking for verification or proof (true/false questions). Napell has pointed out that too often teacher's questions become fixated at the informational level, requiring of students only that they recall bits and pieces of rote-memorized data: "What is the formula for finding the force between two charges?" "What are the years usually ascribed to the writing of the Bible?" "What is the definition of 'quantity demanded'?"[11] Kolcaba adds that "one cannot fully learn how to pursue learning as a goal-directed activity through working exclusively with questions of this type."[12] No more needs to be said about such questioning except to point out that quite a bit of testing in higher education deals with this reductive level.

B) Questions Arising From Informational Understanding. Here students are asked to move beyond the information sought (schema questions) to comprehension and analysis. For example, the history teacher inquires of a student: "From your review of the reasons for the First World War which one seems most important and why?" Here we also are dealing with an informational context, but an appeal is being made to student's analytic ability, as well as recall. Again, follow-up questions on the definition of a drug and its properties might be: How does this drug work in the body? Given a specific diagnosis, what would you do? Suppose the patient is non-compliant? The lab instructor or supervisor of interns is asking the student to lift off the informational base and engage in higher thinking skills: application, evaluation, problem-solving. The instructor pushes, but gently. Questions like these are also called "interpretative" by Kasulis. They are quite commonly used in higher learning.[13]

C) Questions That Open Out to New Questions. Here a gradual or inductive process of questioning takes place, one which leads to moments of revelation (answers) which, in turn, raise new questions carrying their own momentum. The student begins to view the inquiry process as a search which opens up more and more territory. The questioning here can either be convergent or divergent. In the former the student, for example in a scientific discipline, moves toward a synthesis involving closure, but at broader levels. In addressing these questions he learns appropriate strategies for investigation. In the case of divergent questioning, things are deliberately left open-ended.[14] Here the student begins to feel lost, to feel that it's all getting beyond him, unmanageable. Yet the new horizons created by these "unexpected problems" bring a fresh wonder, a unique stimulation. Such questions engage the student in what Kolcaba calls "a dialogue with the unknown."[15] The teacher, and consequently the student, who learns to employ them brings a greater number of inquiry skills into play, those of a more creative nature such as hypothesizing and problem raising.

Two branches of inquiry can develop at this level: The first explores the range of a subject discipline. Answers only lead to new questions and insights. The teacher does not reveal these insights, but galvanizes students to see that they must use their own mental powers to procure them. This activity belongs to what Israel Scheffler calls "the Insight Model of Teaching" wherein the teacher's task "is not to impress his statements on the student's mind for later reproduction," but by making them "instrumental to the student's own search of reality and vision thereof . . . teaching is consummated in the student's own insight."[16] The process also parallels Perkinson's "Darwinian theory of learning" which has the teacher push students to hold a scientific theory only so long as it survives the rigors of examination and questioning.[17] This, of course, is how the scientific enterprise itself proceeds. It also conforms to the picture of Socrates as the paradigm of the relentless questioner, even of his own ideas.[18]

The second branch of inquiry includes those questions which involve a transfer from subject discipline over to the realm of allegiances and attitudes, values and meaning—what is traditionally called "the affective domain."[19] For

example, during a course in American History, a discussion of this nation's
practice of subduing smaller nations and peoples in the Western hemisphere
(exemplified by specific battles, treaties, usurpments) can lead to the question
of how committed we really have been to democracy (a people's right to
self-government), and further to the question of whether a nation that employs
such tactics can hold itself to be a democracy at all. The politically naive
student is moved via this inquiry process to consider a new perspective on
his country along with the patriotic sentiments he has imbibed. All kinds of
hitherto unasked questions may be raised in the student's mind at this point,
leaving him quite confused, yet at the same time curious to explore. From a
cognitive standpoint we are in the evaluative realm. Students are asked not
only to apply political theory and conduct analysis, but to make a judgement
based on possibly new criteria. It is vitally important here for teachers to
keep their questions open and not ask in a way that implies a particular
answer. This type of questioning will take place less often in applied science
and skill oriented courses.

What marks the Inquirer/Catalyst Form is the *tone* of questioning—a tone
that pushes students to deal with questions which catalyze them to grow or
change in their thinking, in their opinions and viewpoints. The teaching
presence is one of challenge. Empathy, beckoning, soft suasion recede to the
background while the spotlight is given over to interrogation, skeptical inquiry, and critical pressure. This kind of questioning is designed to disturb
students' preconceptions and it can range from inquiries in a geology class
that challenge conventional opinion on how continents were formed (and
thus how various species arrived where they did) to questions which overturn
a faulty view of evolutionary theory. In an ethics course, a probing discussion
on criteria for morality can leave students in a quandary as to: Whether such
criteria depend on the society one lives in or have a more universal source;
whether terms used interchangeably (moral and ethical) really mean the
same thing; whether anything—even murder—is always wrong, and so on.
By the end of an hour and a half of discussion in this fundamental area
students can be visibly lost or confused. This is a confusion which the teacher
has deliberately catalyzed. Teaching here fulfills John McDonald's claim of
"fraternizing with three of our culture's villains: ambiguity, ambivalence, inst-
ability."[20] That creating this kind of perplexity is not something encouraged
today in education is attested to, among others, by J. T. Dillon: "In most
classrooms the norm is placid, unrifled procession through the subject matter.
Perplexity is deliberately skirted as an undue disturbance to the students'
rightful state of mind."[21] Yet the fashioning of the critical spirit through
questioning is at the very core of education. One cannot really think unless
one has learned to question and to look at the whole range of questioning.

D) Radical Existential Questions. These are the questions that inevitably
deal with the most profound human values or our metaphysical underpinnings. They often lie at the end of the other questioning processes. For

example, to a philosophy of science class that has just watched a Nova presentation depicting the immensity of the universe the teacher can move beyond the astronomical considerations to address the questions of Pascal: "What is our significance in this immensity? Does it matter what we think or do in a universe of such immeasurable vastness?" Or to a class of drama students that has just watched, read, and discussed at length Arthur Miller's "Death of a Salesman" the teacher asks how they will avoid ending up like Willy Lowman? Students by and large assure each other that their lives will be different. But the teacher does not leave them off the hook. He pushes them to examine the materialistic values of their society, the pace and surface attractions of the "rat race" many of them are just now entering. He clarifies the issue, cuts off escape routes, and pushes them to face the radical question of the meaning of their lives in the contemporary world. This and other similar questions are unanswerable in any conventional sense. Their purpose is to jolt the class out of its superficiality, to catalyze students to look more deeply into the issues that lie at the root of human existence, issues that deal with values and valuing—issues that all reflective humans face. These questions are left open-ended for the student to carry along with them. Or they can be philosophical questions of such depth and generality that each constitutes a whole world of pondering for the student. For example, at the beginning of an introduction to philosophy course the teacher hands out the following list of fundamental questions, which the students will be asked to labor on for the entire semester:

Why?

How do we know anything?

How do words mean anything?

What does it mean to be yourself?

Are there any others?

What makes something right?

What does it mean to love someone?

What is fair?

What is death?

The point is to see education in terms of questions rather than answers. If the Inquirer/Catalyst Form succeeds the student begins to view questioning/ inquiry as a more accurate way of thinking and learning. Postman and Weingartner point out that the teacher who uses the Inquiry Method of teaching measures his success as a teacher by "the frequency with which they [students] begin to ask questions; the increase in the relevance and cogency of their questions; the frequency and conviction of their challenges to assertions made by other students or teachers or textbooks"[22] At my school, one student's recent evaluation of a teacher's inquiry method picks up this thread:

The professor didn't teach the way we think of teaching; he orchestrated the group of "students" to look into themselves, not books, for answers because there were no right answers. This level presented issues not information, beliefs not books, thoughts not things. Instead of answering questions, it questioned answers and asked questions with no answers.[23]

E) Questioning the Questions. This last level of questioning is epistemological in nature and at the extreme pole of the Inquirer/Catalyst Form. It not only questions the presuppositions, but questions the very questions for their own hidden presuppositions. It constitutes the ultimate probing and is probably the final goal of education, which sees past (previous) knowledge as an encumbrance to free thought. The physicist, David Bohm has discussed this form of questioning at some length. He begins by asserting that a human being has to be able constantly to question, with great energy and passion (e.g., as Newton did) whatever is not clear and whatever one suspects may not make sense. But even this is not enough. One has further to question the questions:

For in the beginning these usually contain the very presuppositions that are behind the unclarity and contradiction that led one to question in the first place. One has to do this not once or twice or three times, but rather, it is necessary to sustain such questioning indefinitely, in spite of whatever difficulties and obstacles that one may encounter. This approach or attitude is what has to be communicated in education, that is, to be able to question ceaselessly, without any aggressive wish to demolish things but just simply because one sees that these things have to be questioned.[24]

Bohm goes even further to the epistemological roots of the problem in declaring that such questioning is not an end in itself nor is its main purpose to give rise to answers:

Rather, what is essential here is the whole flowing movement of life, which can be harmonious only when there is ceaseless questioning, through which one can be freed of the common tendency to hold indefinitely to contradictory and confused knowledge that responds actively, to give rise to general disorder in the functioning of the mind.[25]

Most students at this stage may not be ready for such an epistemological quest. Yet they need to be introduced to the possibility through the teacher's inquiry methods. It is wisest to raise issues of questioning questions spontaneously and in the midst of doing something else, such as discussing subject content—a momentary standing back to observe the questioning process itself. Much later on when a student has internalized the entire teaching/learning process he or she will engage in this last level of inquiry as a continual mode of thinking and will view it as the final end of education—what J. Krishnamurti has called "freedom from the known" and in *Things of the*

Mind, "the . . . release from the presupposition of absolute necessity to the excitement of discovery."[26]

STILL TEACHER-CENTERED

Inquiry will be a key element in all of the remaining teaching forms we investigate. But the aspect of Inquiry that is unique to the Inquirer/Catalyst Form is its relative one-sidedness. Inquiry here is less open to discourse than it will be later on. It is the teacher who seeks to probe the student with questions. Instead of seeking a glib response, the teacher wants the question to penetrate and do its work. Even the student's response is mainly pretext for another question. (Students, especially those on Perry's dualistic level, may be bothered that the teacher doesn't provide answers.) Interaction in this form is, then, not one of equals or one of relaxed sharing; nor does it contain the intimacy later forms will reveal. The teacher is definitely the active force: He structures the session, sets the agendas, raises and shapes the questions for the group or individual to examine—though matters are far more flexible and open-ended than in the Presentational Mode. Discussion groups using inquiry techniques in the Inquirer/Catalyst Form are often given format questions structured by the teacher. However, John Clarke points out that even in a sequenced format, for discussion to work, students must "become aware of some unresolved difficulty in the content, They must feel the pressure of their own need to know." It is a function of the Inquirer/Catalyst Form to create this need.[27]

The student is submitting to a process—an initiation to learning—that, hopefully, the teacher herself has long since undergone. It would be hard to imagine calling someone a teacher who has not already been initiated into what R. S. Peters calls "the citadel of civilization" which comprises those "activities, modes of conduct and thought which have standards written into them by reference to which it is possible to act, think, and feel with varying degrees of skill, relevance and taste."[28] Once the teacher is on the inside he or she inhabits a sphere that is almost totally unknown to those (students) who are as yet outside the gates. The fundamental task of teaching, according to Peters, is to galvanize students to enter also into that citadel. But in the act of questioning, teachers initiate the process for themselves again. They reexamine, as did Socrates, questions in the light of their continued growth.

DUAL PRESENCE OF THE TEACHER

The particularity of this teaching encounter is in need of some further explanation. As Inquirer/Catalyst the professor must attempt a kind of fusion of opposites. On the one hand, he is a catalyst to critical thought, to the questioning of assumptions, to self-examination. Like Socrates in this form he may find himself not so much liked as respected—and to some degree feared (although the nature of this fear will be far different than the external physical fear teachers have inspired through the centuries.) His task is to wean, even wrench, the student away from what he holds dear. This is not only discomforting, but threatening to the student's psychological security. So there is danger that the student will turn away and remain within his own world.

Therefore, while the teacher engages in the catalytic process she must also provide some kind of safety net, some manner of protection for letting the student fall too far, too quickly. She already relies on the initial bond of trust created in the previous form. She has increased that trust by surviving the student's testing of her own security. Now the strength of that trust is about to be sorely tested again. During the ascesis, the teacher must somehow let students know they are not totally alone, that some positive force moves along with them through the dark world of confusion they have now entered. The teacher must prod hard enough to sever the student from the familiar, but not so hard as to completely dislocate or shock the student into paralysis. Hence a balance must be found in which the teacher can be present to the student in a dual manner. We could say that while the teaching presence fronts the image of Siva, the destroyer, the underlying hold on the student is that of Vishnu, even Krishna, who while realizing that a hard journey must be undertaken, assures the student that his love and care go with him. However, this second presence must not become obvious to the student or else the catalytic power of the inquiry will be diminished in its force. Thus, Krishna must lurk in the background and underlie the whole process.

The relationship here is somewhat similar to that between parent and offspring when the latter is perched on the brink of adulthood or is about to undertake a ritual whereby he or she will be introduced into a new way of life. The parent must push the offspring—in fact, even set the conditions by which this new learning must come (pushing him out into the water). A short time ago there was the mutual sharing of a familiar world (Inducer/Persuader), then a gradual introduction of new elements into that world. But now comes the necessity for a greater severance, the first cold spray of which will appear to leave the youth adrift without an anchor. But the very powers which have grown stronger in him as a child can now be called into play in this newer world. He needs to adapt them to this new environment. Thus, the rupture is not so abrupt as it first seems.

Neither has the parent abandoned his offspring. His care has been there all the while, but not so visibly or reassuringly that the youth (now coming in to adulthood) can substitute this care for the employment of her own powers. The youth must reach out on her own, she must test her power in this new way. Anything less, the transition cannot take place. The parent, in "forcing" her out, may seem cruel. In pushing her to leave go of the old he is really catalyzing an engagement with deeper forces. Underneath the struggle is a confidence that the child is facing in the right direction, has been prepared and will become stronger as he learns this new course.

Thus, the teaching presence is a firm, loving one, though to the student at first this will not seem the case since it is such a decided change from the previous form. Whereas before, the student's familiar world had still maintained its basic outline though strange elements were being introduced, there is now this new grappling with uncertainties and ambiguities. Now the proportion seems reversed. The teacher reveals a face the student has not observed before, a more serious (yet not less lively) demeanor. To put things honestly, the playful element is now laced with more than a hint of the hard wrestling that will bring knowledge and insight. We are moving into the tough terrain of thought. The student was not quite ready for this. The shock of recognition, the pain and wonder that results from the shattering of the familiar world confuses her for a time. Yet the student does not retreat. The mind is intrigued, though it is dizzy—almost vertiginous—still struggling to take hold. All the time the teacher is adroitly probing, while subtly holding.

Let us supply two classroom examples here, the first out of the world of freshman science: For some time (two-three weeks) the teacher has been empathizing with the new students, refamiliarizing them with general concepts and materials they have previously learned, yet discussing them in ways that are slightly advanced from that former world (high school). The students' past knowledge is rehearsed in a way that, refreshing rather than repetitious, leaves them with a sense of their moorings.[29]

A time comes when that bond of continuity must suffice for the immersion that is now to take place. The students are asked to move from these moorings and set out for fresh territory, gathering in new materials, new concepts building on the old, but at first appearing to jettison them. They are launched into this strange world, given little for the journey except the professor's confidence in the extending elasticity of the mind—while she constantly challenges and tests that mind, seeking to awaken it more fully. Most of the term will be that way until the students finally settles into a broader or deeper mode of study. In fact, every new discipline, every new course involves a similar sequence until the student has absorbed the methods and principles of organization, and the teacher can change into a dialogist or facilitator to commence with more sophisticated and informal activities of learning.[30]

In my second example, an individual one, let me return to the young woman who presented the first draft of her paper in the previous chapter. We have seen that the response of the instructor was one of acceptance and affirmation of the student's unique subjectivity. The teacher had entered the student's world in this example so that he could both understand her subjectivity and build that bond of trust so necessary to the future relationship. Only at the end of the encounter did he suggest (gently push for) change while reassuring the student she could still maintain her world.

Let us assume that the student has begun to redo her paper and has submitted a second draft. The likelihood is that she will not have made the complete changeover necessary for philosophical thinking even on a rudimentary scale. The teacher now becomes more forceful and builds on the suggestions made at the end of the previous interview. He makes inquiries as to the precise meaning of certain terms, probes the student's thoughts, suggests latent contradictions between her ideas on determinism and her postulation of free will. This puts the issue on new ground: The student can't have it both ways; she must relinquish aspects of that former world for the sake of clarity and consistency. Through a series of questions rather than categorical assertions the teacher provokes the student to new thought, which in clarifying what she means, may help her transform her world. She will struggle to express thoughts that were camouflaged before.

Note how the teaching presence in this latest encounter has changed! The student is catalyzed into writing a further version which will be closer to the philosophical paper originally requested. The student may be somewhat chagrined at being challenged this way. She may even protest that she is incapable of carrying such a project off, that the ground is too unfamiliar. (The teacher will tell her that the ideas are already there, needing only to be teased into daylight.) She may feel harried that she has to revise again. But her respect for the teacher, built on the teacher's original acceptance and empathy, will survive the irritation. Above all, the student senses her mind coming alive in a new way. She is intrigued and curious; the radicals are overcoming the conservatives. She decides to redo the paper, clarifying the points raised, clearing up contradictions, jettisoning much original verbiage which, precious in the beginning, now appears irrelevant to her main thesis. So the student sets to work.

Of course, none of this may happen. The student may not respond. Something may have gone awry in the process, confidences lost, too much time elapsed. The burdens of everyday life—work, family matters—take their toll and the student fails to make the effort. Perhaps the teacher, unable to provide the necessary time for the student, settles for less. The chances for success may be even more remote where there is no time at all for individualized attention or when the numbers in a class are so large that the teacher can gain no sense of student growth except through test grades.

RESPONSIBILITIES OF THE TEACHER

Some further remarks need to be made concerning the responsibilities of the teacher in the Inquirer/Catalyst Form, especially when catalyzing attitude and value change in the student. Concern has been occasionally raised in the literature on college teaching about the lengths to which a teacher may be permitted to go in educating for change.[31] Disturbed by claims for the legitimate use of Socratic technique, a teacher may have second thoughts, especially in the area of attitudes and values, when he realizes that upon the tearing away of surface veneer, life often reveals to us what Ernest Becker calls "both the terror and wonder of creation."[32] For example, a student confesses in a philosophy paper that because of the introductory course (and the professor's "devil's advocate" approach to many of the issues in that course) she has lost her belief in the existence of God. In so doing her life has also lost its ballast. The student writes:

My whole life was once based on the single thought that God existed. The starting point for defining myself has now been removed from solid ground. Where now is the logical starting point for my personal philosophy? One cannot hope to arrive at point B by omitting point A.[33]

The metaphysical shock administered by reading materials (Mark Twain, Voltaire, Bertrand Russell) cleverly placed and commented on by the teacher has left the student in a vacuum. She will have to cast off or re-order all the values that followed from that fundamental premise which she unthinkingly accepted. The student may not have been ready for such a shock. She may become depressed, eventually cynical. When students are exposed to works that question the very underpinnings of thought or of value objects most important to them (via Descartes' methodical doubt, Hume's critique of the self, Schopenhauer's ideas on life and death) the more sensitive student may be devastated by being exposed to the terror of existence which lies just underneath the smooth surface of a work like *Candide*. These are the swirling waters that lie in wait for the student from exposure to the Inquirer/Catalyst Form of teaching. In a discussion session involving Twain's *Letters From Earth*, the teacher employs his most provocative devil's advocate technique:

Inst.: I want to know why God, if He is all good and loving, allows such undeserved calamities to take place? (Twain has been talking about disease in the scheme of things.)

Stud.: We can't understand everything God does.

Inst.: But surely you are not going to let Him off the hook with an answer like that!

Stud.: Well, sometimes you just have to accept things.

Inst.: Would you accept these calamities if they happened to you?

Stud.: I -I can't really say. They haven't happened to me.

Ins.: But look here—Twain goes even further. He claims that these calamities are built into creation, that we concede that the Creator is responsible for all this—thus "every trait that goes into the making of a fiend and yet we call Him our father!" What do you think of that![34]

How far should a teacher be allowed to go in taking out the foundations or in opening up chasms underneath a student? To what extent does a teacher have a right to engage in such a procedure? We noted in the previous chapter that the teacher must be scrupulously fair in respecting a student's freedom whether or not to engage in a learning process. We also noted that the very right to teach in specific instances can only be granted by the student and that the teacher may need to remind the student of this fact. In the provocative form of teaching we have just described, when does the teacher's liberty (recently granted) become license?

An answer to this question may lie in the fact that the learning process itself, once entered into, involves change. This is as true regarding the learning of new concepts in a subject discipline as it is in a course involving attitudinal change. And if a person is developing inwardly as a human being, life itself is a journey which involves a continual surrendering of previously held sureties. I don't think we can deny that, once freely undertaken, part of the teacher's *androgogic* mission is to set up contexts for change, be they ones involving principles and concepts or attitudes and values. If Socrates was correct in seeing the first task of education as a reduction to ignorance then there can be no further progress without this taking place, at least to some degree. John Passmore points out that teaching to be critical should not be applied merely to the unthinking performance of a skill within a subject area, but even to the foundation upon which that performance or subject rests:

For to exhibit a critical spirit one must be alert to the possibility that the established norms themselves ought to be rejected, that the rules ought to be changed, the criteria used in performances modified. Or perhaps even that the mode of performance ought not to take place at all.[35]

It is in the Catalyst/Inquirer Form where teaching to be critical is most sorely tested. For one can go too far with radical existential questions, and one can't possibly judge the readiness of every student encountered in the Initiatory Mode of teaching. Thus, if it is the tone and impact of the questioning in the Inquirer/Catalyst Form that sets it apart from the others, it must be the atmosphere created that sets safeguards to letting the questioning go unbridled. The prevailing mood, as in *The Dialogues*, must be one of earnest engagement in the pursuit of truth. If students are given the sense that change, even painful change or admission, means growth in the truth, and that the examined life, no matter how complex or uncomfortable, is more worth living than that which is unexamined, then the enterprise of questioning assumed values and attitudes will have positive worth in the students' minds. This is so even with conventional subject matter or in any discipline where the teacher is trying to catalyze students into new learning. Socrates puts it well when responding to Meno: "We shall be braver and less helpless if we think that we ought to inquire, than we should have been if we thought that there was no knowing and no duty to seek to know what we do not know."[36]

But to assure this outcome the teacher as Inquirer/Catalyst does more than randomly provoke; she must be selective and sensitive, knowing how far to take a discussion group on occasion, when to pull back momentarily, or change direction should matters become too intense. In short, the teacher must not only adopt appropriate methods; she must have internalized her craft and caring so that it is deep and continual, though not obvious or facetious. She must know her students as individuals and gradually become aware of the impact of the classroom dynamic on each of them. This is no easy task; it demands an alertness far beyond that usually called for in conventional teaching situations. As we have seen in the previous chapter, attention must also be given to students' affective needs—especially in tension-creating encounters. Nell Noddings makes this point well when she warns that fidelity to training the intellect must not take place at the expense of affect and emotion, and that in teaching an ethics of caring must prevail which stresses development of the whole person rather than the mind alone.[37] Hence the teacher learns not only how to pace the questioning process and to allow wait time for students to think; she learns also to sense when a pattern of questioning may be emotionally overwhelming.

Above all the teacher will impress upon her students the need to live unanswerable questions, to see them as having long term value. This is particularly true in regard to those question dealing with the most profound aspects of life. The poet Rilke's in his *Letters to a Young Poet* addresses this issue most movingly:

I want to beg you as much as I can ... to be patient toward all that is unsolved in your heart and to try to love the questions themselves ... Do not now seek answers which cannot be given you because you would not be able to live them. And the point is to live everything. Live the questions now. Perhaps you will then gradually, without noticing it, live along some distant day into the answer.[38]

SOCRATES AS INQUIRER/CATALYST

Our ultimate model for this teaching encounter is Socrates. We will see that in both Initiatory and Dialogic teaching Modes, as well as the first form of the Elicitive Mode, the Socratic Method comes into play. Using the teacher-midwife metaphor (since this is how Socrates defined himself in *The Theatatus*) we will see how a different aspect of that metaphor reveals itself with each teaching form. Appropriate to the Inquirer/Catalyst Form is Socrates' comparison of his art to that of midwives who bring on or delay childbirth with primary "potions and incantations."[39] These are equivalent to his probing questions. So, too, the professor administers "shocks" to his students as does the "torpedo fish" of *The Meno* creating perplexity and doubt among his interlocutors.[40] His aim is to help make students aware of their ignorance and in doing so push them toward dialogue or dialectics. Both the original innocent questioning of Socrates and the torpedo fish or incantations belong to the Inquirer/Catalyst Form.

At the same time there is a caring. Socrates as Inducer has already gotten on his hearer's wavelength, having entered their world. In fact, Henry Teloh has shown how Socrates invariably adapts his "logoi" (words, statements, arguments) to the conditions of the "psychai" of the persons with whom he talks.[41] In the beginning he praises, compliments, readies them for a more difficult encounter, one in which they will be brought to reject previous false opinion. This is a form of caring rather than trickery because of Socrates' deep devotion to the mutual search for truth. This Socratic caring continues in the Inquiry/Catalyst Form even as he administers the shocks that create perplexity (aphoria) in his interlocutors.[42] In his fidelity to the search he confirms the best part of his students. He never violates this "metaself" or tosses them unthinkingly to the wolves.

Socrates has thus readied his hearers for a new world of learning, one in which they will more actively and honestly search. That his interlocutors don't always take up the search shows that there is no guarantee that students will accept the challenge presented by the Inquirer/Catalyst Form, no matter how skilled teachers are in their craft.

CONCLUSION

With this model and these principles in mind, the teacher can succeed in bringing about the difficult initiation that is completed with the Inquirer/ Catalyst Form. She will be neither too harsh nor too soft, but will achieve the balance in an engagement that tests both her own resiliency and courage, as well as that of her students. They, in turn, will be more prepared to recognize biases, to open to other viewpoints, to search for new horizons. On a deeper level, they will become activated as learners and begin to take more responsibility for their own progress.

Reading materials in the Inquirer/Catalyst Form, in contrast to those of the Inducer/Persuader, will challenge the students to stretch their minds to house new, unfamiliar, even strange, concepts. The teacher should resist providing easy explanations of material which students do not yet understand, but rather push them forward to examine on their own. Hints, cryptic asides, intimations are the order here, making the student feel uneasy, yet continually curious. Yet the readings should not be entirely unrelated to what has gone before; connections must exist to what is already known. In fact, certain "anchoring ideas," at least in the sciences, should be firmly established in the student's mind before turning to new material or more heterogeneous settings. Material that is totally out of the students' range or absolutely foreign to their experience will probably be incomprehensible even in the Inquirer/Catalyst Form unless the professor supplies an adequate transition.[43]

Evaluation procedures should be of a similar nature. Tests which are challenging and provocative, containing questions which push students to explore, hypothesize, and critically assess are in order here. Objective tests can be designed with these kinds of questions in mind, but essays and papers are more appropriate. Such reading selections and evaluation methods in tandem with the teacher's provocative approach fill out the teaching form and open the student to the possibility of a more active and intrinsically oriented approach to learning, one which involves the student in a deeper level of understanding.

Thus, the Initiatory Mode creates new awareness, a new consciousness of the possibilities of education on the part of the student. The student matures and is ready for a more pivotal involvement in the activities of learning and human growth. He has moved out of his individual world into the general inheritance of a particular civilization. As R. S. Peters puts it, the student is more ready "to work with precision, passion and taste at worth-while things that lie to hand."[44] The teacher, for his part, is prepared to move into a more intimate relationship with the student—one in which they engage each other face to face with more or less equal energies.

INQUIRER/CATALYST

Characteristics of Teacher

- builds on and tests relationship of trust
- afirms student's metaself
- accents moving from known to unknown
- confronts student with new world of learning
- disturbs student's complacency
- creates cognitive conflict in student
- creates a positive tension in the classroom
- provokes student to question assumptions, attitudes, unquestioned values
- catalyzes student to move into more relativistic state
- asks, but doesn't answer questions; raises, rather than solves problems
- emphasizes that students ponder questions rather than seek easy answers
- holds students in firm regard while sounding them out
- acutely aware of questioning's impact on student
- introduces students to thinking skills beyond informational and basic knowledge levels

General Skills

- adroitly uses questioning process—proceeds by degrees
- designs questions which challenge students to think and handle new concepts
- designs questions which challenge students to question assumptions and values
- provides patterning of questioning which students can internalize

- senses when cognitive conflict can be too great
- able to gauge emotional impact of questioning on individuals
- assigns reading materials which move students into new territory
- creates exercises and evaluative procedures that are provocative and challenging

Student Aptitudes

- begins to live with dissonance and conflict both cognitively and affectively
- becomes familiar with questions which require thought and reflection
- learns to question attitudes and values
- expects questions which move one to broader levels of perception
- learns to internalize questioning process
- learns to hypothesize and raise new questions
- begins to question others
- learns to view questioning as essential to learning and knowing
- is more at ease harboring questions that don't have immediate answers
- is more activated to move from known to unknown; learns to connect old knowledge with new
- learns to enjoy challenging reading materials
- achieves a new awareness of learning process
- eager to take more responsibility for learning
- completes move toward intrinsic motivation in learning
- increases respect for teacher

NOTES

1. Barzun, *Teacher In America*, p. 23.
2. DeVito, "Teaching as Relational Development," p. 55.
3. Schwab, "Eros and Education," p. 112. Seductiveness on the part of the student can parallel that same betrayal on the part of the teacher which we discussed in the previous chapter—but its provocative nature merits it being treated here.
4. Ibid., p. 113.
5. Adams, *The Experience of Teaching and Learning: A Phenomenology of Education.*
6. Schwab points out that in some cases provocation won't stop regardless of appropriate teacher response or even disapproval by the rest of the class. There are two possibilities for improvement here: One is psychotherapy for which the teacher is both incompetent and irresponsible. The other is the gradual diffusion of the student's anxiety through exposure over time to the classroom behavior of the teacher. For this "therapy," Schwab claims, the good teacher is preeminently qualified. See "Eros and Education," pp. 113–14.
7. Terry Kirkpatric, "Dartmouth Professor Cries and Bleeds," p. 10.

8. John Wilson, "Two Types of Teaching," in *Philosophical Analysis and Education*, ed. Reginald D. Archambault. (London: Routedge & Kegan Paul, 1968), p. 168.

9. See William G. Perry, Jr., *Forms of Intellectual and Ethical Development in the College Years: A Scheme* (New York: Holt, Rinehart and Winston, Inc., 1970), pp. 89–133.

10. Ramond Kolcaba, "Questions in the Classroom." (Paper presented at Second National Workshop on Teaching Philosophy, Schenectady, New York, August 1978), 7.

11. Sondra M. Napell, "Six Common Non-Facilitating Teaching Behaviors," *Contemporary Education* 47 (Winter 1976): 82.

12. Kolcaba, "Questions in the Classroom," p. 8.

13. Thomas P. Kasulis, "Questioning," in *The Art and Craft of Teaching*, ed. Margaret Morganroth Gullette, pp. 42–43.

14. For the original distinction between both types of questioning see J. P. Guilford, "Three Faces of Intellect," *The American Psychologist* 14, no. 8 (August 1959): 473–476.

15. Kolcaba, "Questions in the Classroom," p. 9.

16. Israel Scheffler, "Philosophical Models of Teaching," in *Reason and Teaching* (New York: The Bobbs-Merrill Company, Inc., 1973), p. 74.

17. Perkinson, *Learning From Our Mistakes: A Reinterpretation of Twentieth Century Educational Thinking*. Especially relevant are pp. 163–169.

18. See Gregory Vlastos, "The Paradox of Socrates," in *The Philosophy of Socrates: A Collection of Critical Essays*, ed. G. Vlastos (New York: Anchor Books, Doubleday & Company, Inc., 1971), pp. 1–21.

19. See David R. Krathwohl, Benjamin S. Bloom, Bertran B. Masia, *Taxonomy of Educational Objectives: the Classification of Educational Goals*. Handbook II: Affective Domain. (New York: David McKay Company, Inc., 1956).

20. John P. McDonald "The Emergence of the Teacher's Voice," *Teachers College Record*, 89 (Summer 1988): 483.

21. J. T. Dillon, *Questioning and Teaching: A Manual of Practice* (New York: Teacher's College Press, 1988), p. 31. Research indicates that 2/3 to 4/5 of the average school day is taken up by questioning - primarily teacher questioning. The basic pattern of interaction is: Solicitation (SOL) by the teacher, Response (RES) by student, Reaction (REA) by teacher. It is quite likely that most of this questioning is not open to creating perplexity. See Pamela J. Cooper, *Speech Communication for the Classroom Teacher* (Scottsdale, Arizona: Gorsuch Scarisbrick, Publishers, 1988), p. 126.

22. Neil Postman and Charles Weingartner, "The Inquiry Method," in *Teaching As a Subversive Activity* (New York: Delacorte Press, 1969), p. 36. The authors' discussion of the inquiry method in this chapter includes techniques that, as we shall see, apply also to the next two teaching forms, Dialogist and Facilitator.

23. Steve Scott, "Written Evaluation of Introduction to Philosophy Course," at the Philadelphia College of Pharmacy and Science, Fall, 1987.

24. David Bohm, "Insight, Knowledge, Science and Human Values," in *Toward the Recovery of Wholeness: Knowledge, Education, and Human Values*, ed. Douglas Sloan (New York: Teachers College Press, 1981), p. 25.

25. Ibid., pp. 25–26.

26. *Things of the Mind: Dialogues With J. Krishnamurti*, composed and arranged by Brij B. Khare (New York: Philosophical Library, 1985), p. 119.

27. See John H. Clarke, "Designing Discussions as Group Inquiry," *College Teaching* (36, no. 4) (Fall 1988), pp. 140–143.

28. R. S. Peters, "Education As Initiation," in *Philosophical Analysis and Education*, p. 107.

29. It is surprising how few college teachers see the psychological necessity for this time period with freshman and only look on it as a grudging chore to be performed due to deficient teaching in high school. Consequently, many teachers approach this task with less enthusiasm and skill than is necessary for setting up the transition from the known to the unknown.

30. The commencement of such activities will depend on students moving, to use Perry's terminology, beyond the early absolutist stages of cognitive and ethical growth. More will be said on this in later chapters. Certainly many freshman would not be ready for these activities. Cf. William G. Perry, Jr., *Forms of Intellectual Development in the College Years: A Scheme*.

31. Most recently, see William A. Reinsmith, "Educating For Change: A Teacher Has Second Thoughts," *College Teaching*, 35, no. 3 (Summer 1987): 83–88. Much of the discussion in the chapter is taken from this article.

32. Ernest Becker, *The Denial of Death* (New York: The Free Press, 1973), p. 283.

33. Elissa Cardoni, Advanced Philosophy Paper, May, 1986, p. 1.

34. Reinsmith, "Educating for Change," p. 87.

35. Passmore, *The Philosophy of Teaching*, p. 170.

36. Plato, "The Meno" in *The Dialogues of Plato*, vol. 1, ed. & trans. B. Jowett (Oxford: The Clarendon Press, 1953), p. 285.

37. Nell Noddings, "Fidelity in Teaching, Teacher Education, and Research For Teaching," *Harvard Educational Review* 56 (November 1986): 498.

38. Rainer Maria Rilke, *Letters to a Young Poet*, (New York: W.W Norton, 1963), pp. 18–19.

39. Plato, "Theatatus," in *The Dialogues of Plato*, vol. 3, p. 244.

40. Plato, "The Meno," *The Dialogues of Plato*, vol. 1, pp. 276–77.

41. Henry Telok, *Socratic Education in Plato's Early Dialogues* (South Bend, Indiana: University of Notre Dame, 1986), pp. 1–22.

42. I should note that Socrates' "caring" has been called into question. Cf. Harrison who argues that Socratic irony and caring about someone may not be compatible. (Joan C. Harrison, "Plato's Prologue: Theatatus," *Tulane Studies in Philosophy* 27 (1978): 121–123.) Also, Socrates may doubt his own ability to care, just as he doubts— in fact, in *The Theatatus* strongly disclaims—that anyone has ever learned anything from him. (Cf. David T. Hanson, "Was Socrates a 'Socratic Teacher'?" *Educational Theory* 38 (Spring 1988): 213–224.) Even before these critics, Gregory Vlastos had pointed out that Socrates was more interested in stating his own perplexities through inquiry than in helping anyone else. (Cf. "The Paradox of Socrates," in *The Philosophy of Socrates: A Collection of Critical Essays*.) However, one must be careful of getting lost in subtleties here. One has only to read *The Apology* to learn of Socrates great concern for the "mental and moral well being" of his fellow citizens. Since this statement and others like it are among his last public words we have no reason to believe that they should not be taken as a final testament. In regard to Socrates' doubt as to whether he is any kind of teacher, we will return to this issue in a later chapter when we discuss the Apophatic Mode of teaching at the far end of the continuum.

43. See Ausubel in Noel Entwistle, *Styles of Learning and Teaching*, pp. 207–209.

44. R. S. Peters, "Education As Initiation," p. 110.

Part Three

Dialogic Mode

The dialogic represents the centerpoint on the teaching continuum. It is the sphere where teacher and pupil come together as equal energies in the interchange. Through the first four forms teaching has moved gradually away from impersonal transmission and distanced presentation until with the dialogic, interpersonal relations are firmly established creating mutuality and a sense of educational intimacy.

At the conclusion of the Initiatory Mode the student has a new view of learning and is prepared to deal with both teacher and classmates in a whole new way. This, of course, does not mean that the student has learned nothing in the teaching encounters on the left side of the continuum, but rather that involvement with the educational process was still extrinsic, sporadic, and somewhat passive—though less so with each succeeding form. Also, it should be pointed out that aspects of the dialogic can be found in previous encounters, but they are subsidiary to the main teaching form of a particular mode, whether Presentational or Intitatory.

With the shift into the Dialogic Mode students are ready to assume a strong and active commitment to learning. They are also able to see education more clearly as a communal process. As Richard Tiberius has put it, when teaching and learning are structured using the dialogic metaphor, "the emphasis is on the interactive, cooperative, and relational aspects of teaching and learning"[1] How far students go here depends on how well the form succeeds.

It is with the Dialogic that the horizon opens onto an increasingly student-centered kind of teaching which, if taken to its limit, will transform both learners and teacher. The teacher's influence on the learner becomes increasingly subtle and refined. A point will be reached at the end of the continuum where the teacher becomes unnecessary as an active force because he or she has been fully internalized by the student. The completion of such a process fulfills the ultimate goal of teaching.

NOTE

1. Richard G. Tiberius, "Metaphors Underlying the Improvement Of Teaching and Learning," *British Journal of Educational Technology*, 17, no. 2 (May 1986): 148.

Chapter 5

Teacher As Dialogist

Education, properly speaking, is an initiation into the skill and partnership of conversation.

Michael Oakescott

The dialogic, to use Martin Buber's phrase, is the "realm of the interhuman," "the sphere of the in between."[1] It involves for the first time "immediacy" of personal encounter and makes mutuality possible. The world created by the Dialogist Form is a vital mingling of persons or significant others wherein reality lies not in one or the other alone, but in relation.[2] The teacher and student have moved through initial contact into the testing phase where reciprocity was established and now into the beginnings of educational intimacy. Its possibilities are described by De Vito:

In a teacher-student relationship, intimacy involves a significant expansion in breadth and depth—we begin to talk about more issues and penetrate more deeply into our individual value structures and personalities. We emphasize perceptions of each other as individuals rather than as roles, responding to each other as unique entities.[3]

Such a characterization obviously assumes a greater equality between teacher and students. The equality here, as MacMurray and others have pointed out, is not that of skills or even functions, but rather of *intent* which helps to insure the mutuality of the relation.[4] Because of this new attitude it is even more apparent that the teacher cannot act on the students as objects or seek to manipulate. Also, because the students have been initiated into learning the teacher can become more personal and matter of fact; she can surrender her external persona and attend to an "authentic meeting" where the desire to think and grow can be more readily assumed as intrinsic to the student. This change in the teacher is equivalent to what Bolton and Boyer have called "reducing her psychological size."[5]

The most obvious sign by which this new alignment is recognized is that the classroom or seminar exchanges are *conversational*. The central activity of dialogic teaching is conversation or discourse wherein the interlocutors mediate the world to each other. Participants in the discourse are ready to talk with one another, to share ideas and viewpoints. For this reason interaction will be more spontaneous than in previous forms. Students may look to the teacher for cues, but when given, the conversation moves right along. At times the teacher will not need to initiate or give cues—things just take off from a communal reading of materials or the addressing of a problem that has been assigned. The teacher is still a force, but not as in the Inquirer/Catalyst Form, a commanding one. Neither does she need to induce students to enter an engagement because the students now see for themselves the rich possibilities of dialogical encounter. And a presentational approach is only occasionally used to supply necessary background or to initiate discourse. Thus, it is kept to a minimum. The teacher's authority should not be as obvious now. He has less the right to speak because of who he is than he had before; more important is what he says. The trust initially established in the Inducer/Persuader Form, having survived the rigors of the Inquirer/Catalyst, is now refined and expanded in this new atmosphere. Reciprocity is increased in the sense that it is constant and ongoing.

The communal sharing necessary to fulfill the Dialogic Form is created out of this occurrence of everyone coming together (to use Buberian terms). The teacher presents the possibility of dialogic encounter to the students; she triggers that specific energy whereby a context is created for meeting. But it is soon taken over by the group and an equilibrium is thus created—a balancing of teacher's address with students response. Gradually, there is a fanning out whereby responses are made not only to the teacher, but increasingly to the group. All become significant "others" for whomever is speaking.

Actually, the strands of the dialogue are fourfold: Teacher with group (group acting as significant other); teacher with each person; group member with group; group members with each other. Each of these threads weaves through the discourse, with the last of these strands gradually taking precedence. It is essential to the Dialogic Teaching Form that its dynamics not rest in a single individual, but in the "meeting" or "the sphere of the in-between." As Buber puts it: "A real conversation . . . is carried out not in one or the other participant, or in a neutral world that encompasses both and all other things, but in the most precise sense between both, in a dimension, so to speak, that is only accessible to them both."[6]

The "both" indicated here does not involve any exclusiveness since all relationships occur within the group. Obviously, students bring to the group many kinds of bonds formed previously. They are not asked to drop or ignore these relationships, but rather to be open to the unique meeting that will take place in the particular educational experience encompassed by the Dialogic.

THE PRESENCE OF THE TEACHER

The most notable quality about the Dialogic Form is the teacher's availability, a specific presence which allows for genuine conversation and address. Through the model of this new availability, the individuals in the discourse can begin to relate to each other as persons. It is the very nature of the Dialogic Form to inspire personal expression and response. The teacher reduces her stature or size, symbolized by the new configuration of the classroom space—chairs in a circle, teacher among rather than apart from the students. The teacher's facial expressions and bodily gestures signify an informal openness, an willingness to be at ease with herself and others. She may even begin a discussion with a personal anecdote, one which humanizes the situation and reveals her own vulnerability in the students eyes.[7]

In a class or seminar where this availability of the teacher is lacking the members are not communal; they function either in isolation or as a completely homogeneous mass. The teacher himself will exist only in his individuality, removed from the others. A variety of egocentric states can be involved here from showboating to speaking with a group that exists only in the teacher's mind. In fact, Gabriel Marcel elucidates four ways in which a person remains unavailable to others: i) encumbrance—preoccupation with self, inability to see the other; ii) crispation—withdrawal into the self as a protective measure against the other; iii) susceptibility—need to be validated by others; iv) moral egocentricity—self complacency, not needing any others. It is easy to see that a teacher exhibiting any of these problems will be unable to function as a dialogist in the classroom.[8]

In contrast, class members who come together with a teacher disposed toward the dialogic find themselves during the process moving beyond separate individualities into personhood. MacMurray has pointed out that the unit of personal existence is not the individual, but rather two people in personal relation. Paralleling the phenomenological thinking of Buber and Marcel, he declares that: "The self only exists in dynamic relation to the other."[9] Thus, the educational encounter created by the Dialogic Teaching Form, fosters the development of the self through relation.

The calling of the students by name reveals the new presence of the teacher; it inaugurates the new relationship between her and the student. The address, the asking here is personal, particularized, and totally open. So, too, listening to the student's response involves that same openness, an access to the sphere of the in-between that both will begin to share. That sphere is neither the one nor the other, but both in concert. Meaning exists in the dialogue itself. One speaks; the other listens. Theunissen, interpreting Buber, puts it as follows: "Instead of the I and Thou as already finished beings, bringing the meeting into being, they must, according to the dialogical approach, themselves first spring out of the occurrence of the meeting."[10]

How different is this form of encounter from that of the Inducer/Persuader where the teacher addresses the student with a formative agenda and the student responds out of a curious vulnerability. The communication here is far from disinterested. As we saw, the instructor listened in order to comprehend the student's world so that he could eventually induce her to move beyond it. True, somewhere within this encounter lies the germ of a different relationship; there is the potentiality for true dialogue. The student perhaps could see this—she may have thought it was really taking place. ("I could really talk to him.") But the teaching form is not that of Dialogist. The "dialogue" was initiated on the part of the teacher to bring about an intended effect. While the teacher has been careful not to be manipulative, there was no real equal exchange.

Neither does the "conversation" in the Inquirer/Catalyst Form involve equal exchange or mutuality. Here the teacher challenged students to dig deeper, to activate, to investigate their own thinking—in fact, to think. In true dialogue there is no more need to provoke or catalyze. The field of discourse has been opened. Conversation between the equally curious replaces those former uneven relationships where it was the teacher's energies that dictated the direction of the educational experience. In the Dialogic Form discussion can be conducted on more neutral ground. Both parties can be presumed equally eager to learn (though the teacher will be, in most cases, better versed—the equality is of intent). The forms of inquiry—a problem to be solved, analysis of facts and materials, clarification of values—all take on the nature of an evenhanded search for enlightenment, for insight and knowledge. And the teacher is participant as well as director of this search.

THE RESPONSE OF THE STUDENT

The teacher's availability allows the student to respond in ways heretofore impossible. This movement from individuality to personhood represents a new educational identity wherein students invest in their own learning and see it not as something to be imbibed from a teacher or at the teacher's provocation. They are more inwardly motivated to think, search, examine. What the student seeks now is a context in which to interact with specific others who are equally motivated. Those others will be found in the discourse made possible by the Dialogic Form. In the students' view the teacher has presented herself as one of the others, yet at the same time a leader who can suggest or even set up structural possibilities within the discourse. They know that the leader will neither impose herself or her teaching, but rather lend a certain focus to the dialogue, indicate avenues of approach, light up unfamiliar areas. In fact, students will resist any attempts on the part of the teacher to revert to previous roles or formats. If they have become fully immersed in the discourse they will treat such behavior as a drag on the dialogic process, even as an insult. Students feels liberated—yet at the same time more responsible, not only for their own progress, but for the continued success of the discourse. The idea that learning can take place in such meaningful and communal ways creates a sense of naturalness, causing class members to wonder why any other type of educational context was ever placed before them. The Dialogic Form in this regard comes as a revelation.

Even in private study the student works within the ambit of the new community which is being fostered by the Dialogic. He does not prepare his work for formal recitation the next day, but rather for discussion, for evaluation and feedback, for the possibility of new insights that will add to the gathering richness of his educational experience. For example, in reading a play in preparation for a class meeting the student quietly absorbs, reflects or even scribbles down reactions before these are shared with anyone else. But even in these solo activities, he knows the main focus of the course will be tomorrow's conversation in which his views will not only be shared, but tested and perhaps broadened. Issues, problems, perspectives will be broached in either free-flowing or directed discussion initiated by the teacher as Dialogist. Even if the teacher pursues a linear sequence of questions, such a procedure is only the foreplay that moves the group into the main discourse. It is this area of the "in between" where students are educationally most alive and where they share in the search (led by the teacher) for understanding. In such a communal environment students function as free relational human beings (persons) where minds and sensibilities can grow. It is the teacher's availability that has set all this in motion.

If students respond to the dialogic presence, while undertaking the background preparation (attentive reading, reflection, necessary written or lab work) a rich learning experience is possible beyond anything they have known from previous teaching forms where they were less active, less intrinsically motivated. The dialogic encounter is possible in almost any subject discipline. In fact, discourse is at the heart of education and is possible anytime people meet in concert (even without a teacher as we shall see in the last form on the continuum) and share a common information base. Among others, Michael Oakescott, in an oft-quoted statement, has expressed this centrality well:

As civilized human beings, we are the inheritors, neither of an inquiry about ourselves and the world, nor of an accumulating body of information, but of a conversation begun in the primeval forest and extended and made more articulate in the course of centuries.... Education, properly speaking, is an initiation into the skill and partnership of this conversation in which we learn to recognize the voices, to distinguish the proper occasions of utterance, and in which we acquire the intellectual and moral habits appropriate to conversation.[11]

The Dialogic Form also allows for surprise since the teacher is not lecturing or challenging the student, but rather opening the way to discourse. In so far as an equality exists and all are creatively engaged in the search, the possibility of the unpredictable and new emerging from within is raised. This is what makes discussion different from recitation. Surprise, new possibilities, are inherent to the Dialogic, as they are to interpersonal relations. In fact, Buber has stated that to deal with the other as other and to let oneself be surprised by him is therefore the same thing.[12] Thus, the dialogic teacher sets up materials with this in mind and keeps them flexible and open-ended. And students, once they give themselves over to the Dialogic Form, come to each new session expecting the unexpected and to achieve fresh insights. This is part of the unique creativity of discourse. We will speak more about this when we come to the final teaching (or non-teaching) form on the continuum.

FORMATS FOR THE DIALOGIC

Two teaching/learning contexts allow for most effectiveness in using the Dialogic Form: that of the group discussion or seminar, and the private tutorial or interview. The present chapter will focus on the first; the tutorial will be covered in the following chapter since the Facilitator/Guide Form is even more central to it.

In the undergraduate college classroom the discussion format allows maximum opportunity for the kinds of discourse spurred by the Teacher as Dialogist. However, it should be kept in mind that although discussion (along with lecture) is the most popular format in education today, the Dialogist Form within the discussion in not nearly as common. As we have seen, dialogue involves a certain equal sharing and mutuality. Most discussions carried on in college classrooms have the teacher taking a far more dominant role than that which is central to the Dialogist Form. So far as this is true, such discussions belong to prior teaching modes. In fact, many "discussions" are nothing more than camouflaged lectures wherein the teacher instructs under the pretense of questioning or conversing.

That which is central to dialogical discussion is true *discourse* which places the teacher in a far less dominant role, and it is the discussion or seminar format that most easily allows dialogue between class members to occur. As DeVito puts it: "The preference for dialogue implies that teachers and students are co-contributors: Both are listeners; both are speakers. Both care for, respect and support each other. Both are learners and both are teachers."[13] In comparing discussions with lecture, one finds that a greater sense of personal discovery is possible in a discussion, for the answers emerge as part of a cooperative enterprise.[14] It is this opportunity for the student to explore and discover through interaction with others that dictates the kind of learning skills that will be acquired.

Paramount among these are the critical skills of analysis, evaluation, and synthesis. Also, applying and experimenting with new ideas, while recognizing one's previous ignorance or partial knowledge, can be the fruit of genuine discourse. All these are learning skills of a different order than those attained in more teacher-centered formats where students imbibe and assimilate information. Even though the teaching forms described in the previous two chapters can generate attitudinal change, only the Dialogic allows for an in-depth perusal of attitudes and a shared examination of issues dealing with values.

However, it is important to stress that the employment of these higher skills presumes an adequate information base. Some common experience or information is essential to making discussions productive and, as Cashin and McKnight point out, "simply sharing ignorance is in no one's best interest."[15] Thus, while it is true that in dialogic discussion class members work toward new insights and ideas, a common experience or a certain shared grasp of principles and concepts is necessary out of which to proceed.

Along with the teacher's failure to be available, the chief obstacle to meaningful discussion is this lack of a common foundation. Eble and others have shown that well motivated students resent not only discussions that are really lectures, but also discussions which contain solely "the half-baked ideas of other students with no corrections from facts, experiences and hard exacting thought."[16] Nothing can be more frustrating for knowledgeable students who are ready to interact than the lack of preparation in other class members. This applies both to a general knowledge base as well as reading materials or problems assigned for a particular class meeting. Teachers have to be firm here in regard to content expectations and course objectives. They must always strive to insure or discover that common base out of which discussion can move.

At the same time, the most interactive discussions, even where a strong knowledge/information base is present, can be often "messy" and inconclusive, tending to lend themselves more to critical analysis than to final solutions. This process has its own intrinsic value by the very fact that the focus is on personal interchange where ideas and values often overlap or clash. Nevertheless, it is possible for a teacher to move a discussion group toward seeing wholes, toward theory construction or reconstruction. One can observe this process in any number of Socratic dialogues, though it is true that such resolutions usually represent temporary plateaus at which the interlocutors rest before new problems arise which plunge them into further exploration. This should not be seen as a defect. On the contrary, such "agon" or wrestling illustrates the probing and growth which is at the very heart of the education process. The special emphasis in the Dialogic Form is that of a *shared inquiry* where students with the teacher quest together in an atmosphere of curiosity and candor. Even the sciences, if taught in dialogic fashion, lose their aura of static certitude and take on an air of the hypothetical and problematic.[17]

Discussion allows students to express and formulate. Perhaps most importantly, when it reaches a certain level the participants share a process of rational deliberation, a philosophical model of teaching called by Israel Scheffler the "rule model." This is the third of three models in Scheffler's schema which leads to the most comprehensive learning experience, one whereby the mind through deliberation, argument, judgement, evaluation, and application of knowledge and insight discovers the underlying principles of any discipline. Scheffler puts it as follows:

Teaching, it suggests, should be geared not simply to the transfer of information [model one], nor even to the development of insight [model two], but to the inculcation of principled judgement and conduct, the building of autonomous and rational character which underlies the enterprises of science, morality and culture.[18]

The discussion format supplies a superb context for this kind of knowledge structuring and shared critical thought, though admittedly it is the most difficult for the teacher as Dialogist to conduct. It may be more applicable to the graduate seminar where the knowledge base must be very strong.

DIFFICULTIES IN SUSTAINING DISCUSSION

A number of educators have pointed out that developing the ability to conduct effective discussion classes is far more difficult than learning to lecture effectively. First of all, not only must the teacher know the discussion topic very well, he must also be familiar with any issues reasonably related to that topic. It is advisable to list possible issues or questions which the students might bring up and to outline possible responses. This will involve more reading and studying.[19]

But it goes beyond the instructor's mastery of content. The way in which teachers use their own knowledge base is what makes the difference between dialogic teaching and the usual teacher-centered discussion. That knowledge is used indirectly, applied adroitly, so as to further rather than short-circuit the sharing taking place. When he speaks the discussion leader adheres to the form and thus rides herd on his tendency to instruct or authoritatively inform.

Teachers who have worked for any length of time in the Dialogic Form do not have to be told about the difficulties involved, even when adequately prepared. Recently, in *Teachers College Record* Sternberg and Martin reviewed three styles of teaching—the lecture-based "didactic" style, the fact-based questioning approach (response questions), and the thinking-based questioning or "dialogical" approach—and while they pointed out that only the dialogical approach encourages genuine class discussion, it is difficult mainly because students in classrooms today are not familiar or comfortable with it.[20] According to their observations of actual teaching when teaching occurred in style 3, the response was almost always the same—silence: "Students were not familiar with or comfortable with this style of interaction, and were unprepared either to do the thinking it required or to take the risks it involved."[21]

What happens, of course, is that the instructors more often than not give in and supply answers to their questions. Often they revert back to the lecture format to relieve the anxiety of discomfort—both their own and the students. Peter Frederick insists that for a vast number of teachers their largest fear lies in facing discussion classes:

The terror of silences, the related challenges of the shy and dominant student, the overly-long dialogue between ourself and one combative student, the problems of digression and transitions, student fear of criticism and our own fear of having to say "I don't know."[22]

The testimony indicates that true dialogic teaching is not very common today because students in higher education fail to move beyond previous modes into a learning atmosphere necessary for shared inquiry—one where the teacher does not induce or even challenge, but rather speaks to the students as initiates who have willingly entered or seek to establish a learning community. This is unfortunate since it means that few educational environments are available for teachers to grow in their craft to the point where they can become dialogic. Mortimer Adler and his associates have pointed this out in regard to Socratic teaching in our schools.[23] However, the purpose of this book is not so much to focus on actual conditions of our educational institutions as to outline and describe the archetype of each teaching form with all its possibilities.

CONCRETE ASPECTS OF DISCUSSION/SEMINAR IN THE DIALOGIC FORM

Leading a dialogic discussion without dominating it requires a high degree of alertness on the part of the teacher. The Brazilian educator, Paulo Freire, has put it well: "It is not our role to speak to the people about our own view of the world, nor even to attempt to impose that view on them, but rather to dialogue with the people about their view and ours."[24]

In opening such a discussion the teacher must initiate and sustain without being overly directive. The following brief transcript from an actual discussion of Shaw's *St. Joan* in a Modern Drama course indicates how this might be done.[25] (It is assumed that students have seen and read the play along with putting their initial reactions down on paper.) The teacher begins in a conversational tone:

T: I found this a complex play. Shaw has one of his characters—I believe it is the king—say that no one ever knew what to make of Joan. I'm not sure how I feel. (Directly to class) What's your overall impression of Joan?

Jean: (assertively) I definitely think she was a saint. Anyone who could do all those things—and then be burned...

Jim: I disagree. She seemed arrogant and full of herself. Saints aren't like that.

T: (To Jim) You agree with the Church's view, then, in the play.

Jim: Yes—she wouldn't listen to anybody...

Anne: (To Jim) I think the Church wanted her out of the way because she listened to God alone. And probably because she was a woman. (Some of the class members nod their heads)

T: I was wondering... (notices Tom) Yes, Tom!

Tom: Did she really live? (pause while teacher looks around)

Ruth: (To Tom) Yes—in the 14th century. We learned about her in history class. She led armies and was imprisoned and burned at the stake.

T: (To group) Yes—Joan of Arc was a historical character. (Reads a brief excerpt from the Encyclopedia Britannica)

Kim: That still doesn't make her a saint though.

Jean: But the miracles prove it. And the voices. (turning to Jim) Jim, you talked about her being arrogant and proud. But wasn't she only obeying her voices?

Jim: Do you think they were really voices. I think it was all in her head.

Mary: I agree with Jim. They were probably hallucinations.

T: (To both Jim and Mary) You mean lots of people hear voices? (Recognizes Jean again)

Jean: (To group) I think we're being too cynical. Do you think Jesus had hallucinations?

Craig: (quite animatedly) Did anyone see "The Last Temptation of Christ?" (Two or three heads nod.)

Kim: You mean the seizures! (Craig nods.)

T: Would one of you explain the connections?

Craig: Well Jesus would hear this voice in his head and then fall down in a kind of epileptic seizure. (A number of voices now—class diverges for a minute.)

Tom: (Voice rises above the noise) Isn't there a part in the play where Joan talks about her voices? I forget where it's at.

T: That should tell us something. Anyone know where that scene is?

Robin: Yes—it's in Scene Five on page 613.

T: Would you read that for us, Robin? Who wants to be Dunois? (Tom puts up his hand. They read somewhat haltingly Joan's explanation of how her voices work, Dunois response, Joan's rejoinder.)

Rita: (After a pause) That's a good point Dunois makes about her common sense.

T: Yes—would a woman with such common sense be having hallucinations?

Susan: There's something else that bothers me. Joan led armies into battle. (turning to Jean) This isn't the usual thing saints do.

Jean: Well, she was following her voices.

Anne: (Agreeing with Jean) Didn't some of the woman in the Old Testament do similar things? (Anne is obviously very well read. Teacher recognizes Peter who has been quiet till now)

Susan: (In lower tone) I still have trouble with the idea.

Peter: I think we might be getting bogged down in her personality. (To teacher) Doesn't Shaw say in his introduction that this play is about the forces of history? (Pause here. Teacher finally responds to Peter)

T: Can you explain what that means?

Peter: Well, it's about evolution...(Peter proceeds to explain his understanding of Shaw's social philosophy behind the play.)

With Peter's explanation, the discussion moves into the more general consideration of the great men and women who appear periodically to move the human race forward. The group will evaluate this idea of Shaw's in the light of their own perceptions and then see how it applies to Joan in the play.

Note here in this opening discussion that the teacher functions both as initiator and facilitator, as well as a member of the group. He tries not to make his viewpoint carry more weight than any of the others. Evidence that he has succeeded is provided by the responses of various students to his remarks. He only uses his background knowledge to back up what another student has said. And it doesn't break the train of the conversation. The purpose here was to begin with a question that fosters diverse opinions, explore these for a while and then move the process into a more general historical context. In this case, one student introduced the larger question which moves the discussion onto a more conceptual level. It should also be apparent, even from this brief segment, that these students are enough at ease with one another to disagree. Only in an atmosphere of mutual acceptance can such disagreements take place without friction.

Another approach where a group is composed of less than twenty is to go around the room for initial statements to begin a discussion. For example, in an introduction to philosophy seminar the teacher could begin the discussion of John Stewart Mill's reading on Utilitarianism (which deals with the greatest happiness principle) by asking everyone to give his or her own definition of happiness. Out of this opening ploy a conversation ensues in which each student listens intently to the other definitions as the teacher or a volunteer class member records the various definitions given. Needed clarifications are sought, differences noted, curiosity piqued—all of which can lead inductively into the central theme of Mill's Utilitarian value system. Starting with these personal ideas of happiness fosters a shared inquiry.

The dialogical approach used here is similar to what Edward Glassman describes as the Participative Discussion where both teacher and students are given a chance to express thoughts and ask questions leading to the enhancement of thinking skills and increased creativity. The key activities for the discussion leader are initiating, asking, sharing, clarifying, creating, and closing.[26] This Participative Discussion is in contrast to what Glassman calls the Directive Discussion where the teacher tells, asserts, models, and asks (i.e. the usual discussion class), as well as the Non-Directive Discussion where the teacher's role is diminished to delegating, consulting, moderating, facilitating. (We will talk about this latter approach in Chapter 6) Thus, the dialogic becomes "a person-centered, participation discussion in which everyone contributes."[27] Cooperation rather than competition prevails, though obviously there will be conflicting opinions.

As Dialogist, the teacher must learn that listening is just as important to the process as speaking. He must also impress this upon the class members. It does not hurt to spend some time at the beginning going through listening exercises to familiarize students with the cycle that is authentic conversation.[28] Students are used to listening (turning on and off) to presentations in large lecture halls and even in a regular discussion class. But listening in a true dialogic manner to what the other has to say is a much more active process. They must be shown, largely through the teacher's example, how to receive what another says in an open manner. They should be brought early in the semester to see as their primary task the genuine understanding of another's statement or point of view. This, along with helping students state as clearly and succinctly as possible their own viewpoints, forms an indispensable foundation for discourse. They must be willing to go so far as empathetic identity. Mortimer Adler explains this in regard to conversation which involves the meeting of minds:

To achieve this, each must forsake partnership with regard to his own position and substitute for it a kind of impartiality with respect to the position taken by the other person...Each person should not only be able to state the position of the others in a manner that the other approves, he should also be able to state the other person's reasons for holding that.[29]

Taking such a position enhances intersubjectivity, that ontology of the inter-human, which is essential for the Dialogic. The process can range from the relatively simple request of the teacher for a restatement of an idea:

T: I think we may have a communication problem here. Jean, see if you can give Jim back the essence of what he is saying.

Jean: (To Jim) You're saying that looked at from the Church's point of view Joan was not only arrogant, but a threat to its authority.

T: Is that it, Jim?

Jim: Well, most of it. But also the fact that its authority was legitimate in the eyes of the people—even Joan.

T: Do you see that Jean?

Jean: Okay, I understand. But Joan never really doubted its authority. She simply said that God came first.

to the far more difficult task of having a student hold at length for a position she is in disagreement with. (The teacher should even attempt to help students identify with the context within which a viewpoint is expressed.) In line with this, Peter Elbow suggests the exercise of "methodological belief" (in contrast to methodical doubt) wherein group members allow themselves to fully experience and try to believe a position before they subject it to analysis or criticism. Elbow applies this to the discussion of a reading:

Imagine five or twenty-five of us sitting around a text. One person has an odd view. We must not just refrain from quarreling with it, we must try to believe it. If we have trouble, we ask for help from the few who do better. We ask them to explain—not defend.[30]

Elbow points out that experiencing our own understanding of a text or of an alien opinion helps us to see how someone else sees. Such an exercise may prove difficult at first, but once class members fully enter into the practice empathetic understanding is greatly enhanced. Women students often can more easily adopt such an approach, especially if they have reached the level of what Belenky and her associates in *Woman's Ways of Knowing* call "procedural knowledge" where in an attempt to achieve a kind of harmony with another person in spite of difference and distance, women try to enter the other person's frame to discover the premises for the other's point of view.[31]

Also important is the effort to distinguish between real and apparent disagreement. In the case of the latter the teacher again needs to lead the way in being tireless to resolve that disagreement. But one should never bring about false unanimity or class consensus in the interests of amicability. One of the most valuable educational experiences available to students is critical disagreement within an atmosphere of mutual acceptance. As numerous educators over the years have pointed out, such tolerance amid diversity of considered viewpoints is the mark of a civilized style. In discussions which are team led it might be good for the two instructors to model such benign disagreement early in the semester.

APPROPRIATE SPACE AND TIME

An appropriate physical environment is crucial to successful discourse. This means an arrangement of chairs so that proper spacing, both psychic and physical, is allowed between participants. Schwab mentions the necessity for "affectively energized discussions" transpiring face to face. The most obvious means of achieving such a physical alignment is the arrangement of chairs in a rough oval. This results in "a curious identification of bodily protection and ego security."[32] Adler suggests the use of a hollow square or large hexagonal table around which participants sit.[33]

However things are set up, the group members must be present to each

other in a way that allows for maximum interchange. Those around one are
not objects, but persons in fluid space. The class functions in a communal
way, while at the same time uniqueness of persons is still fostered. The teacher
is part of the circle. She may be in a center position, but not isolated or
removed from the group. (As the semester proceeds it may be good for
people not to always take the same seats.) Students may need to become
familiar with the teacher in a dialogic context before being able to work fully
with peers. But the teacher will seek to gradually shift the energy flow from
her and those who speak to her out to the group at large as she learns to
listen to their discourse with intense interest and alertness. This is the participatory sharing activated by the teacher's original availability to the group.

Needless to say, except for those few rooms built specifically for seminars,
college classrooms are not constructed with dialogic teaching in mind. Regular setups militate against its possibilities: Chairs set in rows (sometimes
nailed down), a large desk in between student and teacher, blackboards out
of reach of students, inappropriate lighting, vapid surroundings. Dialogic
contexts, thus, often must be created in a makeshift and imperfect manner,
while valuable time is lost in the setting up. Nevertheless, it is essential to
provide some kind of appropriate physical surroundings if dialogic discussions are to be successful.

Sufficient duration also must be allowed for the intricacies of the Dialogic
Teaching Form to take shape. As Adler and others have pointed out, the usual
fifty minute class segment is not enough time for discussions dealing with
substantial issues.[34] Time frames of one and a half hours are ideal to allow
for the complexity of interaction that suits true discourse. What is needed
beyond this is the sense in the group of an ongoing process, of a learning
community being built which transcends the class time. This way issues can
be picked up again and worked at until new levels of insight and participation
are achieved. While the discussion sessions are the focus, much of the growth
and sharing can take place among different members of the group outside
of class. Sustaining this kind of flow through a semester is one of the most
difficult aspects of Dialogic Teaching, especially if one is dealing with students
who have no way of seeing or spending time with each other between classes.

For example, if students are apartment mates or share the same social
grouping, conversations crop up as spontaneous interactions or even as prepared meetings to discuss an assignment for the next day. Typical of the
former is one student's comment about involvement in a philosophy and
values course: "I'd find myself going home and saying to Pete (his roommate
who also took the course): 'What do you think of that?' He'd have a different
opinion than me and we'd argue it for an hour."[35] On the other hand, students
who commute every day will find it more difficult to extend the learning
community beyond the classroom. For this reason there often exists an un-
evenness in those discussion classes composed of students living on campus
and commuters.

THE CENTRALITY OF LANGUAGE

By this point it should be obvious that language can be both bridge and barrier to meaningful discourse. MacMurray has put it most fundamentally: "The ability to speak is then, in the proper sense, the capacity to enter into reciprocal communication with others. It is our ability to share our experience with one another and so to constitute and participate in a common experience."[36]

Certain roadblocks can be removed by helping students early in the discussion process to seek clarification of terms, to qualify, make necessary distinctions, and to aim in general for more precision in terminology. Along with these critical skills, which make dialogue accessible rather than muddled, there are more difficult forms for the group to recognize, subtleties and nuances of speech which are the key to richness and complexity of discourse. Much depends on the linguistic competence of the group that meets together. As we are discovering, high competence in this area represents only one kind of intelligence rather than the sign of general intelligence. But it is especially valuable for discourse.[37]

Equally as much depends, however, on the group's openness to each other which allows rigidities and inhibitions to dissolve. Above all, language, no matter how adroitly employed, should not be separated from the entire person of the speaker. It must be rather the avenue of meaning—not only for ideas, but for attitudes and values. The closer we come to adequately expressing them, to holding them out for the other to see and understand, the more the "in-between," that region of meeting comes alive. But there is more. The placing of silences, of pauses, is crucial. They are all part of language in the larger sense. They further the in-betweenness, the intimacy, letting the group members sense that discourse includes intervals where things are weighed silently, given time to register and be heard. Both teacher and students must learn to become at ease with these intervals. Students in whom what Gardiner calls "the Personal Intelligences" are strong will find these kinds of sensitivities easier to develop. But all the class members must come to see their importance.[38]

A few years ago in an ethics and health care seminar, a group of twenty was discussing the topic of life-sustaining technologies when suddenly the teacher began to share with the class members a wrenching conflict he experienced a few weeks earlier in regard to a decision his family made to stop a respirator which was keeping his mother alive. As the teacher proceeded the words took on a moving eloquence, all the more so as the group sensed the barely suppressed grief which was filling the spaces between the words. It was a supreme moment of sharing—completely on the point at hand—and the issue came alive for the class in a way that would have been impossible via the conventional abstract, impersonal discussion. After a long pause, another class member related how a beloved grandmother had lain for three years in a hopelessly comatose state in a nursing home. A third member talked about a decision his family had made in regard to his father. A fourth brought up a recent case in the news about a doctor/husband putting his dying wife to sleep at her request. Others began to speak. The various types of euthanasia were discussed but set now within the richness of human experience. A casuistic reasoning involving case studies is common in these kinds of seminars. But when group members bring up examples out of their own experience the mood of the room changes, the language comes alive, the discussion takes on a shape and meaning that is personal, yet universal. Along with analysis and other cognitive activities, a session like the above one contains what Menges calls "emotional learning outcomes" which are invaluable and unique to small group settings.[39]

Disembodied, abstract terminology does not promote dialogic understanding, though use of such terms, especially in the sciences, is indispensable. Perhaps this is why so many graduate seminars fail to become authentic dialogues. Specialized discourse, while often necessary, does not have to remain cold and abstract. Given a common knowledge base, participants in a seminar class on any level can share their knowledge as persons rather than as computers or thinking machines. This is not a plea to introduce emotionalizing into science courses, but rather to point out that even science does not have to be disembodied. It is rather a mutual adventure, a unique kind of dialogue involving, it is true, an enormous amount of abstract, often lonely, research. Yet even here genuine scientists are able to see their research in a relational way. They are not so much working with objects as interacting with them and allowing an aspect of the living universe to reveal itself.[40]

Teachers in the sciences do a disservice to their students if in their emphasis on sterile terminology or chemical reactions they fail to introduce them to this humanistic perspective. Not only undergraduate classes, but the graduate seminar, as it is usually conducted today, gives sad testimony to this failure. It is somewhat like the doctor on rounds in the teaching hospital who becomes so intent on discussing a disease state with his staff that they totally ignore the patient who is the living, breathing embodiment of this disease. So, too, science set apart from the context of the human adventure in which it takes place has gotten things out of kilter. More will be said about this, along with the way in which the teaching of science is usually approached, in the concluding chapter.

In short, dialogic teaching is most immediate and fruitful when it involves not only rational deliberation, but deliberation within the context of the interpersonal. In fact, it even has been shown that sound interpersonal development fosters rational deliberation. And we have already spoken in previous chapters about the connection between the cognitive and affective realms. As the Dialogic Mode begins the shift to the right side of the teaching continuum it augments a certain feminization of teaching which will flower in the Elicitive Mode. The teacher moves away from what Noddings has called "the fundamental premise of masculine intellectualism: abstractionism and consequentialism" to a position where "a language of relation guides our thinking in concrete situations."[41] The dialogic discussion reaches its highest potential when enthusiastic participants in an appropriate physical environment with sufficient time through a holistic use of language create a learning community based on common pursuits. This community is nurtured by the teacher, but kept alive by the care of each member of the class for the others.

HANDLING CONFLICT WITHIN DIALOGIC DISCUSSION

It must be understood that the "I" can also stand against a "Thou" and that conflicts will be inevitable even in dialogic discussion. To deny that conflicts will exist is totally unrealistic; to claim that they should not exist is pedagogically naive and an invitation to sterility. Conflicts can threaten the group's progress, even its existence, as a dialogic community. By the same token, if dealt with constructively, they can be a vital part of creative discourse. As Buber has put it, the individual "even when he stands in opposition to the other, heeds, affirms, and confirms his opponent as an existing other."[42] Some conflicts can be explained by misunderstanding or misinterpretation on the part of each participant. Often they can be avoided, as we have seen, by an effort to distinguish between real and apparent disagreement. Still other conflicts can be attributed to overfamiliarity. As time moves on group members may come to know each other too well—which, in reality, means too superficially—in that overattention is paid to the quirks, habits, pretensions, defensive mannerisms of those sitting around us. Participants give up their attempts to care, to see more than meets the eye when someone speaks, to look beneath the surface. Part of the teacher's leadership role in the Dialogic Form is to remind her co-participants that their expectations of each other are becoming too mechanical.

As the relationship grows day to day, week to week, the teacher has begun to see his students more and more from the inside. His viewpoint moves away from the merely extrinsic and utilitarian, away even from the conventional (and universally accepted) "training of minds" paradigm usually thought appropriate for college teachers, to the commencement of an ethical caring which is phenomenological. This means in Nodding's words "a faithful search for understanding of the subjective aspects of experience."[43] Such concern contributes to an appreciation of the total person—the thinking, feeling, willing human being and not merely the more superficial aspects of the other so common in education today. The teacher asks himself: "What does this person reveal in what he or she says? What does he or she really mean?" "What is surfacing with that remark?" Gradually, class members should begin to follow this kind of broader orientation initiated by the teacher's presence. And when they periodically fall back the teacher gently reminds them of this fact and urges them on. It is only within this fuller, more interior perception of the other that conflicts can be creatively dealt with and viewed as opportunities to move to new levels of awareness.

In order to be authentic in this regard teachers must closely examine what they bring from the past to their perceptions of students to make sure that these perceptions are as free from bias as is humanly possible, especially since they are setting out a model for other class members. Without this scrutiny of one's own beliefs and attitudes what seem to be authentic perceptions may in reality be fixed judgements.[44]

Very often cognitive conflict is created in the student by immersion in unfamiliar ideas, and the tension of disagreement tempts the group member either to react defensively or to project this conflict onto other participants. Perhaps the very nature of a course involves conflicts or at least differences in values. An obvious example would be a values seminar where one of the stated objectives of the course is to have the student become aware of perspectives other than his own, including the beliefs and values of other members of the seminar.[45]

Greater diversity within the group creates conflict; the more heterogeneous, the more conflict. Student groups with richly varied backgrounds in regard to race, socioeconomic status, career goals make for a volatile mix, but as Milton points out, it also can make for rich and exciting classes.

Student mix can be one of the most trying factors in maintaining the atmosphere of trust . . . it is also one of the most valuable factors in establishing mutual inquiry. After all, it is especially difficult to learn anything, to grow and expand in understanding, when one is surrounded by people who are carbon copies of oneself.[46]

If the dialogical form is succeeding the trust and reciprocity within the group should be enough to support students through these rough waters. This represents a difference from the Inquirer/Catalyst Form where the support (albeit hidden) comes from the teacher alone. Too often discussion classes fail to reach their full potential or else limp along because the teacher has not been able to shift this responsibility to the rest of the group. Success in bringing about such a shift is enhanced if the teacher helps the class members recognize and deal with diverse traditions and values in the very context of discussion. Conflicts that arise can then become an aid to learning.[47]

On the teacher's part, the realities of power must be recognized. We discussed this issue briefly in regard to a student's vulnerability in Chapter 3. In the Dialogic Mode the power issue will diminish, but teachers should always keep in mind the baggage both they and their students bring to any group session—even where students already have entered the house of learning. Some of these issues may even be brought up and aired during the discourse. However, if true dialogic teaching is taking place, the parties to the discourse will have become more equalized and within this new learning context conflicts should take their natural course which means they will be accepted and handled without undermining the process. Joyce Hocker has made the point that "all power in interpersonal relations is a property of the social relationship rather than a quality of the individual outside of the relationship."[48] If a dialogic atmosphere has been created, the power issue is brought into a proper balance. Collaboration and negotiation are the activities which show that such a balance has been achieved. That such is not often the case is evidence that dialogic teaching is not cultivated much in college classrooms today.

CONCLUSION

Though Dialogic teaching is rather uncommon in academia, its successful mastery can create an indelible educational experience for students, one that can take them far beyond the classroom. It represents that activity by which they begin to take learning into their own hands. There is a timeless element in true discourse, a forgetting of the clock hours in the excitement of shared pursuit. One senses this phenomenon again and again in Plato's dialogues. Kenneth Eble has summed up the ideal discussion as one in which "invisible strings guide a varied vocal group during a period in which most of the participants sense the worth of their own ideas, experience some visceral excitement and arrive at some destination."[49] Eble admits this is a high ideal. To sustain such a process over a semester is even rarer. Wayne Booth documents this rarity when he reflects on his own experience with discussion class, one that is surely shared by numerous teachers in higher education: "I preserve from most courses a memory of only a half-period or two when all—or most—of the students were thinking, every one of them wanting to talk, but all attending to one another, listening, responding, struggling to figure out where all this might lead."[50]

Yet it can happen as is shown by the following description of Joel Jones, made even more incredible by the fact that the group was extremely large:

Several years ago, though, an undergraduate class of over one hundred and forty students (billed and conducted as a "seminar") provided nothing but sheer pleasure, three hours a day, four days a week, for a month. (It was offered during a January mini-semester.) Nearly all of the participants had been students in other classes of mine; most had shared prior classes with others in the "seminar." Sometimes they would lead me, sometimes I them; sometimes one segment of the class would lead another to mutually shared realizations. With this group I never had to refrain from punctuating our dialogue with premature conclusions. Our timing was good; often all one hundred-plus individuals seemed to arrive at the same point together. And if a few of us ever got there first, we did not settle back and revel in our satisfaction; we kept moving with the group and shared in the exultation of the final coming together. That was a rare class, a rare experience conducted under unusually propitious circumstances, but many others have approached it in the quality of their special moments. I know, experientially, that this ideal can be real.[51]

I think it is important to note that all of these students had had Jones before and given his success as a dialogic teacher the new community was created out of a merging of several smaller communities from former classes. This probably explains why, even with such an ordinarily forbidding class size, real discourse took place.

Even so, the fact that encounters like this are more often restricted to "special moments" points up an aspect of the discussion process which lends to it a certain fleeting quality. This is due not only to the demands of time and life's distractions. There may be something inherent in the critical quest itself that makes dialogue creatively incomplete and mysterious. Though Euthyphro has lost his interest in the search for the essence of piety, his point is not wholly without merit when he says to Socrates near the end of the discourse: "... somehow or other our arguments, on whatever ground we rest them seem to turn round and walk away from us."[52] This aspect of discussion is true to the reality of living which can frustrate, in its elusiveness, the person seeking answers. Tied in with this is also the frustration of being right on the edge of seeing a central truth—and then turning aside as in *The Euthyphro*. The teacher, like Socrates, refuses to "tell" the group. She would like them to make the discovery for themselves.[53] But then the moment is lost as the discussion moves on. Add to this the limitations and complexities of human nature. Mortimer Adler puts it well:

At the same time we should not expect too much. Human beings—creatures of passion as well as of intellect, with minds that are often clouded by their feelings, and with all the other limitations to which their fallible minds are subject—must be satisfied with some measure of approximation to the ideal and not inordinately seek its complete realization, at least not at any given time or place.[54]

It is good to remember these things not only in regard to dialogic discussion processes, but to interpersonal relationships in general.

SOCRATES AS DIALOGIST

The best known aspect of Socratic teaching is in the Inquirer/Catalyst Form where the method is a relentless questioning of the student similar to the "elenchus" used by Socrates.[55] As we have seen, the effect hoped for is a "breaking through" whereby the student seeks to become more actively involved in learning. However, the elenchus is only part of the Socratic method. It prepares the interlocutor for the mutual search that can take place once students have come, at least to some degree, to recognize their ignorance. Such a recognition, if achieved without destroying the attitude of trust, brings with it a strong curiosity which will make the student more active in the search. For example, in *The Meno* a point is reached where through elenchus Socrates has moved the young man from a certain mental sloth and overconfidence to an attitude of genuine concern for the quest, even though that concern will be short lived. As Kenneth Seeskin in his recent study of Socratic method puts it, "Socrates puts out a helping hand: they will now inquire into the nature of virtue together."[56] This is the invitation to dialogue where the participants can work toward attaining "a clearer picture" of the reality they are discussing.

A number of interesting similarities crop up between Socrates' activities in the early dialogues and the Dialogic Teaching Form as described in this chapter. Perhaps the most important is that Socrates, through his new method, rejects the accepted pedagogy of his time wherein the teacher (poet, sophist, Athenian elder) transmits the logoi (content) to passive pupils for memorization and reproduction. Instead, Socrates sought to engage his interlocutors. He abhorred long speeches (lectures) because the listener must remain passive and is not able to question or analyze.[57] In dialectic there is a passing back and forth, a testing of opinions wherein the participants can search together actively.

So, too, the dialogic teaching form moves beyond previous teacher-centered forms and involves the class members in an active discourse wherein growth in all the participants becomes possible. Socrates a number of times in the early dialogues claims he is also testing himself and needs to see more clearly. Thus, his function is similar to that of a discussion or seminar leader who is not a teacher in the ordinary sense, but as Adler puts it in describing Socratic method for the modern classroom, "merely the first among equals in a joint effort to reach a goal that is shared by all."[58]

Secondly, Socrates is person-centered in that he focuses on both the character and beliefs of his interlocutors. In this sense he involves the whole self. Even more, Socrates adapts his method to the "psychai" of the persons he faces.[59] We have already seen that identifying with the student's world is of key import in the Inducer/Persuader Teaching Form. But as dialogist Socrates sustains this approach all through the dialogue in which the person is allowed (even urged) to be himself and say what he really thinks. In short, the interlocutor will be asked, as Teloh puts it, "to give an account of his life, that is, of his core beliefs which direct that life."[60] Of course, Socrates' notion of personal relationships is not as all embracing as that described for the Dialogic Teaching Form. But given the modes of address for that time in Athens, these similarities are strong enough to bear a comparison.

Thirdly, Socrates' "availability"—his modeling and example—creates the possibility of dialogue. However, as we have noted with the dialogic teacher, this availability, while indispensable, does not insure that a discourse will take place. What Socrates presents are opportunities; he does not force his interlocutors to enter dialogue, and they are more likely to participate if they have survived the rigors of the elenchus (Inquirer/Catalyst).

Fourthly, the conversations which take place in the early dialogues rarely supply definitive answers, but instead usually leave the discussants in a state of "aphoria" (perplexity). Such an outcome is intended by Socrates in so far as he does not see it as his task to supply conclusions or answers. This would be to revert back to the transmissive type of education so common in his time. Socrates refuses to take the authoritarian approach because he does not want to stifle dialectic. He seeks rather to allow the participants to see and discover for themselves. And such discoveries imply a transformation.[61] It is also important to remember that Socrates himself claimed not to know, to be a fellow searcher. Thus, he says to Critias in *The Charmides*: "Critias, you act as though I professed to know the answers to the questions I ask you, and could give them to you if I wished. It isn't so. I inquire with you ...because I don't myself have knowledge."[62]

This attitude of mind is the same for dialogic teachers whose task is not to supply answers, but rather to lead and share in the search. They, as does Socrates, give direction, or at the most, fertile suggestions pointing to possible paths of inquiry which again, as in the Dialogues, occasionally lead to dead ends. The discussion will often break off without the kind of closure students are accustomed to in lectures. Group members will leave in midair, in perplexity, full of ruminations, possibilities. Adler points out that though good discussions presume a common knowledge base the important questions that arise in a seminar are those to which there is no "right" answer.[63]

Deliberations of this nature call for a certain openness and commitment on the part of the participants. For this reason Socrates tried to steer the dialectic away from turning into contests in which one or another of the participants wins. He was seeking something much more enduring—an adventure involving in the words of Kenneth Seeskin, "The honesty to say what one really thinks, the reasonableness to admit what one does not know, and the courage to continue the investigation."[64] That he often did not succeed in this endeavor is sad, but not surprising, given the atmosphere of ancient Athens—one in which male citizens of leisure were trained in verbal jousting before an audience. Thus, in sparring with Socrates interlocutors such as Critias, who had a reputation to preserve, were more concerned with not looking like fools than with an intellectual exploration regardless of the consequences.

So, too, dialogic discussions, as we have stressed, can founder when participants lose sight of the real purpose for the coming together, when deliberations turn into matches of gamesmanship rooted in ego-boasting or when they turn acerbic, separating students into islands of distrust. Plato claimed that it is only where people ask and answer questions in a spirit of benevolence and without envy that philosophical discussion can take place.[65] Such a spirit should be easier to create in the Dialogic classroom where it can be assumed that most class members will be more willing than many of Socrates' interlocutors to share and question without allowing conflict to degenerate into animosity. The maintenance of a communal atmosphere is all the more likely if the group has an equal number of women who are often repelled by the competitive jousting and posturing more common to males as they seek a more supportive educational environment.[66]

We have already pointed out the importance of listening in good discourse. A number of Socrates' interlocutors fail to engage in dialectic because they lack this ability. Polemarchus and Thrasymachus in *The Republic* will not listen although the latter accuses Socrates of the same failing. Just as in modern discussion classes, the reason for this lack of attention is often that class members are set in their ways, more interested in holding to their positions than opening themselves to the possibility of change. Sometimes there are other causes: Callicles and Nicea lack sufficient knowledge; Critias and Protagoras have reputations to protect. Henry Teloh points out that Socrates' most complete and successful elenchus is with Meno's slave—probably because he has no vested interest in the topic and could come to it without bias.[67] So, too, very often in higher education it is the simple, unsophisticated student who will grow the most through dialogue.

Finally, a number of recent commentators point out that Socrates frequently fails in his pedagogic efforts to sustain dialectic.[68] Part of the reason, as we have seen, lies in the agonistic spirit of Greek society. Another cause lies in natural distractions or unexpected interruptions that take place in any discourse. Though Plato's dialogues are artistically crafted, they retain that element of everyday reality that makes them so concrete. Also, limitations of human character are an important factor. Socrates seems more committed to the search than most of his interlocutors.

So, too, in dialogic discussion we have outlined the obstacles that can prevent or shortcut success. We have noted that environments in higher education today almost militate against the Dialogic Teaching Form. Beyond this, we have noted something in the very nature of the critical quest that renders discussion incomplete even when all other conditions are met. This may be due to the "aphoria" created in the discussants. Yet for Socrates such perplexity and unfinishedness are the result of his teaching method, a method he refused to compromise because to do so would be to cut off the process of testing and examination.

Dialogic discourse, like all human relationships, cannot be wrapped up and tied together in neat little packages as can teaching in the more didactic modes. Even in those discussions where a climax is achieved, it only holds until the next time the discussants meet. Group members are left to continue the pursuit on their own as they singly or in concert assume more and more responsibility for their own learning. The teacher has been successful here if he has catalyzed this shift and then opened the students to a testing of their own opinions in the waters of the common discourse.

In closing this brief addenda on Socrates, one difference should be pointed out between the procedure in the early Dialogues and that of contemporary dialogic discussion. In the Dialogues, though a number of participants come together, actual dialectic usually takes place between Socrates and one other interlocutor. Often Plato has different characters argue with him in succession. In the Dialogic Teaching Form we have seen that the teacher attempts to shift the emphasis away from that kind of prolonged encounter, though brief tête-à-têtes between individuals take place within the context of the general discussion.

Still and all, even in the Socratic dialogues a learning community is present because the energies are not limited merely to the two interlocutors but fan out to all those who are listening and avidly following the discourse. Socrates' encounters with his interlocutors are dialogic because there is shared inquiry.

DIALOGIST

Characteristics of Teacher

- available and open
- initiates discourse and shared inquiry
- both directs and participates
- reduces psychological size
- shifts energy flow from self to group
- listens attentively
- inspires personal response
- creates mutuality and cooperativeness
- keeps materials flexible and open ended
- thoroughly knowledgeable in subject area
- aware of diversity of class members

General Skills

- initiates and sustains discourse effectively
- able to induce group interaction
- employs own knowledge indirectly in interests of group discussion
- employs questions oriented toward shared inquiry
- allows adequate "wait time" when questioning
- makes use of student remarks to move discussion on
- helps group distinguish between real and apparent misunderstanding
- employs exercises in skills of empathy

- creates opportunities for students to take positions different from their own
- gives students practice in clarification and precise usage of terms
- opens students to richness and subtleties of discourse
- moves group to function on both cognitive and emotional levels
- probes learning materials in more detail
- moves group members to see dialogue as communal knowledge sharing
- increases own awareness of each student's unique subjectivity
- works on reducing own biases in regard to students
- helps group to recognize and deal with diversity in backgrounds and values

Student Aptitudes
- intrinsically motivated to engage in discourse
- takes equal responsibility for success of discourse
- comes alive as person through relation
- practices higher learning skills via discussion
- converses from adequate knowledge base
- sees discourse as natural way of learning
- able to state own position clearly
- able to clarify and distinguish among terms
- learns to examine subject material and issues in more detail
- becomes aware of both cognitive and affective aspects of learning
- learns to identify with positions of other class members
- comes to view learning as open ended process
- appreciates communal aspect of learning

NOTES

1. Martin Buber, "Elements of the Interhuman," in *The Knowledge of Man*, ed. Maurice Freedman (London: George Allen & Unwin Ltd., 1965), pp. 72–87.

2. "The Philosophy of Dialogue as the Counterproject to Transcendental Philosophy: The Dialogic of Martin Buber," in Michael Theunissen, *The Other: Studies in the Social Ontology of Husserl, Heidegger, Sartre and Buber*. (Cambridge, Mass.: MIT Press, 1984), p. 274.

3. DeVito, "Teaching As Relational Development," p. 55.

4. John Mac Murray, *Persons In Relation* (London: Faber and Faber Limited, 1961), p. 158.

5. Charles K. Bolton and Ronald K. Boyer, "One-Way and Two-Way Communication Process in the Classroom," *The Teaching-Learning Monograph Series*, vol. 1, no. 1 (Cincinnati: Institute for Research and Training in Higher Education, University of Cincinnati, 1971), p. 4.

6. Quoted in Theunissen, *The Other*; p. 277.

7. See Ohmer Milton and associates, *On College Teaching: A Guide to Contemporary Practices*, (San Francisco: Jossey-Bass Publishers, 1985), pp. 69–71.

8. McGown, *Availability: Gabriel Marcel and the Phenomenology of Human Openness*, pp. 11–17.

9. MacMurray, *Persons in Relation*, p. 17.

10. Theunissen, *The Other* p. 280. Buber's term "interhuman" is for Marcel the "intersubjective," i.e. "a community rooted in ontology without which human relations would be impossible." (cf. *Availability*, p. 43).

11. Michael Oakescott, *Poetry as a Voice in the Conversation of Mankind: An Essay* (London: Bowes & Bowes, 1959), pp. 10–11. See also R.S. Peters, "What Is an Educational Process" in *The Concept of Education*, pp. 21–22.

12. Theunissen, *The Other*, p. 310. Elizabeth Douvan also points out that the unexpected is intrinsic to the concept of interpersonal relationships. Except in cases of disloyalty we react with surprise and delight. Elizabeth Douvan, "Interpersonal Relationships: Some Questions and Observations," in *Close Relationships: Perceptions on the Meaning of Intimacy*, ed. George Levinger and Harold L. Raush (Amherst: University of Massachusetts Press, 1977) p. 18.

13. DeVito, "Teaching As Relational Development," p. 53

14. Wilkenson, "The Varieties of Teaching," p. 6.

15. William E. Cashin and Philip C. McNight, "Idea Paper no. 15: Improving Discussions," *Center For Faculty Evaluation & Development* (Manhattan, Kansas: Kansas State University, January 1986): 2.

16. Eble, *The Craft of Teaching*, p. 61. See also Wilbert J. McKeachie, *Teaching Tips: A Guidebook for the Beginning College Teacher*, p. 38; Ohmer Milton and associates, *On College Teaching*, pp. 71–72.

17. Perkinson, *Learning From Our Mistakes: A Reinterpretation of Twentieth Century Educational Theory*, p. 177.

18. Israel Scheffler, "Philosophical Models of Teaching," in *Reason and Teaching*, p. 77.

19. Cashin and McKnight, *Improving Discussions*, p. 2.

20. Robert J. Sternberg and Marie Martin, "When Teaching Thinking Does Not Work, What Goes Wrong," *Teachers College Record*, 89 (Summer 1988): 555–78. See also, Mary Lynn Crow, "Teaching as an Interactive Process," in *New Directions For Teaching and Learning: Improving Teaching Styles*, p. 54.

21. Steinberg and Martin, p. 561.

22. Peter Frederick, "The Dreaded Discussion: Ten Ways to Start,' *Improving College and University Teaching*, 29, no. 3 (Summer, 1981): 109. Research evidence also documents the paucity of highly interactive discussions involving most of the students. See Robert J. Menges, "Instructional Methods.'

23. Mortimer J. Adler, *The Paideia Proposal: An Educational Manifesto on Behalf of the Members of the Paideia Group*, (New York: Macmillan Publishing Co., 1982). In particular, the author's comments on what he calls Level Three of Schooling: Understanding through Maiutic or Socratic Questioning and Active Participation.

24. Paulo Freire, *Pedagogy of the Oppressed* (New York: The Seabury Press, 1970), p. 85.

25. Transcription from Modern Drama Course at Philadelphia College of Pharmacy and Science, September 25, 1987.

26. Glassman, "The Teacher as Leader," in *New Directions For Teaching and Learn-*

ing: Improving Teaching Styles, p. 34. Glassman points out that the class can take equal responsibility in gathering learning materials and even in setting up evaluation procedures. Here the activity of negotiation takes shape led again by the teacher.

27. Ibid., p. 34.

28. Practical guidelines and exercises for attitudes in listening can be found in Robert Bolton's *People Skills: How To Assert Yourself, Listen to Others, and Resolve Conflicts* (Englewood, N.J.: Prentice Hall, Inc., 1979), pp. 27–77.

29. Mortimer J. Adler, *How to Speak How to Listen* (New York: MacMillan Publishing Company, 1983), p. 161.

30. Peter Elbow, *Embracing Contraries: Explorations in Learning and Teaching,* pp. 260–261. For exercises in improving students perceptions of others and their contexts, see Kenneth Bullmer, *The Art of Empathy: A Manual for Improving Accuracy of Interpersonal Perception* (New York: Human Sciences Press, 1975). For a discussion of how to write papers which empathize with opposite points of view, see Richard E. Young, Alton L. Becker and Kenneth L. Pike, *Rhetoric: Discovery and Change* (New York: Harcourt, Brace & World, Inc., 1970), pp. 273–90.

31. Mary Field Belenky et al., *Woman's Ways of Knowing: The Development of Self, Voice, and Mind* (New York: Basic Books, Inc., 1986), p. 101.

32. Schwab, "Eros and Education," p. 122.

33. Adler, *How To Speak How To Listen,* p. 173. Donald and Alice Stone suggest a number of innovative arrangements to accommodate numbers larger than twenty. See "The Seat of Power," *Carnegie Mellon Magazine* (Winter 1988): 12–18.

34. Adler, p. 173; Eble, *The Craft of Teaching,* p. 62; Ohmer Milton et al., *On College Teaching,* p. 65.

35. William A. Reinsmith, "Humanistic Education in a Professional-Technical School: An Advanced Humanities Course" (D.A. diss., Carnegie-Mellon University, 1982), p. 152.

36. MacMurray, *Persons in Relation,* p. 60.

37. See Howard Gardner, *Frames of Mind: The Theory of Multiple Intelligences* (New York: Basic Books, Inc., 1985).

38. Ibid., pp. 237–76. Gardner has not specifically made the application to dialogic discussion, though his book does contain a chapter on the Education of the Intelligences. However, I believe the applicability is obvious.

39. Menges, "Instructional Methods," p. 574.

40. One scientist who takes this exact approach is Barbara McClintock. See the chapter, "A World of Difference," in Evelyn Fox Keller, *Reflections on Gender and Science* (New Haven: Yale University Press, 1985). In speaking of McClintock's research Keller notes: "Indeed, the intimacy she experiences with the objects she studies—intimacy born of a lifetime of cultivated attentiveness—is a wellspring of her powers as a scientist." (p. 164)

41. Nel Noddings, "Fidelity in Teaching," *Harvard Educational Review* 56 (November 1986): 499.

42. Buber, *Pointing the Way* Torchbook Edition (New York: Harper & Row Publishers, 1963), p. 238. Joseph DeVito states that if a class is without conflict it is probably dealing with insignificant issues. See "Teaching As Relational Development," p. 57.

43. Noddings, "Fidelity in Teaching," p. 501–502.

44. See Bullmer, *The Art of Empathy.* Bullmer points out that interpersonal perceptions are really "inferences concerning the emotions, intentions, attitudes, traits,

and other internal properties of the perceived person. In this sense, since so many human properties are internal rather than external and cannot be observed visually, persons are not so much perceived as they are judged." (p. 1)

45. Reinsmith, "Humanistic Education in a Professional-Technical School," p. 48.

46. Milton, *On College Teaching*, p. 78. Special attention must be given to students from minorities who are new to college experience—though by the time they are exposed to the Dialogic teaching form these students may have been matriculating for a while. Nevertheless, these students may have deeply embedded feelings about how they have been treated in the past. See Milton, pp. 79–80.

47. Ibid., p. 78.

48. Joyce Hocker, "Teacher-Student Confrontations," in *New Directions For Teaching and Learning: Communicating in College Classrooms*, p. 77.

49. Eble, *The Craft of Teaching*, p. 64.

50. Wayne Booth, *The Vocation of a Teacher*, p.260.

51. Joel Jones, "The Art of Teaching: An Act of Love," in *New Directions For Teaching and Learning: Communicating in College Classrooms*, p. 89.

52. Plato, "The Euthyphro," in *The Dialogues of Plato*, vol. 1, p. 320.

53. Vlastos shows how Socrates takes exactly this tack with Euthyphyo, how he leads him to the point where he can see for himself the right answer. But Socrates refuses to tell Euthyphro this answer not because he does not think Euthyphro's soul worth saving, but "because he believes there is only one way to save it and that Euthyphro himself must do the job by finding this one right way, so that he too becomes a searcher." See Gregory Vlastos, "The Paradox of Socrates" in *The Philosophy of Socrates: A Collection of Critical Essays*, p.14

54. Adler, *How to Speak, How to Listen* p. 165–166.

55. "Elenchus" literally means "to examine, refute or put to shame." See Kenneth Seeskin, *Dialogue and Discovery: A Study in Socratic Method* (Albany: State University of New York Press, 1987), p. 1. The emphasis in the Inquirer/Catalyst Teaching Form is on examining.

56. Ibid., p. 25.

57. This use of a new method by Socrates in the early dialogues is explained by Henry Teloh, *Socratic Education in Plato's Early Dialogues*, pp. 1–23.

58. Debbie Walsh, "Socrates in the Classroom: Strategies for Enhancing Critical Thinking Skills," *American Educator*, 9, No. 2 (Summer 1985): p. 22.

59. Teloh, *Socratic Education in Plato's Early Dialogues*, p. 1. Teloh calls this "the *Phaedrus* principle."

60. Ibid., p. 16.

61. For Socrates and the "transformative" tradition of teaching, see Philip Jackson, *The Practice of Teaching*, pp. 125–137.

62. Quoted in Vlastos, "The Paradox of Socrates," p. 9. Vlastos goes on to assure us that this is not an example of Socratic Irony, but rather that side or aspect of Socrates in which he assumes the role of fellow searcher.

63. Walsh, "Socrates in the Classroom," p. 22.

64. Seeskin, *Dialogue and Discovery*, p. 3. I have used the terms "dialogue" and dialectic" here interchangeably though I realize that the latter has come to imply more a confrontation or testing of opposites. However, the root meaning of the words is similar.

65. Seeskin, p. 112.

66. See Belenky, et. al. "Toward an Education For Women" in *Woman's Ways of Knowing: The Development of Self, Voice, and Mind*, pp. 193–213.

67. Teloh, *Socratic Education in Plato's Early Dialogues*, p. 12.

68. Seeskin, pp. 13–17; Teloh, pp. 20–23; Vlastos, pp. 12–17.

Part Four

Elicitive Mode

Active commitment to learning on the part of the student has already resulted in sustained dialogic encounter involving equal energies between teacher and students. Now things can move solidly to the right side of the continuum where teaching becomes increasingly student-centered. In the Elicitive Mode the teacher's overt activities decrease while those of the student gather momentum. The task has shifted to that of assisting the student's learning. Dressel and Marcus articulate this vision very well: "A teacher's commitment to learning and a sense of excitement in pursuing that commitment must be accompanied by an abiding awareness that in the long run, it is what the learner does rather than what the teacher does that really counts in teaching."[1]

Henceforth, the teacher's presence is one of helping the student bring knowledge to birth, not through extrinsic persuasion or the "bells and incantations" described by Socrates in *The Meno*, but in a more interior way, a way that has been made possible through the relational and centering activities of the Dialogic Mode. The teacher will be softer, more yielding and supportive, suggesting, evoking, guiding, witnessing the student's growth. This is not meant to suggest that the teacher's task is easier. True, she may be less obvious and pervasive, but the Elicitive Mode requires more subtle skills than those involved in previous modes. Genuine mid-wifery is the act of helping students articulate what is already within. As one student put it on a evaluation form for an undergraduate drama course: "The instructor made me feel as if I was learning everything on my own and that he had no hand in it."[2] Such activity calls for a close watching, a delicate feel, a further feminization of the teaching act, if you will.

It is in the Elicitive Mode that the student's energies are refined. On the one hand, immersion in group work is even more spontaneous and cooperative; on the other, something is being drawn out of the communal which enriches the personal quest. Also, teacher and learner begin to relate in a new way. It is in this mode that—to employ Sylvia Ashton-Warner's term— a certain "espousal" takes place,[3] one involving a more selfless giving by the teacher and a grateful acceptance on the part of students exemplified in their blossoming out into total independence.

NOTES

1. Paul L. Dressel and Dora Marcus, *On Teaching and Learning in College: Reemphasizing the Roles of Learners and the Disciplines* (San Francisco: Jossey-Bass Publishers, 1982), p. XIX.

2. Anonymous student evaluation of Modern Drama Course, at the Philadelphia College of Pharmacy and Science, Fall, 1988.

3. Ashton-Warner, *Teacher*, p. 210.

Chapter 6

Teacher As Facilitator/Guide

You cannot teach a man anything; you can only help him to find it within himself.

Galileo

STUDENT-CENTERED LEARNING

This chapter begins with the fundamental statement that all real learning is directed from within. Sooner or later the teacher as well as the learner must come to realize this. Throughout the history of pedagogy holistic educators have always viewed the teacher's task as that of assisting the inner energies of the child. Henry Perkinson's description of the Montessori classroom shows this clearly:

The Montessori classroom is a free environment, a place where the student is free from a "judgmental" teacher, a place where the student is free to disclose his present knowledge. The teacher approaches the child in an invitational mode, encouraging him to talk, to act—to demonstrate his present skills and understandings.[1]

Montessori and others have gone even further to suggest that the teacher's most important work is to observe children carefully and to learn from them. In fact, the acute observer will see not only how complex the child's inner world is, but that the children are impelled from within to use body, mind, and feelings to interact with the world outside of them.[2]

On the secondary and college levels this same truth holds. The teacher's first task is to set up contexts in which the student's inner energies can focus properly. Speaking to this issue, Perkinson describes how the teacher helps students to articulate and then improve on the knowledge they already have:

"So the initial step is to create an environment where the pupil feels free to disclose that knowledge. In a free environment, pupils are not ashamed of their present knowledge, nor are they afraid to reveal it, to make it public."[3]

Thus, the teacher reaches a point on the continuum where preparation has been made for an entirely new type of encounter, one in which she responds rather than initiates or directs. This shift should not be misunderstood. The teacher does not simply do the student's bidding or fade away into the woodwork; her rechanneled energies, though non-invasive, are crucial in creating the formats and boundaries within which the students, either individually or in concert, carry on their learning experiments. The teacher's presence acts in an even more intimate way than in the Dialogic Form, but that presence is not as obvious, as we shall see. Paradoxically, the teacher's expectations for the student have grown. Those students who are moved to take responsibility for their own learning will be much more in touch with their inner powers and thus make new demands on themselves. Through a facilitating presence the teacher corroborates and strengthens this new view of the learning self.

The delicateness of the blend here can be gleaned from Ken Macrorie's interview in *Twenty Teachers* with Sam Bush, a woodworking instructor who teaches prep school boys. Bush starts the process by reflecting back to the student the responsibility that is his: "A boy comes to me, and asks to build a chair. Right from the first I put all the decisions on him. What kind of chair—narrow? low? modern? dark brown? At first that approach usually throws the boy, but he recovers and we start drawing."[4] Bush then follows the student's progress, commenting, questioning in order to hear him support his ideas:

I do this so he will feel we are working from *his* impetus, that his decisions are taken seriously, and because often his ideas are better than mine...At this time I make suggestions that I think will be improvements, without being overpowering. If I tell him outright that he *has* to do a certain thing, he will do it, but he will also hate me for stealing his project. (pp.4–5)

This theme of working with the student in a non-invasive manner, yet expecting quality work, punctuates all of Bush's dealing with his pupils: "I tell them all the required capacities to do the work exist within them, waiting to be released by their struggling." (p. 5) Bush will aid in their struggling, but he will not take over their struggling for them—he will not do their work for them or substitute his vision for their own. Neither will he lecture or tediously tell. Any instruction that he does give is in keeping with the inner vision the student is pursuing. This is the essence of the Facilitator/Guide Form. Bush puts it perfectly: "I'm trying to draw out what is in the boy rather than pile it on him." (p. 8)

In another chapter of *Twenty Teachers* Macrorie observes how two teacher-enablers working together with a small group in a college math classroom assiduously follow rather than interfere with their students' energies. His running commentary reveals the essential dynamic of the Facilitator/Guide Form:

As I sat there, I realized that John and Bill aren't directing the groups, rather teaching from behind the lines. [The groups are working at the board] Bill is on tiptoes in mind and body, watching, waiting for moves that advance toward the answer. He tightens his lips, nods his head, his whole body saying, "That's it! That's it!" And then his lips form, "Oh no!" (p. 62)

Bill whispers to Macrorie that the hardest thing is to hold back and let the students struggle: "When they are learning there are so many physical re-actions in the room. When they're not, the room can be lifeless." (p. 62) This method of holding back allows the teachers to watch students thinking mathematically."

Facilitative teaching involves a kind of enthusiastic restraint that allows students the freedom to grope, to take wrong directions, reverse fields, and try new approaches. The teacher often functions in this form as a coach, providing critical feedback. But such activities are only facilitative when they move out of a different conception of the educational task than is usual in higher education. Again, Perkinson puts the matter well when suggesting that the actual methods, strategies, and tactics used will best come "from practicing teachers who have reconceived education as a procedure of growth instead of a process of transmission."[5]

Perhaps the most complete demonstration of how the facilitative dialogue works between teacher and student is provided by Donald Schon in his discussion of the design process in an Architectural Studio.[6] In this context, master/teachers work with apprentice/students on a kind of graduate level, thus insuring that intrinsic motivation for design is already there. Nevertheless, students exhibit varying degrees of self-confidence and inner sureness. Schon shows at length how relationships can get off on the wrong footing and revert to more conventional modes of master telling the apprentice how she *should* be conceiving a design task or what he is doing wrong on a project. But when things go well—usually in a situation where the instructor is quite skilled as a coach and guide—the results can be dramatically different. The following extended encounter between Dani and Michal provides an excellent example:

Dani presents Michal with an opportunity to learn how to practice where "practice" is conceived as exploration and testing of alternative means of producing the qualities of product she finds appealing. She is invited to attend to her own appreciative judgements, surfacing preferences she might otherwise ignore or suppress. (p. 152)

Yet, Dani is also able to help his student move into a firmer vision of her work without being invasive:

In the same process by which Dani encourages Michal to produce what she likes, he guides her through a discipline in which appreciation regulates experimentation. Implicitly, he leads her to see the kind of objectivity achievable in a practice experiment—a kind that is dependent on her subjective preferences: she can judge for herself independent of mere opinion, whatever she has succeeded in realizing the qualities she says she wants. (p. 152–53)

Here Dani functions as dialogist, facilitator, guide—even co-learner—and instead of imposing his view upon her releases her to see and choose more clearly her own design. In fact, Schon says that Dani seems here to have entered into a kind of contract with Michal, the elements of which seem to be as follows:

She should step into the situation, advocating the qualities she wants to produce; Dani will accept Michal's preferences, without trying to impose his own on her. Michal must become an experimenter, testing out alternative ways of achieving her goal. Dani will become her coexperimenter, helping her figure out how to do what she wants, demonstrating for her how she might achieve her goals. Michal must judge her own work—and Dani will join her in judging it—on the basis of her success in producing what she intends. (p. 153)

We see here quite clearly that the energies lie with the student, that the teacher not only assumes the student accepts responsibility for her own progress in learning (note that Sam Bush has to remind his prep school students), but allows her to initiate her preferences. He then urges her to move ahead and use the freedom to try options—that is, not be afraid of the trial and error process. Dani will assist, even work with, his student. He may even show her some possible moves, but he will never take the reins out of her hands. Finally, in a kind of partnership both teacher and learner, working within the form the student has chosen, will judge the success of her intent. Robert Kloss, using the metaphor of coach for teaching, recalls John Dewey's admonition on the learning process:

It is this procedure, it seems to me, that Dewey [1974] had in mind when he declared of the learner that "He has to see on his own behalf and in his own way the relations between means and methods employed and results achieved. Nobody else can see for him, and he can't see just by being 'told,' although the right kind of telling may guide his seeing and thus help him see what he needs to see." [7]

How different this dynamic is from that of the teaching forms on the left side of the continuum. We can also note how an atmosphere of educational intimacy has been created and sustained. Still, a decided shift has taken place even from the centering energies characteristic of the Dialogic Form where, through the teacher's impulse teacher and student(s) equally shared the sphere of the "in-between." Now, a new sphere has been created, largely by the student, and the teacher begins to work within it. Moving along with the student's energy flow, the teacher assists, coaches, offers feedback, and when necessary, challenges. But most importantly, he works within the student's line of vision. Over a quarter of a century ago, Sylvia Ashton-Warner spoke of this process in regard to her Maori children as one in which the teacher releases and then goes with the organic growth inside the child, where " . . . the latent energy, the element that so severely opposes a teacher when imposing knowledge, is here turned on what they are doing. It's an energy that is almost frightening when released."[8]

So too, what Donald Schon calls a kind of learning contract cements the new relationship between teacher and learner, one which avoids the usual problems that arise between an overly directive instructor working with an inwardly directed student:

Sitting next to Michal in the presence of a shared problem that originates in her intentions, Dani escapes the dilemma of how to convey negative information to her without triggering her defenses. Information that might otherwise be seen as negative can now be seen, realistically, as helpful to her efforts to achieve her goals.[9]

Such progress in the learner is achievable for the educator who operates successfully as Facilitator/Guide.

OBSTACLES TO CREATING STUDENT-CENTERED LEARNING

If, as we have said in the last chapter, dialogic teaching is difficult today in higher education, attempts to sustain student-centered learning through a facilitative teaching form in conventional classroom settings can be even more daunting. A number of reasons exist for this. The first has to do with how students perceive their teachers in the university setting. In *Embracing Contraries* Peter Elbow has discussed this problem at some length. He claims there is a crucial contradiction in the role of almost every institutional teacher, one that prevents our being genuine allies of the student:

We are both credit-giver and teacher. As credit-giver we are the hurdle the student has to get over; as teacher we are the person who helps the student get over the hurdles. It is very common for teachers to imply that they are more truly allies of the student than this contradiction permits.[10]

As long as the teacher makes the final evaluation of a student's progress and that evaluation is non-negotiable (as it is in most higher education contexts) her efforts as facilitator are somewhat mitigated. Added to this is the fact that, as Elbow's quote implies, the vast majority of undergraduate students view their educational process as a series of mine fields to be traversed rather than as forms of knowledge to be entered into. Because of this those teachers who attempt to be facilitative often do so in a superficial manner, to help student's overcome institutional hurdles on their way to a diploma. Exaggerated grade consciousness may be the most pervasive disease among students in higher education today—a direct outcome of our intense emphasis on the vocational aspect of learning. It is one thing to view a grade as tangible evidence of educational growth or mastery of knowledge; it is quite another to see grades as ends in themselves, purely as status symbols or tickets to graduate school or better employment opportunities.

Elbow, to an extent, gives in to these realities when he speaks later of using facilitative teaching (functioning as an ally) as a counterpoint to the institutional or gatekeeper role the teacher is forced to play. He views the alternation here as a kind of dialectic between opposing forces:

But how, concretely, can we best function as allies? One of the best ways is to be a kind of coach. One has set up the hurdle for practice jumping, one has described the strength and tactics of the enemy, one has warned them about what the prosecuting attorney will probably do: now the coach can prepare them for these rigors. Being an ally is probably more a matter of stance and relationship than of specific behaviors.[11]

Though this sounds very much like "teaching to the exam" we recognize the Facilitator Form here. But the level and extent of its employment are nowhere near as deep as the encounters between master and apprentice depicted in Donald Schon's study, *Educating the Reflective Practioner*. That is because the student's motivation is not as intrinsic.

The second obstacle to true facilitative teaching flows from the first. Because of their educational immaturity students will often resist a teacher's attempts to place responsibility for learning on their shoulders. One of the main tenets of this book is that unless students have been initiated in some manner into assuming such responsibility they will not be active participants in seeking knowledge. Consequently, they will not readily respond to a facilitative teacher, especially one who attempts to use the form fully. The necessary encounter will simply not take place. The pedagogical dust bin of academia has its share of abortive attempts to employ facilitative teaching methods before students were ready or circumstances allowed. As Anne Toppins points out, years of traditional academic experience condition even graduate students to be passive, dependent learners.[12] Certainly, most undergraduate students today expect the teacher to be the active force in their education. Even students who at first seem to welcome the kind of self-reliance facilitative teaching offers can have trouble handling such responsibility once it is assumed.[13]

Another daunting obstacle to employment of the Facilitator/Guide Form is the time it takes to sustain student-centered learning. Doing so entails a flexibility that normal classroom schedules don't allow. Once you invest the learning process fully in the student the rigid nature of our educational system becomes apparent. Activated students are highly individualized, they exhibit different learning styles, need to work at their own pace and want much more control over how and when they will work. Except for open labs, optional recitations, and opportunities for individual conferences during professor's office hours (where the teacher's time is often constrained by research demands), undergraduate education in American universities is not conducive to such openness.[14] Everyone is more or less expected to assemble, absorb, and reproduce in lockstep fashion.

Finally, because of institutional constraints and lowered student expectations, most teachers today in higher education have little opportunity to present themselves as Facilitator/Guides and thus, can't gain much experience in the form. Testimony to such a condition is provided when one observes how much class time teachers spend talking both to and at their students, often in monologic fashion. This is largely true even in formats which are ostensibly meant to be facilitative.[15] As we stressed at the beginning of the chapter, learning to teach in a student-centered manner involves a redirection of the teacher's energies, one which places her at a different vantage point in the educational process. She must learn to move off center, to retreat, to open out—often wordlessly—to the student's initiative. It can be very difficult for a person used to teacher-centered instruction to suddenly make the switch to the Dialogic or Elicitive Modes. The shift more often takes place gradually, in keeping with the teacher's inner growth (a disenchantment with conventional teaching forms) and the good fortune of having students eager, or at least ready, to take responsibility for their own learning. Even where the shift is made in this fashion the teacher can encounter deeper, more phenomenological problems. Gordon Chamberlain has put this well:

One of the problems is that of intersubjectivity. Whenever a person is concerned, or employed, or required, to help another person learn something, both helper and learner are involved in all the problems of the two subjectivities, of a common world but different life-worlds, of attempting to discern the meaning which the other is trying to communicate.[16]

We saw in the Inducer/Persuader Form how indispensable it is for the teacher to relate to the student's world. In the Facilitator/Guide Form the relating is much deeper and more prolonged. It becomes paramount for the teacher to understand where his students are, as well as the authenticity of their efforts to grow. Only in this way can he be sure he is serving their needs rather than an image he has constructed from his own desires and plans. If the teacher has already made a concerted effort to free himself from perceptual biases in regard to his students, success is more likely in facilitative teaching. At the same time the student must be clear about the identity of the teacher and what his role will be.

FACILITATIVE TEACHING AND THE ADULT LEARNER

It comes as no surprise, then, to learn that the Facilitator/Guide Form can be most successful among adults who return to higher education with considerable inner motivation. At the same time, working with such students allows for the most flexibility in setting up time tables and adapting to individual learning styles.

Over the years, Malcolm Knowles probably has written most extensively about the adult learner. In what he calls "a new approach to learning" Knowles has proposed an "andogogical model" wherein assumptions are set forth totally at odds with those of traditional pedagogy.[17] One immediately notes that these assumptions are the same ones necessary for employing the Facilitator/Guide teaching form:

• The learner is self-directing
• The learner enters into an educational activity with a greater volume and quality of experience
• Adults engage in learning activity because they have experienced a need to know or do something in order to be more effective in some aspect of their life
• Though some external motivation is usually present—a better job possibility, a salary increase—the more potent motivating forces are internal[18]

These assumptions lead directly into what is known as "contract learning." We have seen that Schon uses the term in regard to the relationship established between master and apprentice in the architectural studio. But this contract is unspoken and usually informal. In the androgogical model a formal negotiable contract is established between teacher and learner, one that has to do with course design, learning objectives, sequence of learning units, and type of teaching. Here the teacher facilitates in a broad basic way, assisting adult students right at the beginning in laying out their educational plans. (The androgogical model finds the term "facilitator of learning" preferable to the conventional word "teacher.") Though adult students also often negotiate the content of their course design, emphasis is put on the overall process of individual learning. In fact, Knowles defines contract learning as "an alternative way of structuring a learning experience ... Instead of specifying how a body of content will be transmitted (content plan), it specifies how a body of content will be acquired by the learner (process plan)."[19] Within this broader realm is where the facilitator's main tasks come into play.

One of the most important of these tasks is what Knowles calls "climate setting"—both physical and psychological. The physical climate is similar to that created in the small seminar which will be discussed later in the chapter. Even more important is the psychological climate—one of mutual trust and respect, collaborativeness, supportiveness, openness and authenticity.[20] We have seen that trust and respect are part of the mutuality that goes into the Dialogic Mode. They are equally indispensable in facilitative teaching with adults. The foundation for such trust and respect is the positive regard the teacher shows for each person in the class. Collaborativeness and support are also central to working with adult learners since sharing will be constantly taking place not only between teacher and students, but among the students themselves. Adults will discover that for many kinds of learning activities peers are the richest resource, and thus an atmosphere of cooperation must offset the competitiveness that is most often the rule in traditional undergraduate—even graduate—education.

Knowles mentions that he opens all his courses and workshops with exercises that put participants into a sharing, mutually supporting relationship. These will be especially helpful to those students who are somewhat insecure about returning to college. For example, in the first session the class can be divided into groups of four or five with each group discussing the actual resources of its members: Who knows what, or who has had experience doing what? Through this exercise even the most insecure individuals will realize early on they have something to offer. At the same time collaborative, I-Thou relationships are being established rather than competitive, adversarial encounters.[21]

A climate of openness and authenticity is crucial in androgogy, and probably easier to sustain in facilitative teaching since the learner from the outset is viewing the teacher in a different light. And since the teacher assists and aligns herself with the student's educational plan, the usual resistance factor so common in more teacher-centered forms will be absent. Lastly, Knowles stresses creating a climate of pleasure—that is, learning as a gratifying experience. A number of qualities we have discussed under the Inducer/Persuader Form come into play here: the adventure of learning, the excitement of discovery, playfulness, and humor. The difference is that this sense of pleasure is not conveyed by the teacher alone, but mutually shared (even generated) by all in the pursuit of their educational goals.

One of the most important and innovative activities in Adult Learning involves having participants diagnose their own learning needs. The Facilitator/Guide here works with the student on a much broader level than in the usual undergraduate classroom where the teacher or the department has designed the objectives and learning activities beforehand. The process deals with what Knowles calls "felt needs" (internal to learner) and "ascribed needs" (societal and organizational); it often involves facilitator and learner in complex negotiations.[22] Here students can tap their considerable reservoir of life experience and translate into skills already attained. From this vantage point the student now has a better idea of what he or she needs to learn, and this vision can be placed within the even larger context of one's life direction. Admittedly, diagnosing one's learning needs and negotiating a course design out of these needs presumes a certain knowledge base and educational maturity on the part of the student, which is why such activities are more successful with the older learner. At the same time, negotiation may also require communication skills never used before in the student's educational career, though here, too, some transfer may be made from the student's working life. For example, both parties must work not only at deciding what course objectives should be met, but *how* and in what time frame they will be met. What responsibilities lie with the students and, once these have been defined, what are the teacher's obligations? For their part, teachers need to help learners identify learning patterns from past educational experiences and then discuss ways in which these patterns can be adapted to materials in the present course.[23] To achieve this kind of interaction the teacher will have to move into line with the student's vision of his experience.

The broad structuring activities discussed above are more easily carried out in disciplines like education, health care, humanities and social sciences. Courses in hard sciences are more difficult to set up in this fashion, though it has been done, almost always with students in their upper years or on a graduate level. Students must have enough of a previous knowledge base to recognize what they need or want to learn.[24]

Such facilitative activities can take place with students on a junior or senior level where the educational environment permits such negotiations to take place. But more often in courses where learning contracts are used a mitigated schema is involved, one in which students do not assist in designing learning materials, but only select those materials which encompass the level at which they choose to perform. Students may also meet with the teacher throughout the semester to discuss whether the selected goals are being met.

FACILITATIVE TEACHING AND STUDENT LEARNING STYLES

After long neglect research on how undergraduate students read, study, and learn in an academic setting is finally getting through to practitioners in higher education. Though much of it is quite recent and as yet somewhat indeterminate, the research is forcing an increasing number of educators to become conscious of what always should have been obvious—the importance of accommodating teaching methods to students' levels and styles of learning.[25]

We have pointed out already that facilitative teaching is often met with resistance by students who simply are not yet willing or able to take responsibility for the kind of learning that such teaching requires. An appreciation of the variety of student approaches to learning would certainly be helpful—one might even say indispensable—in deciding whether the Facilitator/Guide

Figure 6.1
Student Orientations Toward Studying

Orientation	Value	Motive	Strategy
Personal meaning (Factor I)	Personal development as overall goal of education	Intrinsic-interest in what is being learned	Work satisfying only if personal meaning established by relating new information to existing knowledge
Reproducing (Factor II)	Vocational preparation as main purpose of university	Extrinsic-need for qualification or fear of failure	Limit activities to those demanded (syllabus-bound) Learn by rote
Achieving (Factor III)	University as a game providing competition and opportunities to show excellence	Achievement-need for success	Structuring, organizing work, meets deadlines, plays the game (to win)

Source: Noel Entwistle, *Styles of Learning and Teaching*, p. 102.

teaching form can be effective within a given situation. However, Noel Entwistle points out that to date, "there has been little research into the effects of matching or mismatching teaching with learning style—a variable which has more direct relevance to attainment than any measure of personality."[26] Entwhistle does indicate work done by Pask that suggests what common sense would dictate—that extreme teaching styles could be markedly disadvantageous to pupils with a mismatched learning style.[27]

One research finding that applies quite readily to the Facilitator/Guide Form is that done by John Biggs of Australia which suggests a framework for understanding various dimensions of the studying process. Biggs's framework is shown in the adopted format in figure 6.1.

Here we have three orientations to learning adopted by student learners. We can easily see that in the orientation toward personal meaning facilitative teaching could be used fully. In fact, this is similar to the learning commitment we have been discussing above in reference to the adult student where the four basic assumptions for the androgogical model are set forth. The teacher assists and guides the learners to design and carry out educational goals that they have set for themselves.

The reproducing and achieving orientations are much more common in universities; they allow for facilitative teaching, but in a mitigated manner. For example, the student who needs to learn vocational skills may make use of the teacher as a coach, as well as for critical feedback. But in so far as the orientation is merely reproductive the student's motivation is extrinsic and the teacher, in reality, may find himself functioning more as a drill-master, persuading from the outside. Of course, this would not be the case where learning of a skill is tied in with inner growth or personal meaning—which is probably the case with Sam Bush's prep school students (Macrorie), as we saw earlier.

Again, students who view college education as a game or competition for success, credentials, and the like (achieving orientation) allow for facilitative teaching to the degree that it can help them over the hurdles that the institution or the teacher himself has set. The teacher here becomes the ally that Elbow talks about in his dialectic of contraries. But there is probably little intrinsic motivation to learn.

Future research and its application to the practice of teaching seem promising. Perhaps in time it will be possible to connect a specific teaching presence, not only with student readiness and maturity, but also with cognitive learning styles. However, it must be remembered that cognitive processes are only part of the whole person and it is this whole person, this autonomous "other" to whom the teacher is always present. More will be said about student approaches to learning in the concluding chapter.

WOMEN AND FACILITATIVE TEACHING

It is interesting to note that much of the educational research on how students learn in undergraduate education has been done with males.[28] When one looks more closely at women learners it becomes clear that the Facilitator/Guide teaching form may be attuned to their developmental needs. We have already briefly noted in discussing the Dialogic Mode that moving to the right side of the continuum represents a certain feminization of the teaching act, away from what Noddings calls "the fundamental premise of masculine intellectualization" to where "a language of relation guides our thinking in concrete situations."[29]

Yet as a number of feminist educators have pointed out, most of the institutions of higher education in America have been designed and continue to be run by men. It does not take much acuity to observe that a connection may exist between this fact and dominance of teaching forms that deal mainly with the presentation of abstract "masculinized" knowledge. In such environments women have traditionally had to "master the masculine mode" (Noddings). Yet such a mode may be foreign to their deepest nature. Jane Roland Martin has observed how the ideal of the educated person as portrayed by a host of male educational theorists and philosophers, most notably R. S.

Peters, "coincides with our cultural stereotype of a male human being. According to that stereotype men are objective, analytic, rational"; they are interested in ideas and things; they have no interpersonal orientation; they are neither nurturant nor supportive, empathetic or sensitive."[30]

The authors of the 1986 study, *Woman's Ways of Knowing*, have documented certain definite traits as well as vulnerabilities woman learners bring to higher education, among which are: a lack of self-confidence as learners; the need for teachers who are affirming; a desire for learning that is shared and collaborative; a need to be accepted earlier into a community of learners than is usually allowed by the male academic establishment.[31] Most important among their needs is that of validation of their inner worth since as one woman puts it: "Self-approval has been so far pushed down it couldn't come back by itself." (p. 197) The authors found that it is not enough for these women to be told that they have the potential to become knowledgeable; they need to be assured that they already know something, that the tools for learning are already inside them. In keeping with these insights learning is more meaningful for women when it starts from personal experience, when they can be brought to see things out of their own eyes rather than someone else's. These students were more at home with learning experiences that move from concrete and particular to the abstract and general. Thus, an inductive approach to learning (which is common to Dialogic and Facilitative teaching) is preferable to the deductive "theoretical rattle of men." (p. 203) The assertion of authority and a pontificating from out of professional expertise is offsetting to women. The lecture communicating predigested knowledge from an omniscient academic mind is not an avenue to learning for these female students. Almost all of them are more comfortable with teachers who share with them the vagaries in their own thinking process. The authors coin the term "teacher-midwife" to describe the teaching presence with which these women feel the most affinity:

The kind of teacher they praised and the kind for which they yearned was one who would help them articulate and expand their latent knowledge: a mid-wife teacher. Mid-wife teachers are the opposite of banker teachers. While the bankers deposit knowledge in the learner's head, the midwives draw it out. They assist the students in giving birth to their own ideas in making their own tacit knowledge explicit and elaborating it. (p. 217)

This depiction picks up on Paulo Freire's portrayal of traditional teaching and education as "banking education" where the teacher's role is "to fill" the students by making deposits of information which he considers to constitute true knowledge.[32] Such teaching "anesthetizes" in the same way anesthesia is administered to a woman in childbirth—so she becomes a spectator rather than a participant in her own learning. The teacher (in a male mode) like the physician, usurps the woman's natural role. He gives birth to the baby (which is really his) with an "array of technological devices." In contrast, mid-wife teachers focus on their students' own knowledge:

They contribute when needed, but it is always clear that the baby is not their's but the students . . . The cycle is one of confirmation—evocation—confirmation. Midwife-teachers help students deliver their words to the world, and they use their own knowledge to put the students into conversation with other voices—past and present—in the culture.[33]

It should be apparent that all of the qualities described above characterize the Facilitator/Guide teaching form where the teacher is midwife to the students' energies. The facilitative teacher is affirming, supportive, and becomes even a collaborator as we have seen in Schon's description of the interaction between Dani and Michal. Above all, facilitative teaching assumes that knowledge is latent in the learner and the teacher's task is to draw that knowledge out.

THE ALVERNO EXPERIENCE

One of the best known alternatives to the male-dominated educational model reigning in most universities today is a small liberal arts college in Milwaukee founded and staffed largely by women. Until recently almost all the students were women in the traditional undergraduate range, but over the last decade the school has increased its outreach to older students so that now over seventy percent of its matriculators are adult learners. Alverno has become most widely noticed throughout the educational community for its work on outcome assessment, but its main emphasis is on what the school calls "self-directed undergraduate study."[34] Students usually choose Alverno for many of the reasons annunciated by the women students interviewed in *Woman's Ways of Knowing*.

It is also interesting that these women, like most college students at first, have not perceived the locus of learning as inside themselves. Thus, they share problems common to most learners upon entering higher education. As Loacker and Doherty point out, they do not understand that the learning process will change them or, suspecting that, cannot imagine how that change will take place. They have yet to experience learning as an active, self-transforming process. Emily, a returning housewife, reflects that even older students are not always ready at first to focus on what one brings to the learning experience: "It took me that whole first semester to get acclimated to concentrating on my abilities rather than just on content."[35]

Gradually, and with continued guidance in self-assessment the student gathers confidence in her inner powers. Jean, a younger student, articulates nicely the shift taking place and the feeling of empowerment it brings:

When I came here I thought that everyone had the knowledge, and I had to find the people who had the knowledge in order to get brains, education, talent. As I struggled through this learning process, I realized that the stuff is inside me—and that people can help me bring it out and hone it down so its rough edges are gone, and considerably expand it.[36]

The teacher's employment of the Facilitator/Guide Form is crucial to this unfolding on the part of the student.

An interesting question arises here as to whether women might be open to student-centered learning much sooner than men, of whether they can take responsibility for their own learning earlier. While this could be true especially of older students, we have seen from the Alverno experience that at first most of them are as unaware of this possibility as any other undergraduate. Thus, even at Alverno the educator takes much of the initiative in the early stages of the learner's movement toward self-direction. (Teaching forms on the left of the continuum are not absent.) It is only gradually that the learner begins to take full responsibility for shaping and evaluating her own learning. Eventually, the student through continual assistance and guidance becomes an independent learner negotiating with the facilitative teacher. But she has now reached the point where she defines as many of the learning terms as the teacher does. As Loacker and Doherty, describe it: "At every stage it is the learner who exerts the critical initiative, from negotiating for her internship to defining its learning goals and measures, from evaluating both her performance and her learning to setting new directions for both."[37]

Another question could be asked as to whether women teachers by nature are also more at ease when present to their students as Facilitator/Guides. While this would seem at least probable, there is certainly no doubt that women students prefer teachers who exhibit characteristics common to this form. And most of the teachers discussed positively in the interviews conducted by the authors of *Woman's Ways of Knowing*, as well as those mentioned by students at Alverno, were, in fact, women. Probably more research needs to be done in this area.[38]

FACILITATOR/GUIDE AND GROUP WORK

The Facilitator/Guide teaching form is crucial for students who are set up (or seek on their own) to learn in small groups. In these contexts the element of individualism and competition, so much a part of traditional university education, can be replaced by a spirit of cooperation. The term commonly used to describe this approach in group work is "collaborative learning" and has been appearing more frequently in the literature on teaching over the last decade. The teacher's role here shifts in the manner described at the beginning of this chapter. Sheridan, Byrne, and Quina put it as follows: "In the collaborative process the teacher's influence recedes and becomes more indirect. The teacher becomes an organizer and facilitator instead of the central actor, and relinquishes the role of authority figure."[39]

Implied in this new teaching presence is a distinctively different approach to traditional patterns of classroom control. Essentially, the teacher is willing to share his control. Such sharing allows for an inductive learning process on the part of the students and requires that the teacher reconceive his presence in working with small groups. Thom Hawkins, describing what he calls "the parceled classroom" in the context of a writing course, sums up this change:

Group teaching requires teachers reorder their instructional priorities so that they can approach group situations with an attitude that will allow them to function in ways that will incubate and sustain student discovery...You must use a facilitating inquiry approach while the groups are in session because your job during that period of time is to listen and understand, not to talk and explain.[40]

Of course, cooperative learning environments don't just happen, especially in undergraduate education. They must be cultivated and built up to. Most often there are preliminary steps in creating effective group work which set the stage for collaboration. In these early stages a teacher takes a more directive approach. Particularly, in situations where students are not used to disciplined group work teachers will function as task-setters and classroom managers; they may often need to train students to use interactive skills. (Much of this has been modeled in the Dialogic Mode.) Getting students acclimated to certain parameters so that they can more easily work in a cooperative way is, according to Wiener, what distinguishes collaborative learning from mere group work.[41] For example, the teacher may be very active in creating an "involvement stage" where students get used to the rules for group work and begin to understand their roles. A "transition stage" follows where students become more comfortable in confronting each other and handling feedback, as well as examining diverse perspectives. Finally, there is the "working stage" where the group begins to function autonomously. Here the teacher recedes and becomes fully present to the group as Facilitator/Guide.[42] Edward Glassman describes this as Stage 3 in the evolution of discussion groups where the teacher is no longer asserting and telling, or even encouraging and negotiating, but starting to let go of the leadership. Other, more subtle skills, now come into play. The teacher uses what Glassman calls "facilitating and delegating leader behaviors" where he listens and supports the discussion group in its effort to learn through discussion. He calls discussions of this type "non-directive" in that they become totally student-centered.[43]

Glassman demonstrates how this stage is reached in an undergraduate biochemistry class. After being divided into independent learning groups of eight to ten, students are informed that the teacher will be responsible for the "content exercises" during the first six sessions. (Students meet for three consecutive hours once a week.) From then on the groups are expected to take over the class with respect to determining content and generating exercises, at which point the teacher will be available as a "process guide and resource consultant."[44]

During the first six weeks students, with the teacher in a more directive role, learn a considerable amount of biochemistry and genetics along with being trained (through structured exercises) in group interaction and the use of learning groups to teach. At no point, however, does the professor lecture. Since most of the students in Glassman's class are seniors, some motivation and a certain educational maturity can be assumed. At the end of the six weeks the teacher "recedes" and assumes the non-directive facilitator presence. The teacher's role here is that of resource consultant: i) He does not answer questions or give opinions pertaining to content, but rather refers students to other sources (persons, books, articles). Thus, he is not perceived as the only expert present; ii) He does not judge or evaluate student performance prematurely. The students are therefore free to risk and learn from their mistakes; iii) He allows the students to self-motivate. He does not entertain, tell jokes, perform, cajole, enthuse, or use charisma. Thus the responsibility is placed on the students for their own learning.[45]

In his role as guide to the processes of group interaction Glassman views his responsibility as one of "facilitating creativity, independence, and self-direction in the learners"[46] He achieves this through short exercises involving group dynamics. Finally, at the end of the course, Glassman involves the group in open-ended evaluation processes with the teacher. There are no written exams.

In courses like the one above where written exams are given students could work in small groups to design questions from different content areas, thus creating a pool of questions, some of which would actually be used in the exam. Small groups could also be used to work on "practice exams" perhaps guided by a teaching assistant.[47]

Though these teaching roles may seem somewhat more impersonal than the encounter between individuals and teachers (enablers) described in Macrorie's *Twenty Teachers* or Schon's Architectural Studio, the outlines of the Facilitator/Guide teaching presence are clearly discernable. Collaborative student-centered learning can be carried on in any number of courses throughout the disciplines. But teachers, irrespective of their disciplines, find that creating facilitative encounters is always easier among students (usually older) who are familiar with the process of working together than with younger students who have been trained to work as isolated individuals. However, as we have seen, even adult students need to be prepared for collaborative learning.[48]

EXAMPLE OF A FACILITATIVE GROUP SESSION

Occasionally, special situations arise wherein a teacher can be present as Facilitator/Guide throughout a structured learning process. I experienced this in the summer of 1989 when I was asked to be part of a symposium on Ethical Issues in Geriatrics at my college for students attending the 35th Congress of the International Pharmaceutical Students Federation.[49] My task at the conference was to conduct a three hour seminar on euthanasia and the elderly. The student population—gathered from all over the globe—was in its upper years and highly motivated. (The seminar itself had been self-selected.) Given these advantages, I was able to assume their readiness to participate in a specific learning process and perhaps even a general knowledge base. Before the seminar I informally spent some time with these students who themselves had been with each other for the previous five days in a cordial atmosphere. Thus, when the symposium began a certain dialogical intimacy had been achieved and we were able to move right to the "working stage."

I explained to the eighteen people gathered in the seminar that the purpose of the session would be threefold: To help participants achieve a correct understanding of the types of euthanasia; to give them an opportunity to discuss ethical implications of allowing older people the right to die; to find out if the practice of euthanasia varied according to cultures or nationality. I told them that the method used would be the inductive case-study approach wherein participants would function within small groups of six and try to move toward consensus regarding their specific case. Each group would appoint a recorder and then systematically discuss key questions that the teacher would write on the board. Points for discussion would be the following:

a) to enumerate all elements of the case (each group given a different case)

b) to analyze and weigh the issues involved

c) to decide whether actions taken were right or wrong and by what standards

d) to give reasons for judgement made by the group

e) to prepare a consensus report

f) to allow for a minority report (if necessary)

I allowed fifty minutes for deliberations within the groups and then forty-five minutes for each group to make its report, followed by brief general discussion. Afterwards we brought the different points of consensus together via a general discussion. Then I induced them to summarize the different types of euthanasia and apply some formal moral theory. Finally, time ran out before we could fully observe the role of cultural differences in approaches to euthanasia in the elderly.

The seminar turned out to be a concentrated exercise in collaborative learning which rather successfully accomplished what Olmstead lists as the two main purposes of well-handled group discussions: That students gain new insights into a problem by hearing many different viewpoints and by having their own ideas criticized; that they learn new ways of behaving to which they [might become] committed because of group discussion and decision.[50]

For my part, after setting out the purpose and method, and distributing the case studies, I became completely facilitative, moving around the room, listening and observing the specific groups, occasionally clarifying a point in the directions, supporting a particular group's effort, suggesting they return to a specific point if I saw a decision getting off track. But mostly, I let the groups work on their own—which they seemed eager to do. As different groups made their reports I wrote their conclusions on the blackboard and then asked leading questions meant both to draw them toward seeing commonalities in their responses and to open up new avenues for discussion. Though sorely tempted, at no point did I ever try to impose my view on the group. As synthesizer I tried to follow Harvey Wiener's notion of the task: "The teacher should lead the class to consider the similarities and contradictions in the recorded points of view and should unite them all, if possible, into a larger vision . . . "[51]

Students' written responses to the seminar were quite positive. The most common thread in these responses was that they enjoyed being active participators in, rather than passive recipients of, learning. In my mid-wifery to their learning, I experienced a certain abdication of power which, though it produced some anxiety in me at first, left me deeply satisfied. It was a teaching encounter that, heretofore, had taken place all too seldom. Yet I found this non-intrusiveness, this subtle art of indirection, as students groped together toward a clearer understanding of euthanasia and its ethical implications, to be teaching of a more artful kind. But I hasten to reiterate that only a number of converging factors (student maturity and motivation, along with a friendly atmosphere) made such a teaching encounter possible.

THE SMALL SEMINAR

The seminar can be conceived as an act of specialized discourse among a few—most often on a graduate level. I mentioned in the previous chapter that the graduate seminar, as it is usually conducted today, is more like a recitation: impersonal, sterile, and utterly lacking in educational spontaneity or intimacy. The typical scenario is one where a student presents her research during which she is questioned and critically reviewed (or more appropriately "grilled") by peers and faculty. Some discussion ensues, often among the faculty members present; there is a disagreement over a subtle point, the straining out of a gnat. The seminar environment presents opportunities for professors to contest, judge, parade their pedantry—in short, do everything that utterly destroys authentic dialogue. Often abstract jargon of the discipline pervades the room as if disembodied machines were speaking to each other. In the midst of all this sits (or stands) the terrorized student, watching the seconds on the wall clock tick more slowly than she ever dreamed they could.

We must remind ourselves that dialogic teaching is only fruitful when it involves rational deliberation within a context of the interpersonal. Spontaneity and reciprocity are essential. Everything discussed under dialogic teaching applies to the small seminar. All the conditions for discourse must be present. However, the tutorial (graduate) seminar, in its ideal form, holds certain requirements that move the teacher into the facilitative presence since the learning there is even more student-centered. In the small tutorial session the task of the tutor is to be present to his or her students in such a way as to engender the most informed, thoughtful, challenging learning experience, and one that is equally shared among the group members. The students' information base is absolutely assumed here; they must be familiar with the intellectual structure of the discipline, as well as bring to the seminar sessions certain intellectual (and linguistic) abilities that allow them to discourse fluently and in some depth.

If, for example, the group is working on a common text, students must be able to demonstrate their understanding. The two indispensable skills for handling texts on a graduate level are the writing of a precis and a critique of the material. The one involves the power of concision, the other that of creative analysis.[52] These skills are the foundation out of which any further elaboration, application, or evaluation must flow. It is in these latter activities that the subtle skills of the Facilitator/Guide come into play. The teacher must phrase questions in such a manner as to allow the group to lift off from the information and share their insights. Again, the dual goal of entertaining varying perspectives and of working toward a general consensus should be in the facilitator's mind. More—she wants to assist students in their further internalization of the methods and values of the specific discipline. Thus, the teacher's main task is not that of grading students' presentations, or judging their performance. This alone (quite common on the graduate level) does not begin to mine the potential for growth in learning that the small seminar offers. It is of more value that the teacher function in what Noddings calls the "perceptive/creative mode", one in which questioning is undertaken to draw out the student's knowledge and understanding given in a way that helps the student see her discipline holistically.[53]

Equally as important is what Maurice Broady calls the "Social-Psychological Structure" of the seminar. Since the deliberations within the group will be quite thorough and intense it is important to personalize the surroundings and to promote as much informality as possible. As Broady puts it: "The heavier the intellectual demands which a tutor expects to make of his students, the more desirable such informality becomes."[54] This is all the more reason why an impersonal, stilted atmosphere must be avoided.

It is the teacher's task to lend coherence and continuity to successive seminars without being invasive or too directive. At the other extreme is the diffusive, aimless circling which takes place when the seminar has no sure guiding hand. Needless to say, given these factors, facilitating the small tutorial seminar is a most difficult art form compared to which the lecture is relatively easy. Yet once learned, the rewards for both teacher and student are educationally far more satisfying. Unfortunately, very little training is provided for academics in the art of conducting the small, tutorial seminar.[55]

In *The Vocation of a Teacher* Wayne Booth gives a personal accounting of how a small seminar (though somewhat larger than what we have described) works when things go well. His group consists of nine advanced graduate students, moving toward their dissertation in English Literature. After five weeks Booth describes them as "a living, thinking body, not just the isolated, individual competitors that they sometimes were in January."[56] The seminar has now reached a point where each student must present a draft "chapter" or "article" for discussion and criticism. Booth notes his reactions to the proceedings:

Today we had the first of these sessions, as Terry Martin led a discussion of his essay on the rhetoric of Donne's Devotional Sonnets . . . All 8 seemed to have read his essay with some care, and they pushed Terry, courteously and firmly, on the needless sprawl of his potentially powerful essay: its failure to focus its readers early on a clear question or problem, and its various other weaknesses. I was at no point fully relaxed, feeling unsure whether we were hitting him too hard (everybody objected to something or other) or not hard enough (he's so good that he should be pushed to become really outstanding).

As we were drawing to the end, Lisa said, "I'd like to ask Terry whether he found this session helpful or just destructive?" He looked surprised: "Oh, I thought it was wonderful. I really learned a lot." And I felt that he had.

So I came home thinking. "At last. they're making it. It'll be one of the better runs."[57]

Booth also mentions that most of the students in the seminar were women.

RESULTS OF STUDENT-CENTERED TEACHING

The most obvious benefit of student-centered teaching is the full activization of the student's energies. This alone, provided those energies are focused, will mean that the student will be more involved in the learning process. In theory, as McKeachie has pointed out, student-centered teaching may have its drawbacks when it comes to achieving low level cognitive goals. When certain determinate information is involved the instructor-focused learning models are probably more efficient. Also, student-centered teachers who emphasize group work can have their effects undercut if the group sets for itself lower standards of achievement than academically acceptable to the teacher.[58]

Where groups operate in a collaborative learning context a number of beneficial effects accrue: Students have opportunities to develop not only interpersonal relations, but they get to see each other as resources for mutual learning. At the same time, through group interaction, they can practice the higher intellectual skills of inquiry, problem solving, and evaluation. Along with the opportunity to conduct reality-testing of their own ideas, there ensues a greater tolerance for diversity and ambiguity.[59] Facilitative teaching enhances creativity to an extent not possible in previous forms since the learning process is now centered in the student.

On the debit side, much time may have to be spent initiating activities, setting up learning tasks, as well as allowing for individual learning styles and specific groups to gel. An uncertainty principle operates whereby a teacher cannot have the assurance and control that is possible in more structured, one dimensional situations in which definite concepts or skills are to be demonstrated. (Both individualized and collaborative learning wreak havoc in a department dedicated to covering syllabi in lock-step fashion.) Student-centered learning de-emphasizes traditional use of tests and grades and in many cases students share responsibility for evaluation.[60] As we saw with dialogic discussion, a lack of closure or "finishedness" is often the case, not only in group interaction, but in regard to a student's inner progress. Every concept or skill expressed is immediately caught up in the spiral of new questions and goals. Endings and new beginnings coalesce. Thus, learning and group objectives, though valuable in a procedural way, are rather useless when it comes to the deeper aspects of the learning process.

Perhaps the most common advantage cited over the years in the literature on student (or child)-centered education is the opportunity to engage in what theorists have called "learning by discovery." The main assumption is that whatever students come to or discover on their own will be better integrated and remembered. This is also the kind of learning that a Facilitator/Guide teacher encourages. Jerome Bruner has characterized this kind of teaching as the "hypothetical mode" which corresponds to the teaching forms on the right side of the continuum.[61] However, it is easy to misunderstand the term and make learning by discovery mean something that the student does out of the blue without the teacher's assistance. Learning by discovery does not take place in a vacuum; in traditional education it moves out of some structure or hypothesis set up by or negotiated with the teacher. As Bruner makes clear, new knowledge or facts are rarely "discovered" in an uncharted sea of ignorance. If they appear to be discovered in this way, it is almost always due "to some happy hypothesis about where to navigate. Discovery, like surprise, favors the well-prepared mind."[62]

R. F. Dearden, discussing learning in young children, speaks of "planned experiences" in which the teacher contrives or structures situations in such a way as to allow appropriate discoveries to take place by the children.[63] This comes near to describing the Montessori method. Such a description, of course, would be entirely too constraining for adult learners who return to the classroom with a wealth of life experience and can negotiate a learning contract with teachers present to them as Facilitator/Guides. But even here some conceptual model or structure of discourse is presumed out of which discovery and educational growth can emerge. The more knowledge, though it be latent, that lies within students, the more they will be able to structure their own learning experiences in which the act of discovery will be paramount. The point is that the teacher, (whether external to or internalized by) the learner, directs the discovery; it does not take place in an aimless fashion. Dearden puts it well:

The stress is on the individual's mastery of knowledge, so that throughout all this teacher activity what the teacher says is specific enough to focus attention and effort in the desired direction, but at the same time open enough to leave genuine discoveries still to be made, discoveries which the teacher can be reasonably confident will be made on the basis of what he knows has already been learned in the past and the deliberate guidance he is now giving.[64]

This leads to one of the central conundrums in all of learning with which we will end this chapter.

SOCRATES, THE FACILITATOR

We have discussed Socrates' presence as catalyst and dialogist in previous chapters where we suggested that both activities form part of his mid-wifery, the task of creating "aphoria" and engaging interlocutors in shared inquiry. The third aspect of his maiutic role becomes evident when Socrates, as Facilitator/Guide, actively assists others to bring to light their own tacit knowledge and to recognize its implications. Gilbert Highet, in discussing the tutorial system throughout Western education, has pointed out that for Socrates teaching was not merely asking a series of questions, with the aim of exposing the pupil's ignorance or piercing his own pretensions:

He had a positive end in view, although that end was concealed from the pupil. He wanted to make every pupil realize that truth was in the pupil's own power to find, if he searched long enough and hard enough, refusing all "authoritative" statements and judging every solution by reason alone.[65]

The method sounds similar to that of Sam Bush in guiding the aspirations of his wood-working students ("I'm trying to draw out what is in the boy rather than pile it on him."), as well as other facilitative teachers referred to earlier in the chapter. As we noted, Socrates had varying degrees of success;

more often than not he failed in getting his interlocutors to follow their ideas all the way through. He was successful in his encounter with the slave boy where his questioning process is definitely that of a guide drawing latent knowledge into the light. In fact, Socrates is at pains to point out to Meno that here he is guiding rather than instructing: "Mark now the further development. I shall only ask him, and not teach him, and he shall share the inquiry with me: and do you watch and see if you find me telling or explaining anything to him, instead of eliciting his opinion."[66]

However, it must be admitted that the slave boy does not offer any extended insights or comments on his own, something that an adult learner would do in his interaction with a facilitative teacher. The knowledge may be there, but so hidden that Socrates must create the structure within which the boy's responses lead to the revelation of what he knows. Also, because he is a slave it is unlikely that the boy will pursue this new found knowledge or seek for a teacher (Socrates!) to continue in this vein. What places Socrates squarely in the Elicitive Mode is his overall attitude to teaching and learning which forms one of the main dilemmas of *The Meno*. Previous to the slave boy sequence, he and Meno have been discussing whether virtue can be taught, and then how learning can happen at all:

Men. And how will you investigate, Socrates, that of which you know nothing at all? Where can you find a starting point in the region of the unknown? And even if you happen to come full upon what you want, how will you ever know that this is the thing which you did not know?
Soc. I know, Meno, what you mean; but just see what a tiresome dispute you are introducing. You argue that a man cannot inquire either about that which he knows, or about that which he does not know; for if he knows, he has no need to inquire, and if not, he cannot; for he does not know the very subject about which he is to inquire.[67]

Socrates temporarily escapes from the dilemma by positing the immortality of the soul and thus, the doctrine of recollection. If this be the case then the true task of the teacher can never be to *impart* but to *elicit* from the pupil what he already knows, albeit in a recondite way. And so ensues the episode with the slave boy.

Whether the soul's preexistence and the implications for learning are an adequate explanation is not so important to us as the stance such a conviction causes Socrates to take regarding his teaching method. As we pointed out in the previous chapter, Socrates was rejecting the transmissive pedagogy of his time in favor of one which served the process of dialectic. This new teaching presence was one which helped participants come to see and discover for themselves. It became the foundation for what Philip Jackson calls the "transformative" method of teaching in the Western world.[68] Socrates' dedication to a manner of teaching that we have called shared inquiry and facilitative is absolute. Though he may often fail for reasons already noted, he can see no other way to proceed:

Some things I have said of which I am not altogether confident. But that we shall be better and braver and less helpless if we think that we ought to inquire, than we would have been if we thought that there was no knowing and no duty to seek to know what we do not know—that is a belief for which I am ready to fight, in word and deed, to the utmost of my power.[69]

Thus, we see here the origin of the view that knowledge resides in the learner, though he may not know he knows. Sufficiently initiated into the community of discourse, students will take responsibility for their educational growth, in the service of which the teaching form becomes that of Dialogist and Facilitator/Guide. We conclude this chapter as we began it, noting that all real learning is student-centered.

FACILITATOR/GUIDE

Characteristics of Teacher

- respects and affirms individual learner
- non-invasive and indirect
- responsive to student's initiative
- corroborates student's new view of learning
- moves into student's line of vision
- flows with student's energies
- allows student to struggle
- adjusts to student's learning style
- continually aware of student's experience
- draws student out
- confirms value of life-experience of student
- holds high expectations for student

General Skills

- sets up contexts for active learning and discovery
- assists students in diagnosing learning needs
- asks leading questions to draw out knowledge already existing in student
- assists student in laying out educational plans and learning objectives
- inductive—moves from particular to general, from concrete to abstract
- able to create and sustain group learning activities
- knows when to structure and when to allow free play
- able to provide and encourage critical feedback

- able to delegate and shift control to students
- moves students toward collaborative rather than competitive learning
- creates exercises that foster communication and mutual support
- creates exercises in small group dynamics
- creates learning activities that involve students in higher learning skills

Student Aptitudes
- sees center of learning inside oneself rather than in external authority
- becomes fully activated and makes new demands on learning self
- experiences a need to learn
- able to follow own line of vision with assistance from teacher
- able to diagnose own learning needs
- able to tap into past experiences and apply to present circumstances
- able to create general educational goals as well as specific learning objectives
- uses higher learning skills: analysis, problem-solving, application, synthesis
- able to evaluate own learning
- able to fuse internal needs with institutional requirements
- moves toward personal meaning orientation
- able to work productively in small groups
- sees fellow students as resources for mutual learning
- appreciates diversity of group members
- able to disagree articulately with other group members
- contributes toward consensus within the group
- able to summarize and critique reading materials
- able to connect ideas in different reading materials
- able to create new synthesis from disparate ideas
- able to constructively criticize ideas and presentations of others
- at ease in presence of ambiguity and open-endedness
- views learning as on-going

NOTES

1. Perkinson, *Learning From Our Mistakes*, p. 96. Along with Maria Montessori (1870–1952), other pioneering educators who focused on the inner energies of the child were Johann Pestalozzi (1746–1827), Friedrich Froebel (1782–1852), and Rudolf Steiner (1861–1925).

2. Margaret Yonemura, "Shared Visions and Common Roots: Montessori, Pratt, and Steiner," *The Educational Forum*, 54, no.1 (Fall 1989): 59.

3. Perkinson, *Learning From Our Mistakes*, p. 171.

4. Ken Macrorie, *Twenty Teachers*, p. 4.

5. Perkinson, *Learning From Our Mistakes*, p. 185.

6. "The Architectural Studio As Educational Model For Reflection-in-Action," in Donald A. Schon, *Educating the Reflective Practitioner: Toward a New Design For Teaching and Learning*. (San Francisco: Jossey-Bass Publishers, 1987), pp. 41–157.

7. Robert J. Kloss, "Coaching and Playing Right Field: Trying on Metaphors for Teaching," *College Teaching*, 35, no. 4 (Fall 1987): 137.

8. Ashton-Warner, *Teacher*, p. 64.

9. Schon, *Educating the Reflective Practitioner*, p. 154.

10. Elbow, *Embracing Contraries: Explorations in Learning and Teaching*, p. 88. Jerry Farber makes a similar point in discussing the tyranny of the grading system in a more recent article in *College English*. See Jerry Farber, "Learning How To Teach: A Progress Report," *College English*, 52, no. 2 (February 1990): 136.

11. Elbow, p. 156.

12. Anne Davis Toppins, "Teaching Students to Teach Themselves," *College Teaching*, 35, no. 3 (Summer 1987): 95

13. McKeachie, *Teaching Tips*, p. 60.

14. An obvious exception would be the Personalized System of Instruction (PSI) where students can work at their own pace with textbooks and other readings, supplemented by study guides. While PSIs have been quite effective in promoting individualized learning they are firmly grounded in behavioristic reinforcement theory and can not substitute for the interpersonal relations that are created by the Facilitator/Guide form. For a discussion of mastery learning and self-paced modules see K. Patricia Cross, *Accent on Learning*, pp. 75–110. Also, Michael J. Dunkin and Jennifer Barnes, "Research on Teaching in Higher Education," in *Handbook of Research on Teaching*, ed. Merlin C. Wittrock, pp. 756–759.

15. See Roland Huff and Charles R. Kline, Jr. "Using Peer Group Instruction to Teach Writing," in *The Contemporary Writing Curriculum: Rehearsing, Composing and Valuing* (New York: Teachers College Press, 1987), p. 134.

16. J. Gordon Chamberlain, *The Educating Act: A Phenomenological View* (New York: University Press of America, 1981), pp. 23–24.

17. Malcolm S. Knowles, "The Art and Science of Helping Adults Learn," in *Androgogy in Action: Applying Modern Principles of Adult Learning*, ed. Malcolm S. Knowles (San Francisco: Jossey-Bass Publishers, 1984), p. 9–12.

18. Knowles, *Androgogy in Action*, p. 12. Knowles does stress that what creates an orientation which is intrinsically motivated is usually life, task, or problem-oriented rather than learning for learning's sake.

19. Malcolm S. Knowles, *Using Learning Contracts: Practical Approaches to Individualizing and Structuring Learning* (San Francisco: Jossey-Bass Publishers, 1986), pp. 39–40.

20. Knowles, *Androgogy in Action*, pp. 14–16.

21. Malcolm Knowles, *The Adult Learner: A Neglected Species* (Houston, Texas: Gulf Publishing Company, 1973), p. 118. See also any number of exercises in David W. Johnson, *Reaching Out: Interpersonal Effectiveness and Self-Actualization* (Englewood Cliffs, N.J.: Prentice Hall, 1972). In particular, Chapter 3.

22. Malcolm S. Knowles, *Androgogy in Action*, p. 17. See also, Jean Sheridan, Anne C. Byrne, and Kathryn Quina, "Collaborative Learning: Notes From the Field," *College Teaching*, 37, no. 2 (Spring 1989): 50.

23. See Anne Toppins, "Teaching Students to Teach Themselves," p. 98.

24. See, for example, David J. Boud and M. T. Prosser, "Sharing Responsibility For Learning in a Science Course—Staff-Student Cooperation," in Knowles, *Androgogy in Action*, pp. 175–87; Also, Edward Glassman, "Teaching Biochemistry in Cooperative Learning Groups" *Biochemical Education*, 6, no. 2 (April 1978): 35.

25. Two quite recent books that treat or discuss student learning styles: Noel Entwistle, *Styles of Learning and Teaching: An Integrated Outline of Educational Psychology For Students, Teachers, and Lecturers*; to a lesser degree, Joseph Katz and Mildred Henry, *Turning Professors into Teachers: A New Approach to Faculty Development and Student Learning* (New York: MacMillan Publishing Company, 1988). K. Patricia Cross pointed out in 1981 that research on cognitive styles has been going on in this country for some twenty-five years in psychology laboratories, but the research has not been widely applied to educational problems. See *Adults As Learners*, (San Francisco: Jossey-Bass Publishers, 1981), pp. 112–113.

26. Entwistle, *Styles of Learning and Teaching*, pp. 237–38.

27. Ibid., p. 238. For disparity in student responses to a particular teaching mode see Richard Tiberius, "Metaphors Underlying the Improvement of Teaching and Learning," 150. Again, K. Patricia Cross expresses reservations on the wisdom of matching student learning styles with the teaching resources of the institution—especially through automatic computerized matching. See *Accent on Learning*, pp. 132–133.

28. For example, see Roy Heath, *The Reasonable Adventurer* (University of Pittsburgh, 1964). William G. Perry, Jr.'s well known study *Forms of Intellectual and Ethical Development in the College Years: A Scheme* is largely male oriented. The only recent research carried out with woman students alone is that of Ference Martin at Gothenburg (See Entwhistle, *Styles of Learning and Teaching*, pp. 75–76.) For a critique of the male oriented studies of Piaget, Kohlberg, and Erickson, see Carol Gilligan, *In a Different Voice: Psychological Theory and Womans' Development* (Cambridge: Harvard University Press, 1982.)

29. Noddings, "Fidelity in Teaching," 498.

30. See Jane Roland Martin, "The Ideal of the Educated Person," *Educational Theory* 31, no. 2 (Spring 1981): 102.

31. Belenky, et al. *Woman's Ways of Knowing*, pp. 190–213.

32. Freire, *Pedagogy of the Opressed*, p. 63.

33. Belenky, et al. *Woman's Ways of Knowing*, pp. 218–19.

34. Georgine Loacker and Austin Doherty, "Self-Directed Undergraduate Study," in *Androgogy in Action: Applying Modern Principles of Adult Learning*, ed. Malcolm S. Knowles, p. 102.

35. Ibid., p. 114.

36. Ibid., p. 111.

37. Ibid., p. 118. Rough parallels to Perry's developmental sequence (for men) are drawn by the authors of *Woman's Ways of Knowing* in regard to women in education. The movement is from Received and Subjective Knowledge through Procedural Knowledge to Constructed Knowledge. Some of these stages have dual or even disparate phases. It would be at the Procedural Knowledge stage where the female (usually older) student begins to take responsibility for her own learning. See Belenky, et al. *Woman's Ways of Knowing*, pp. 35–151.

38. The thesis that woman teachers are more interested in the interpersonal dynamics of teaching than men is given some anecdotal credence by Kenneth Eble's

observation: "In a dozen years of speaking to hundreds of faculty groups assembled to discuss teaching, I have been struck by the fact that women faculty attend in greater numbers in proportion to their numbers on the faculty than men. Less confidently, I would say that these women faculty often show a more intense interest in teaching and a greater responsiveness to its widest dimensions than men." See *Aims of College Teaching*, p. 52.

39. Sheridan, Byrne, and Quina, "Collaborative Learning: Notes From the Field," p. 49.

40. Thom Hawkins, *Group Inquiry Techniques for Teaching Writing* (Urbana, Illinois: National Council of Teachers of English, 1976), p. 11.

41. Harvey S. Wiener, "Collaborative Learning in the Classroom: A Guide to Evaluation," *College English*, 48, no. 1 (January 1986): 54. For the importance of clarity in designing group work see Elizabeth G. Cohen, *Designing Groupwork: Strategies for the Heterogeneous Classroom* (New York: Teachers College Press, 1986), pp. 92–93. Also, Mary Lynn Crow, "Teaching As an Interactive Process," in *New Directions for Teaching and Learning: Improving Teaching Styles*, pp. 48–50.

42. These three stages are articulated by Roland Huff and Charles R. Kline, Jr., "Using Peer Group Instruction to Teach," in *The Contemporary Writing Curriculum: Rehearsing, Composing, and Valuing*, pp. 138–140.

43. Glassman, "The Teacher As Leader," *Improving Teaching Styles*, p. 36.

44. Edward Glassman, "Teaching Biochemistry in Cooperative Learning Groups," *Biochemical Education*, p. 35.

45. Ibid., p. 35.

46. Glassman, "Teacher As Leader," p. 34.

47. For a fuller explanation of how small groups can be used to create exams see Michael Strauss and Toby Fulwiler, "Writing to Learn in Large Lecture Classes," *Journal of College Science Teaching*, 19 (December 1989/January/1990), pp. 158–163.

48. For a sobering account of a teacher's lack of success in an English 102 class, see Mary Rose O'Reilley, "Exterminate...the Brutes'—And Other Things that Go Wrong in Student-Centered Teaching," *College English*, 51, no. 2 (February 1989): 142–146.

49. "Ethical Issues in Geriatrics," 35th IPSF Congress, Philadelphia College of Pharmacy and Science, August 15, 1989.

50. J. A. Olmstead, *Small Group Instruction: Theory and Practice* (Alexandria, Va.: Human Resources Research Organization, 1974), p. 92.

51. Wiener, "Collaborative Learning in the Classroom: A Guide to Evaluation", p. 59.

52. Maurice Broady, "The Conduct of Seminars," in *Teach Thinking By Discussion*, ed. Donald Bligh (Great Britain: The Society for Research into Higher Education and NFER-NELSON, 1986), p. 159.

53. Nel Noddings, *Caring: A Feminine Approach to Ethics and Moral Education* (Berkeley: University of California Press, 1984), p. 23. See also "Fidelity in Teaching, Teacher Education, and Research For Teaching."

54. Broady, "The Conduct of Seminars," p. 156.

55. Broady suggests some kind of apprenticeship system: "The best method of training young teachers in seminar method would be to institute some kind of academic apprenticeship, in which they would be assigned to the seminar of a more experienced tutor, who would be responsible for explaining and discussing critically

what he was doing in the seminar and why he was doing it that way." (pp. 161–162) Though Broady is writing primarily in regard to the British university I see no reason why it can't be applied to the American graduate school.

56. Booth, *The Vocation of a Teacher*, p. 274.

57. Ibid., pp. 274–275.

58. McKeachie, *Teaching Tips*, p. 46.

59. Sheridan, Byrne, and Quina, "Collaborative Learning: Notes From the Field," pp. 49–53; Also, Mary Lynn Crow, "Teaching As An Interactive Process," pp. 41–55.

60. McKeachie, *Teaching Tips*, p. 47.

61. Jerome S. Bruner, *On Knowing: Essays for the Left Hand*, (New York: Atheneum, 1976), p. 83.

62. Ibid., p. 82.

63. R. F. Dearden, "Instruction and Learning by Discovery," *The Concept of Education*, ed. R. S. Peters, p. 144.

64. Ibid., p. 150.

65. Highet, *The Art of Teaching*, p. 188.

66. Plato, *The Meno* in *The Dialogues of Plato*, p. 285.

67. Ibid., p. 277. Donald Schon uses this section of *The Meno* to parallel the "impossible" problem the student has in needing to look for or understand something without knowing what that something is. The teacher of course cannot tell her, or more properly he can, but she will not understand. See "The Paradox of Learning to Design" in *Educating the Reflective Practitioner*, pp. 82–95.

68. Philip W. Jackson, *The Practice of Teaching*, pp. 120–128.

69. Plato, *The Meno*, p. 285.

Chapter 7

Teacher As Witness/Abiding Presence

Not the professor, but the artist is your true school master.
Caldwell Cook

In 1985, Daniel Duke, director of an educational program at Lewis and Clark College, decided to refamiliarize himself with the elementary school classroom. He asked to serve as a part-time teacher's aide to a fourth grade several days a week for a period of one year. During that time he noted how different his administrative perspective had become from that of the classroom teacher. Most notable was the difference in perception of students. He observed, for example, how he tended to focus on collective experiences in the classroom and whether a program was being implemented effectively, while the teacher's central focus was on the quality of her relations with individual students. Duke commented that if the class worked to him, "the result was a coherent symphony"; if it worked to her, "there were 30 enjoyable recitals."[1] Whether an observer could hear a symphony was not of primary importance to her.

Duke also became aware of how important the task of listening was for the effective teacher:

I was also reminded of how much children liked to be listened to—what we tell children is probably of less value in the long run than what we allow them to tell us. The chance to be really heard, not just allowed to speak, requires children to organize thoughts and feelings and to convey them to another person. What could be more central to the educational process?[2]

The line between the teacher helping or assisting and simply being present to receive or absorb the learner's energies divides the two teaching forms of the Elicitive Mode. This all but last teaching encounter on the continuum is one in which the teacher witnesses the student's growth and serves as an abiding presence.[3] If there is a key to this transition it has to be in the heightened confirmation of the student's concrete individuality. Though the teacher may have set up the environment and created structures for learning, she gradually moves into a totally receptive frame of being. Things are allowed to happen within the student and the teacher is simply there, with total alertness, to absorb and reflect the student's often volcanic energies.

Several times in her classic work, *Teacher*, Sylvia Ashton-Warner provides the reader with evidence of this wonderful process, one where, as she puts it, "the drive is no longer the teacher's but the children's own" and where the teacher is at last with and not against "the stream of the children's own inexorable creativeness."[4] Her comments in regard to the process of organic writing by the children show quite clearly the teacher presiding as Witness. After musing on the unexpected revelations that spill out of the Maori young from writing into talk, Warner stresses that the teacher not interfere in any way: "You never want to say that it's good or bad. That's got nothing to do with it. You've got no right at all to criticize the content of another's mind ... Your only allowable comment is one of natural interest in what he is writing ... "[5]

This is to *witness*—all in keeping with the idea of allowing children to move in complete harmony with the inner laws of their own growth. The idea of assisting and then witnessing this inner flowering is common to the great innovative pedagogical movements such as the Free Tolstoy schools in Russia during the nineteenth century, A. S. Neill's Summerhill school in England in the twentieth, and the Montessori and Waldorf schools throughout the world. And though there are general laws which apply to all children, the inner flowering is highly individualistic—the teacher adapts whatever "methods" she uses to the individual child.

Teachers capable of this kind of concrete personalization also exist in higher education. In *Twenty Teachers* Ken Macrorie describes teaching with the well known teacher/researcher James Britton at the Bread Loaf Graduate School of English in Vermont during the summer of 1982. During that time he noticed that Britton was a tremendous listener who focused entirely on the minds and lives of his students. Many of the comments on Britton came from his students who were awestruck by his ability to move out of himself and be totally curious about their diverse worlds:

He was so excited about us. "You're from Wyoming, and John, you're from Michigan and run dog teams!" John would start talking about dog teams, and I—being from Alaska—started saying what I knew about that, and Jimmy wanted to know everything, how many dogs, how you get them together, and what kind of sled. I told him what I knew because I had worked at different dog races and live in a small town where you all help out with them. It was so easy to talk with him. He did that for the entire evening. With Eileen, it was about her teaching experiences because that's what really comes to her, and with Roger it was Wyoming. And Bill Noll—Jimmy talked to him about Vygotsky the psychologist because he knew that Bill was interested in him and the structure of the language. It was incredible.[6]

In identifying with their worlds, Britton is obviously far beyond the Inducer/ Persuader Form, for the intrinsic motivation of the young teachers in this writing program can be assumed. He is engaging them in extended personal narrative which will work into their own writing. But they still need to become more confident of themselves as writers and as persons. And Britton is able to bring the best out of them by this special touching, this vital personal interest and ongoing receptivity to aspects of their world. In turn, the teacher-students will learn the secret of drawing their own students out. As one of them put it: "You can see from what he does that you have to let students express who they are without making a judgement if they are to write comfortably."[7]

THE ONE TO ONE CONFERENCE

Full individualization can take place in the one to one tutorial/conference or the independent study where students have taken over entire responsibility for their learning, yet still want the teacher's presence. Though I and others use the terms "private tutorial" and "independent study" interchangeably, the former is often used to denote more teacher-centered functions. Robert Menges has pointed out that the individual tutorial session all too easily becomes either a recitation in which the professor conducts an oral quiz of a single student or a monologue in which the professor lectures the student on the fine points of the subject at hand.[8] Independent study connotes a student-centered activity, especially after the outline and basic parameters of a project are agreed upon by student and instructor. So it should commence in the Dialogic Mode and move on from there. According to Dressel and Thompson, "Independent study is the student's self-directed pursuit of academic competence in as autonomous a manner as he is able to exercise at any particular time."[9] As the student progresses in her work the teacher or tutor will act as Facilitator/Guide and eventually, if the student becomes completely independent, as Witness/Abiding Presence to her efforts.

The difference between facilitative and witness teaching could be seen as one of degree. Both forms act in the service of the student's learning energies. But in the former the teacher still functions as enabler whereas in the Witness teaching form the emphasis is entirely on the student's exertions. The teacher is no longer pushing, or making it possible for something to happen, or even actively assisting in the student's learning. Rather, the teacher lets go as the student totally assumes control of the learning process and begins to internalize the teaching function itself. In the process a new encounter is

established. Wilkenson puts it well when he says that "The 'structured dialogue' between teacher and student common to all now becomes a silent,
inner dialogue where the student acts the teacher's part, offering self-criticism
and self-encouragement."[10] The teacher is still there, of course, but as a
confirmatory presence to these proceedings. Neil Whitman, in his definition
of the tutorial method emphasizes this passivity of the teacher and draws a
contrast with the preceptorship where it is the student who is completely
passive. In the former the student does and the teacher observes, whereas
in the latter the opposite is true.[11]

An exemplar of the Witness/Abiding Presence teaching form can be found
in the one-on-one conferences conducted over the years by Donald Murray
of New Hampshire College. In his 1979 article, "The Listening Eye: Reflections
of the Writing Conference" Murray describes in vivid detail his individual
encounters with college students about their writing.[12] Like Ashton-Warner
and others, he points out that while in the beginning the teacher establishes
the climate (tone) and overall structure, the learning and knowledge come
from the students. He emphasizes "underteaching" and not teaching what
his students already know. He offers the reader this classic statement of the
Witness teaching form:

The other day I found myself confessing to a friend, "Each year I teach less and less
and my students seem to learn more and more. I guess what I've learned to do is to
stay out of their way and not to interfere with their learning."[13]

It is important to point out that Murray's approach to teaching represents
a kind of "conversion" or "enlightenment," and only began to take place a
good way into his teaching career—after he found himself stuck in more
teacher-centered modes. In short, we could say he has moved up the continuum. Once he got beyond the avid-lecturer form, Murray used inquirer
techniques in asking his questions, became dialogic in his conversations with
students, facilitative in helping them clarify things for themselves. But he
discovered that centrally (finally) he has become a listener. He found that
his questions become unnecessary because his students have already asked
them before they came: "They have taken my conference away from me.
They come in and tell me what has gone well, what has gone wrong, and
what they intend to do about it." (p. 159)

Given these energies, Murray began to question the usefulness of his role
in the conference—he felt especially guilty in regard to those who have to
travel so far for fifteen or twenty minutes. Though his concerns proved
groundless, he remained mystified. His students assure him it is important
for them to hear what he has to say: " 'But I don't say anything', I confess.
'You say it all.' They smile and nod as if I know better than that, but I don't."
(p. 159)

Like Britton, Murray's ability to focus totally on the individual student's world is the key to his success in the Witness/Abiding Presence teaching format. And in so doing he elicits from them what they often didn't know was there. Such a teaching form has to be the most subtle of all. Still, Murray confesses that he is haunted by the "paranoia of his profession" where if the teacher is not doing most of the talking he is not doing his job: "I confess my fear that I'm too easy to a colleague, Don Graves. He assures me I am a demanding teacher, for I see more in my students than they do—to their surprise, not mine." (p. 160)

Murray is obviously doing something unusual in his teaching. He has reached a point of educational intimacy with his students that is rare within the confines of higher education. Yet he feels anxious and somewhat uncertain—as one often does when finding himself exploring new territory in a chosen field. Ashton-Warner expressed similar feelings of guilt and isolation in her work with Maori children.[14]

We also see from his description that in these conferences his students have appropriated the learning process—there is almost a raging desire to learn, to grow. Murray's chief concern now is to stay out of the way, to let things happen. He recalls that in his younger days when he was a boxer he learned to counter-punch. This may be what he is doing now, he says— circling his students, trying to shut up: "It isn't easy—trying not to interfere with their learning, waiting until they've learned something so I can show them what they've learned . . ."[15] He points out that the writing, the language, the knowledge is theirs. They write to discover what they know. He does not want to interfere with that. He is there for them to use as a sounding board, to think out loud. Here we see how learning as discovery works in highly motivated college students. The learner—completely individualized by the teacher's interest and caring—feels free to operate on all frequencies, to learn and grow within a teaching presence that silently confirms what is happening. Murray tells the reader that he professionally edits and makes suggestions (always showing more than one option) only near the end of the process, after the author has found something to say and a way to say it. The conference with Andrea exemplifies this perfectly:

Out comes the clipboard when I pass the paper back to her. She tells me exactly what she attempted to do, precisely where she succeeded and how, then informs me what she intends to do next. She will not work on this draft; she is bored with it. She will go back to an earlier piece, the one I liked and she didn't like. Now she knows what to do with it. She starts to pack up and leave. I smile and feel silly; I ought to do something. She's paying her own way through school. I have to say something.

"I'm sorry you had to come all the way over here this late." Andrea looks up surprised. "Why?"

"I haven't taught you anything."

"The hell you haven't. I'm learning in this course, really learning." (p. 162)

This student's energies are now oceanic, coming full force from inside. The teacher is there, not so much to channel, but to absorb and mirror for the student her success. The teacher has become masterful (perhaps unconsciously) at what Heidegger calls "letting learn."[16] Those who reach this stage are engaging in a most delicate art—an art which is, in fact, artless.

Also, the teacher's presence here allows the student to be most creative, to make connections—to learn for surprise. Perhaps it is all surprise. Perhaps it is not really teaching. As Sylvia Ashton-Warner put it: "But I don't call it teaching: I call it creativity, since it all comes from them and nothing from me."[17]

A teacher feels privileged to be part of this energy and has a strange sense of sharing an enterprise that transcends her. Teaching in this sense becomes mysterious; the teacher's "non-doing" paradoxically brings a feeling of fulfillment unlike that in the previous forms. Her "influence" has markedly decreased, yet in another way it is more refined, subtle, unself-conscious. Becoming totally student-centered, the teacher is moving toward a certain egolessness. Nowhere in the teacher-training programs are candidates ever prepared for this kind of teaching form. Probably there is no way to prepare them. But at least aspiring, and even practicing teachers, should be told that such encounters can take place. Then they would be apprised of the full range of teaching possibility.

TEACHER AND LEARNER AS EQUAL SUBJECTIVITIES

A few of the teachers described by students in *Woman's Ways of Knowing* are similar to James Britton and Donald Murray in that they are vitally interested in their students' ideas. In a section titled "Portrait of a Connected Teacher" Candace reminisces about an English professor at the woman's college she attended who was intensely interested in everybody's feelings about things: "She asked a question and wanted to know what your response was. She wanted to know because she wanted to see what sort of effect this writing was having. She wasn't using us as a sounding board for her own feelings about things. She really wanted to know."[18]

Here an important point needs to be stressed about which there should be no misunderstanding: The teachers described above do not merge their identity with that of their students. They remain very much their own unique selves. Focusing on another student's person and world is not the same as abandoning one's own vision. Two subjectivities still exist here. Rather it means not treating one's own experience of the student's framework as primary. Candace is clear about the distinction in regard to her English teacher:

As a teacher she believed she had to trust each student's experience, although as a person or a critic she might not agree with it. To trust means not just to tolerate a variety of viewpoints, acting as impartial referee, assuming equal air time to all. It means to try to *connect*, to enter into each student's perspective.[19]

This distinction between subjectivities is rendered very well by Martin Buber's notion of "inclusion." Brian Hendley, writing on "Martin Buber and the Teacher/Student Relationship," sees it as "the embracing of the other, putting yourself in his position and seeing things from his side as well as your own."[20] Inclusion, therefore, does not abolish the distance between oneself and the other. Rather, in Buber's words, it is "a bold swinging over into the life of the person one confronts, through which alone I can make him present in his wholeness, unity and uniqueness."[21] This activity is evident in the Witness/Abiding Presence teaching form, for when done impartially it requires that the teacher act not from herself and her idea of the pupil, but from the pupil's own reality. This is more than merely sympathy or even the empathy described in the Dialogic Form. And it can be extremely difficult to achieve.

Nell Noddings stresses the same theme when she points out that caring "involves stepping out of one's own personal frame of reference into the other's."[22] From a phenomenological standpoint we are concerned not only for our own consciousness (that of subject) but also with that of the one we encounter: "The 'object' of consciousness is [also'] a subject, another consciousness."[23]

In order to concretize what is meant here, Noddings (in *Caring*) offers a graphic example of a young man who hates mathematics and shows how the teacher might move herself away from the usual dedicated teacher's frame of reference into a new kind of understanding. She begins with her reflection on the initial encounter: "He tells me that he hates mathematics. Aha, I think. Here is the problem. I must help this poor boy to love mathematics, and then he will be better at it..."[24] After realizing that this aim, noble though it might be, has not really taken into view the boy's subjectivity, she shifts now to a more "inclusive" perspective, one that involves her in a new way of reflecting: "What matters to me, if I care, is that he find some reason, acceptable in his inner self, for learning the mathematics required of him or that he reject it boldly and honestly..." (p. 15)

Once having made this shift in her perspective the teacher is now able to resist more conventional procedures and create a presence which is truly inclusive.

When I think this way, I refuse to cast about for rewards that might pull him along. He must find his rewards. I do not begin with dazzling performances designed to intrigue him or to change his attitude. I begin, as nearly as I can, with the view from his eyes: Mathematics is bleak, jumbled, scary, boring, boring, boring...What in the world could induce me to engage in it? From that point on we struggle together with it. (pp. 15–16)

Here obviously the student has not yet appropriated his own learning. But the teacher in moving over to the boy's point of view has placed it totally in his hands, allowing him full freedom to accept or reject. He, in turn, still sees her as the mathematics teacher with her own identity and interests. But he also realizes that she is truly focused on him, and she will not attempt to manipulate his state of mind. She is present to him in a new way. No guarantees. How rare is this kind of teaching encounter!

We mentioned briefly in the last chapter how a teacher has to deal with the inherent problem of two subjectivities trying to discover the meaning which the other is trying to communicate. This problem should diminish in the Witness teaching form since by this stage the teacher is present to the student's world in total receptivity as the student has assumes complete charge of the learning process. Once this mutual shift has been accomplished the potential for misunderstanding is minimized. That said, however, it is still true that no one ever sees another's world exactly as it exists to the student. The very fact that two subjectivities co-exist involves a certain irreducible separateness. Surrounding these subjectivities, however, is what Philip Jackson calls a certain "presumption of shared identity" which must remain unquestioned to some degree for social interaction to become a possibility.[25] Even Edmund Husserl pointed out that while the fields of memory and perception present to each consciousness are different, there is something "intersubjectively known in common." Husserl continues: "...we come to understandings with our neighbors, and set up in common an objective spatio-temporal fact-world as the world about us that is there for us all, and to which we ourselves none the less belong."[26]

TEACHER LEARNS FROM STUDENT

Buber has made it clear that he believes inclusion is one-sided in that the student is not capable of a similar shift of perspective. Hendley, in his article, questions whether things can't be two-sided—especially in the higher stages of education where teacher and students become partners in a common activity. He argues that if education means allowing a part of the world to affect the student through the medium of a teacher, why rule out the possibility of the teacher being affected by the students as well?: "Is he to be thought ineducable? Do we really feel that as teacher we have nothing more to learn from our students?"[27]

Donald Murray and James Britton would support this view strongly. Murray talks about the fact that he is learning more from his students than they from him, of how he has been instructed in other lives, heard the voices of students they themselves have not heard before, shared their satisfaction in solving the problem of writing with clarity and grace.[28] We have no reason to think that this is not the case—and once teacher and student become co-learners as a constant rule then teaching has moved into its Apophatic Mode, as we shall see in the next chapter. In actuality, there is probably no firm dividing line in these last stages of the teaching continuum. Just as students find themselves more and more internalizing the teacher so, too, teachers find themselves becoming learners. We have in this mysterious teaching presence an outgrowth and deepening of the new relation between teacher and learner that was initiated with the Dialogic encounter. What began with the sharing of a common sphere where both subjects exude equal energies had shifted to the teacher working facilitatively within the students sphere, and now to this further stage where the teacher is wholly present (often in silence) to the student's advancing progress without losing his own unique identity. Full concretization also has taken place here. The teacher is no longer focusing on students in general, or on just any student, but on this particular student in this particular concrete situation. And that focus is one of totally alert receptivity.

However, for educational intimacy of this sort it is not necessary to establish deep, lasting, time-consuming personal relationships with every student. What I must do, says Noddings, "is to be totally and non-selectively, present to the student—to each student—as he addresses me. The time interval may be brief but the encounter is total."[29] There should be no confusion here if educational intimacy is distinguished from the intimacy of close friends or of lovers. The bond between teacher and student is unique while it lasts, though it certainly can be overlaid with the tapestry of other relationships.

The French phenomenologist, Gabriel Marcel, has explored the terms "presence," "availability," and "openness" in ways that can be applied to the teacher as Witness/Abiding Presence. In *Presence and Immortality*, he reflects that "When the other is present, he renews us in some way and makes us more fully ourselves than we would have been alone."[30] In another place: "Presence breaks forth as a response to the act by which we open ourselves to receive."[31] This last statement is especially relevant to the inner attitudes of teachers discussed in this chapter who are "available" to their students without sacrificing their own identities, and then find their students flowering or breaking forth. Though the kind of openness indicated here may be unusual things can happen spontaneously when a teacher and student are so disposed.

Again, we have Marcel's idea that the realization of the self is a gift of another, perhaps of many others. Educationally, these sentiments can be applied to teachers who find in their students what they themselves fail to find, often just by being totally present to their student's educational needs. Witnessing, accepting, confirming at this phenomenological level brings students fully into themselves—in a sense, gives them their individuality. And teaching by means of total receptivity and acceptance increases intimacy to the point where the teaching presence is no longer outside, but internal to the student. Marcel writes: "The rapport which is granted with another acts on us, not as an outside cause, but as an inward principle which develops us from within."[32] It is this totality of attention from the teacher, this swinging over into the student's perspective that internalizes the teaching principle for the student and finally makes the extrinsic teacher dispensable.

DISTANCING OF TEACHER AND STUDENT

A huge paradox begins to appear toward the end of the Elicitive Teaching Mode. While the teacher is achieving the special intimacy (often unspoken) of the Witness form, the student, by this very fact, is achieving a heightened awareness of his or her own inner freedom and autonomy. The purpose of the teacher all along has been has been to open students to their own freedom, in Van Cleve Morris's phrase, "to waken learners to themselves as learners and seekers and creators of their own truth."[33] The teacher as Witness allows and applauds the student's complete emancipation; she should feel most fulfilled when she observes this phenomenon. For her androgogical task is coming to an end. Here the teacher has given herself to the extent that students, far from imitating her, move out on their own. Instead of giving birth to replicas of herself (an extremely immature ideal in teaching), the teaching act has issued forth in men or women who stand free, who can distance themselves from the external teacher who first encountered them on their educational journey. As Van Cleve Morris puts it:

It is the distance that makes the student a mature self, a free, self-moving subjectivity. When that individual stands apart and alone, awake to his existing, aware of his freedom, responsible and in charge of his own life, he will see for himself why he may, for the first time, be called *authentic*.[34]

Thus, any "role-modeling" on the part of the teacher will be that of the authentic seeker. This second aspect of witnessing is that of the educator who has set out on his own journey to learn and to grow. To be a teacher in the fullest sense is always to be learning anew, to be always following one's own path. It is the modeling of what William Adams has called "the metaself." That metaself calls to the development of the metaself values in the learner.[35] What is meant here goes far beyond competence in one's field or subject matter (though these are obviously important). Highlighted in the student's mind is not so much the teacher's love and enthusiasm for her subject (which we saw in earlier teaching forms) but something more profound: The teacher's trajectory of commitment to the larger aims of life despite the cost. Philip Jackson speaks of this "personal modeling" as one of the chief characteristics which identify the teacher in the "transformative tradition":

For it is essential to success within that tradition that teachers who are trying to bring about transformative changes personify the very qualities they seek to engender in their students. To the best of their ability they must be living exemplars of certain virtues or values or attitudes.[36]

The teacher who gives witness to this kind of growth impresses on his students the need to continue their own. Here is why the separate identity of the teacher can never be lost. Such was the witness given by Socrates. That which most impressed the readers of those dialogues (as it must have impressed his interlocutors) was his absolute commitment to the search for truth and to the wonder of learning. It is this witness, this special presence, this "way of being" of a teacher that also stays with the learner forever.[37]

GROUPS ON THEIR OWN

Teachers who in their own work with groups have moved from being directive to facilitative have already shifted the energies away from themselves. It now remains to allow the groups to function almost totally on their own. For this the teaching presence is passive and extremely non-invasive. Contrast, for example, a discussion in which the teacher acts as facilitator to one where the group is allowed complete autonomy. In Chapter 6 we saw how the teacher (Glassman) structured cooperative learning groups among seniors for a biochemistry class. He viewed his responsibilities as that of "facilitating creativity, independence, and self-direction in the learner."[38] We saw him in the preliminary stages function as task-setter and manager, creating an involvement stage. When after six weeks the groups began to function fairly autonomously (working stage) the teacher receded and became present to the group as Facilitator/Guide. He moved from encouraging, assisting, negotiating to delegating, and finally to resource consultant where he let students work largely on their own. In these latter stages he began to listen and confirm. Evaluation took place with the teacher in an open-ended process and there were no written exams.

The teacher's use of the Facilitative Form is clear in the above excerpt. In contrast, a discussion with the teacher functioning as Witness might take place in a graduate level seminar where students with an already rich data base share ideas based on their research or disagree over interpretations of experiment results. The professor, having set the parameters of the seminar in the beginning of the semester, or even longer ago, now sits totally alert, observing, listening, even asking an occasional question to clarify a point (if no one else does), perhaps taking notes. But the group does not wait to hear her contribution to the discussion, nor do students have a need for her to perform the usual facilitative tasks. They don't even need her active encouragement. If she is conversant with or even an expert in the field, the group will be acutely aware of her presence and the fact that she is taking everything in.[39] But they are allowed complete freedom to express themselves and deal with each other. And if the professor has established a dialogic atmosphere previously a community will already exist where, in John MacMurray's words, "each cares for all the others and no one (merely) for himself."[40] Such an atmosphere is admittedly ideal, but learning communities can exist which approximate this ideal, where the teacher simply remains as witness to these activities—absorbing, refracting, silently confirming—while the students, in charge of the seminar dynamics, are learning on their own. The difference is that the professor does not facilitate the students' independence and creativity. (One of the students may actually handle the discussion.) She merely observes them operating on their own and joins in the flow.

Joseph Axelrod, in *The University Teacher As Artist*, renders portraits of two "evocative" student-centered teachers who allow group discussions to take place on an undergraduate level in what is tantamount to the Witness/Abiding Presence Form. Both teachers have reached a point in their growth where their focus is on the whole person rather than just on the student's mind or the acquisition of skills. (Axelrod calls these teachers "student-as-person prototypes." (p. 14) Thus, they individualize their students—even within the group. Their ability to listen and take in the proceedings is also very much in evidence. Axelrod comments on one professor's teaching presence which he tells us represents a transformation from previous less student-centered forms: "Sometimes it seemed as if he [Professor Abbot] would sit in his place at the table and say almost nothing for an entire class period, only occasionally adding an "uh-huh" or a "yes" to the discussion." (p.116)

Professor Abbot took notes at these sessions and after two or three weeks would use them as the basis for a "lecture" where he commented, not on his own ideas, but on what students were reading and thinking. Axelrod tells us that these occasional lectures represented a departure from his former style, but any observations he had about literary subjects or methods he related to his students' concerns.

The other professor, Barton Persey, used the same approach and also saved his comments for special lecture sessions, while remaining relatively quiet during the other discussions, occasionally functioning as resource person and traffic manager. Axelrod records a brief conversation with Peter Moorhead, one of Persey's students, in regard to the teacher's apparent non-involvement:

Interviewer: I noticed during the class that Bart didn't do very much talking. Does he often just sit at the table taking notes without saying anything for a long time?

Peter: He usually says something.

I: I don't mean just calling on students or saying "That's fine" or something. I'm talking about the way he lets the students do practically all of the talking.

P: He wants *us* to talk, and he lets us talk.

I: Suppose he didn't come to class at all. Suppose he just wasn't there some day. Would it make any difference to you?

P: It certainly would.

I: But what's the difference between not being there at all and being there but not saying anything—the way he did today? Isn't it pretty much the same thing?

P: It's not the same at all. He doesn't have to *say* anything. Just having him there is important to us. (p. 36–37)

We see here, indeed graphically, the teacher as a silent abiding presence in the classroom or seminar room. The group functions on its own, but the students feel very strongly the value of Persey's presence.

Learning within the group, however, at least in undergraduate contexts, may have its limits for those individual students who are growing more rapidly than the others. William Adams notes how students with very developed "metaselves" may grow beyond the students in discussion format and wish to go totally on their own—or one on one, person to person, with a metaself teacher. He admits that a teacher can convey a sense of metaself values to a group interacting with each other, but full metaself interaction can only take place privately.[41] So too, Van Cleve Morris suggests that "the group, for all its cognitive, problem-solving capabilities in educational situations, cannot completely tune to that frequency of interhuman communication which is effective and emotional in character."[42] While this may be largely true in terms of educational intimacy, we have seen that mature participants in a truly dialogic group encounter one another on levels other than cognitive when there is sympathy and caring. However, it must be admitted that this kind of holistic and cooperative group learning in the competitive atmosphere of higher education today is not common.

When individuals leave a learning group it does not mean they are renouncing community. It means, more likely, that either they are ready to seek a broader, more meaningful learning community or for the time being need to nurture learning within themselves. There is always the need for a balance between the personal and the communal in education. What's more, at this advanced stage of learning, whether the student is working alone or in tandem with others, he is always part of an invisible community, the voices of which speak to him constantly through books, ideas, experiments and indeed nature itself. To be deeply engaged in learning is to advance in both solitude and concert with others.

SELF-EVALUATION

At this stage of the learning process any evaluation of the student from an extrinsic source will be meaningless. We noted in Chapter 6 that teacher and student often negotiate together the learning agenda. When the terms of the learning contract are fulfilled a certain grade or accomplishment level will be assigned. The energies for learning are coming from within the student; the teacher assists, guides, clarifies, and even confirms. But in the Witness/ Abiding Presence Form the student must be the chief repository of any critical assessment. The student is internalizing the teaching function, and so learning and evaluation come from the same source; both will be a natural process of discovery, review, confirmation, redirection, new discovery, and so on. Self-evaluation is witnessed and confirmed by the teacher. For Donald Murray evaluation and reevaluation take place as the student moves through different versions of her paper. At a certain stage he will offer editorial comment, but he will not judge the piece. He does not need to. We have seen that Schon's example of Dani and Michal in the previous chapter shows the teacher joining in the act of judgement based on what the student has already ascertained: "You must judge your own work—and I will join you in judging it—on the basis of your own success in producing what you intend."[43]

The point is that at this stage the criteria for evaluating qualitative work and true growth lie inside oneself. The teacher or any other external evaluator can only corroborate the learner's judgement. And once the student has reached this stage we can be sure that she will have no more keen and demanding critic than herself. When one has totally invested in one's own learning, dishonesty and half measures are instantly recognized. For she is looking inside—the only place where the real teacher resides.

In so far as one must function within the structure of higher education for more utilitarian ends, grading in some fashion probably cannot simply be abandoned. Both Noddings and Adams see grading as necessary only in so far as others need to be informed about a student's progress. Given this need, the teacher can get caught between what Noddings calls "the employment community and faithfulness to the student."[44] Thus, the conflict between credit-giver and teacher, between gatekeeper and ally we have already discussed.

Even here, though, the difficulty may be more apparent than real. For in the Elicitive Mode the caring teacher has been working with the student all along in negotiating the transfer of the evaluation process to the student. As Noddings puts it: "The teacher who values her student as subject will be concerned with his growing ability to evaluate his own work."[45]

In this second form of the Elicitive Mode, the teacher as Witness confirms the level of competency or growth to which the student has brought himself. Obviously, when specific competencies are involved there may be external agencies which need to give their stamp of approval. And the student will learn to adapt to these so that he can help himself in society. But in this last stage the superficial levels of academic progress can give way to more profound aspects of educational growth. And these aspects are not measurable according to the usual external criteria. Quite often institutional structures are not relevant to this kind of learning; they can even become obstacles to the student's further progress. The truth is that the deeper dimensions of learning evidenced in the Witness/Abiding Presence encounter are not only exceedingly rare within the system of higher education, but actually transcend it—and in the process may subject that system to rigorous criticism. For the student has above all reached the point where his self-evaluation is part of a larger questioning process which is constant, even relentless. He searches now, as all true learners must, not so much for answers but for ways to nurture an attitude of being that is both critical and creative. This will necessitate not only asking questions which rise up from within, but questioning those very questions in order to make sure they are the right ones. Such an attitude can be imbibed from intensive work over a period of time within a particular discipline. As one absorbs a field of knowledge, one also internalizes a particular habit of thought and hopefully of questioning. But this is not enough. One must see outside and beyond that field to a larger universe where all fields interconnect. It is here that the great questions of life, beyond any subject discipline, are asked. For the learner seeks what Krishnamurti calls true intelligence rather than intellect. And such intelligence is often far different than what is tested in the institutions of higher learning:

We have made examinations and degrees the criterion of intelligence and have developed cunning minds that avoid vital human issues. Intelligence is the capacity to perceive the essential, the "what is"; and to awaken this capacity, in oneself and in others, is education.[46]

The teacher has long ago initiated this process of self-discovery in the student. The learner, now following the current of her own trajectory, has begun to seek integrated understanding or meaning (Krishnamurti). Life as a whole spreads out before her and whatever specific discipline she has entered, whatever knowledge she has gained, is now viewed within this broader arc. In these latest encounters the teacher watches and is present. But a time comes when even that confirmatory presence is no longer needed. With the learner fully emancipated the task of teaching comes to an end.

NOTES

1. Daniel Duke, "Understanding What It Means to Be a Teacher," *Educational Leadership*, 64, no. 2 (October 1986): 31.
2. Ibid., p. 32.
3. Some of the qualities that I have placed within the Witness/Abiding Presence Teaching Form are often thought of under facilitative teaching. For example see McKeachie, *Teaching Tips*, pp. 59–60. I have no hesitation in breaking into two forms what many educators see as one. This is not to say that listening does not go on in facilitative teaching. But in the Witness form it is absolutely central.
4. Ashton-Warner, *Teacher*, pp. 92–93.
5. Ibid., p. 57.
6. Macrorie, *Twenty Teachers*, p. 179. James Britton has written two highly influential books in the field of Writing Theory: *Language and Learning* (Baltimore: Penguin Books, 1974) and *The Development of Writing Abilities (11–18)*, written with Tony Burgess, Nancy Martin, Alex McLeod, and Harold Rosen (London: Schools Council Publications, 1975).
7. Ibid., p. 177.
8. Menges, "Instructional Methods" in *The Modern American College*.

9. Paul Dressel and Mary Magdala Thompson, *Independent Study: A New Interpretation of Concepts, Practices, and Problems* (San Francisco: Jossey-Bass Publishers, 1973), p. 1.

10. Wilkinson, "Varieties of Teaching" *The Art and Craft of Teaching*, pp. 8–9.

11. Neal Whitman, "Choosing and Using Methods of Teaching," *NSPI Journal*, (June 1981): 17. It should be pointed out here that Whitman's perception of the tutorial is not shared by all educators. Many—perhaps most—view the teacher as much more active in the tutorial relationships, even to the point of imparting instruction.

12. Donald M. Murray, "The Listening Eye: Reflections on the Writing Conference" in *Learning By Teaching: Selected Articles on Writing and Teaching* (Portsmouth, N.H.: Boynton Cook Publishers, Inc., 1982), pp. 157–163. Originally published in *College English*, 41, no. 1 (September 1979).

13. Ibid., p. 158. Murray's writing conferences are fairly unique. Most of the literature on the Writing Conference describes teacher/student relations in terms of earlier teaching forms on the continuum. Even where the student is extremely active in the conference the teacher acts as facilitator or coach rather than as witness. Cf. Muriel Harris, *Teaching One to One: The Writing Conference* (Urbana, Illinois: National Council Teachers of English, 1986) Also, Thomas A. Carnicelli, "The Writing Conference: A One To One Conversation," in *Eight Approaches to Teaching Composition*, ed. Timothy R. Donovan and Ben W. McClelland (Urbana, Illinois: National Council of Teachers of English, 1980), pp. 101–131. However, Charles Duke in a 1975 article, "The Student-Centered Conference and the Writing Process" (*English Journal*, 64, pp. 44–47) advocates a teaching style similar to Murray's, one that is Rogerian.

14. Ashton-Warner, *Teacher*, p. 103.

15. Murray, "The Listening Eye: Reflections on the Writing Conference," p. 160.

16. Ignacio L. Gotz, "Heidegger and the Art of Teaching," *Educational Theory*, 33, no. 1 (Winter 1983): 8.

17. Ashton-Warner, *Teacher*, p. 52.

18. Belenky et. al., *Woman's Ways of Knowing*, p. 225.

19. Ibid., p. 227.

20. Brian Hendley, "Martin Buber on the Teacher/Student Relationship: A Critical Appraisal," *Journal of Philosophy of Education*, 12 (1978): 142.

21. Ibid., p. 142.

22. Nell Noddings, *Caring*, p. 24.

23. Noddings, "Fidelity in Teaching," p. 501.

24. Noddings, *Caring*, p. 15.

25. Jackson, *The Practice of Teaching*, pp. 26–27.

26. Edmund Husserl, *Ideas: General Introduction to Pure Phenomenology* (New York: Collier Books, 1962), p. 95.

27. Hendley, "Martin Buber and the Teacher/Student Relationship," p. 144.

28. Murray, "The Listening Eye: Reflections on the Writing Conference," p. 157.

29. Noddings, *Caring*, p. 180. See also, Richard E. Hult, Jr., "On Pedagogical Caring," *Educational Theory*, 29, no. 3 (Summer 1979): pp. 237–243.

30. Gabriel Marcel, *Presence and Immortality* (Pittsburgh: Duquesne University Press, 1967), p. 153.

31. McCown, *Availability: Gabriel Marcel and the Phenomenology of Human Openness*, p. 42.

32. Ibid., p. 45.

33. Morris, *Existentialism in Education: What It Means*, p. 152.

34. Ibid., p. 154.

35. Adams, *The Experience of Teaching and Learning: A Phenomenology of Education*, p. 38.

36. Jackson, *The Practice of Teaching*, p. 124.

37. Peter Abbs refers to Socrates when he talks about the teacher's need to be an image of "authentic being" for all those in his charge: "The teacher himself embodies what it is to create, to think, to contemplate. In and through his being he represents education as a passion for meaning and a way of relating to the entire universe." See Peter Abbs, "Education and the Living Image: Reflections on Imagery, Fantasy, and the Art of Recognition," in *Toward the Recovery of Wholeness: Knowledge, Education, and Human Values*, ed. Douglas Sloan (New York: Teachers College Press, 1981), p. 122.

38. Glassman, "Teaching Biochemistry in Cooperative Learning Groups," p. 35.

39. The excerpt quoted in Chapter 7, Wayne Booth's *Vocation of a Teacher* (p. 274) from a literature seminar for advanced graduate students, could possibly be seen as an example of the Witness teaching form.

40. John MacMurray, *Persons in Relation*, p. 159.

41. Adams, *The Experience of Teaching and Learning*, p. 130.

42. Morris, *Existentialism in Education*, p. 101.

43. Schon, *Educating the Reflective Practitioner*, p. 153.

44. Noddings, *Caring*, p. 194. Noddings makes the distinction between evaluation and grading. The latter, she notes, "is an intrusion upon the relationship between the one caring and the one cared for." (p. 193)

45. Ibid., p. 196.

46. J. Krishnamurti, *Education and the Significance of Life* (San Francisco: Harper & Row, 1981), p. 14.

Part Five

Apophatic Mode

Chapter 8

Teacher As Learner

The great teacher is the one who wants to become obsolete in
the life of the student.

Jacob Neusner

But this rough magic I here abjure
I'll break my staff,
Bury it certain fathoms in the earth,
And deeper than did ever plummet sound
I'll drown my book.
(Prospero, *The Tempest*, Act V)

THE DISAPPEARANCE OF TEACHING

There comes a moment in an androgogical relationship when a teacher who
has seen a student accept full responsibility for her learning realizes that he
is not needed any more, that even the most non-invasive teaching presence
is an encumbrance to the learner. This gathering insight can be viewed in
terms of a shifting of power and it carries with it both pain and pleasure.
Peter Beidler expresses it well:

If I am doing my job by the end of the semester my students are independent of me.
I strive every semester to give my students power, even though when I succeed I
inevitably disempower myself. I hate that feeling of powerlessness at the end of the
semester. And I love it.[1]

While Beidler, unless he is working with exceptionally motivated students,
describes this end of semester state more as an ideal than a reality, he puts

his finger on the conflict of feeling a teacher may have within himself when he sees that he is committed to a process that will result in making him completely dispensable. Thus, teaching at its most successful renders itself obsolete. It is this Van Cleve Morris points to when he discusses teaching in the existentialist mode: "Such teaching succeeds by doing itself out of a job. It succeeds by becoming unnecessary, by producing an individual who no longer needs to be taught, who breaks loose and swings free of the teacher and becomes self-moving."[2]

Donald Vandenberg broadens the view and applies the idea of dispensability to the whole educational process. In "Phenomenology and Educational Research" he states bluntly that the goal of educating is to put an end to itself.

The aim of educating is to be able to stop educating. The underlying purpose of all specific acts of educating is to cumulatively make it possible to put an end to educating, to enable youth to finally leave the pedagogic relationship entirely and for good. The aim of educating is the development of the adult who exists independently of any pedagogic relation, that is, the independent student.[3]

This independence, this final breaking loose, when it happens, represents the full internalization of the teaching process by the student and should be the occasion for joy. That self-activating energy which began in the Dialogic Mode has accelerated with every successive teaching encounter until the student can be "self-taught." There is no more need of an extrinsic other and, in fact, for such a teaching presence to persist is a kind of absurdity.

Joseph DeVito, in applying developmental relational stages to teaching, speaks of a movement beyond "Intimacy," that of "Deteriorization" and "Dissolution." But these are not to be viewed negatively as in romantic relationships. DeVito stresses that in the teaching situation this stage has a more positive tone, representing a normal and healthy developmental process in which "the student is preparing to separate from the mentor, not unlike the bird leaving its nest."[4]

Indeed, the student may be the one to make the final break. Dimly realizing that the bond with the teacher has fulfilled its usefulness he seeks a way to dissolve the tie. This can happen in any number of ways: He may show diminishing interest in the encounter; he may simply stop coming; she may subtly signal that anything the teacher says in a pedagogical way is unwelcome. She may ask the teacher to become a friend or through natural evolution show her readiness to meet the teacher on new ground, as an equal partner.[5]

More often, however, it is the teacher who signals the student that the relationship is over. The prescient teacher sees the end coming; she prepares herself and her student. She becomes more passive, more non-invasive, more a listener, a simple presence. Donald Murray uses the phrase, "the pilgrimage toward unteaching" which can be the journey of a semester or of many years.[6] Such a state can be reached in formal higher education when the androgogical relation has been moving toward self-direction all along. Loacker and Doherty describe this last stage in a learning contract as one where the student has "a practical understanding of her own learning and a demonstrated ability to guide it that is in kind, if not yet in degree, equal to that of her educators."[7] In fact, she is now "a junior peer" and her own educator. The authors assure us that true teachers are gratified to see their students reach this point—"all in their own individual way"—but it is also at this point that they prepare to take their leave.[8] Obviously, much more is meant here than the simple ceremony of graduation.

In more informal circumstances the final sundering may come as a surprise to the student. The teacher gives him a gentle push which may at first be disconcerting. Some reflection will put the matter in focus. The student will realize consciously what he has subconsciously known ever since he began to take over his own learning. Thus, the teacher's leave–taking is the unveiling of a final educational reality. Quite often the break is unspoken and mutual between the two parties. They move away from each other, simply desist and have no urge to come together again as teacher and learner. This is the stage of "Dissolution" which according to DeVito represents the physical separation of student and teacher. Dissolution also makes it possible for each of the two parties to formulate new relationships, ones that hold possibilities for new learning.[9]

Prospero in *The Tempest* could perhaps symbolize the artist-teacher who reaches a point where he "abjures his magic," the pretension to teach in any way. Even the art which had become "artless" in later teaching forms on the continuum is now renounced. For the learner has no need of it and can, in fact, find it an obstacle to further progress. Perhaps the most striking remarks ever made on the abjuration of teaching are those of Carl Rogers in a paper presented at Harvard over three decades ago to an audience of forty progressive teachers:

It seems to me that anything that can be taught to another is relatively inconsequential and has little or no significant influence on behavior . . . I have come to feel that the only learning which significantly influences behavior is self-discovered, self- appropriated learning . . . As a consequence of the above, I realize that I have lost interest in being a teacher.[10]

Rogers had reached a point in his teaching career where (somewhat like Murray) he realizes that since learning is self-appropriated, any attempts "to teach" are futile. He further points out that his past teaching may have been counterproductive to the students' efforts: "When I look back at the results of my past teaching, the real results seem the same—either damage was done or nothing significant occurred."[11]

Perkinson points out that when Rogers uses the word "teacher" in his remarks he is speaking of "transmission teacher" which would correspond to the forms set out in the early stages of the continuum.[12] My sense is that Rogers meant his remarks to apply even to more student-centered teaching, especially since he describes his audience that day as "made up of forward-looking college teachers, many of whom were using discussion methods in their classes."[13] His discovery obviously had been an unsettling one and from his own testimony the sharing of his dismay proved highly disturbing to the majority of his audience. But he tells us that a few individuals gradually spoke up and admitted their experience had led them to similar conclusions which they had never dared to voice.[14]

I have been suggesting that on a continuum of teaching encounters ranging from teacher-centered at one pole to student-centered at the other there comes a phase at the far end where a teacher simply terminates his or her androgogical efforts. He does so because he realizes the student no longer has any need of him. And to stay on, to want to hold on or "teach" in any way is a futile and even damaging exercise of pedagogical energy (whether active or passive). Whether the teacher gives up the "pretention to teach" as a final act in a developmental sequence or as the result of a more enlightened insight into the nature of learning (Rogers), both still point to the same reality in the end: Non-teaching. They differ in that teachers who moves into such a stage less abruptly, or "non-violently" if you will, do not look back at their previous teaching efforts with as much disdain as Rogers does. On a closer examination, however, the difference may not be that great since moving to a more student-centered teaching form always makes clear to one the limitations of a previous form. Contained in those limitations may be a harm factor if the teaching presence underestimated a student's readiness to take a more active role in learning. It is even worse if the teacher misused the form and destroyed any eagerness to learn on the part of the student. I believe what Rogers and Murray mean when they use the word "harm" or "damage" is that by their actions they reinforce the student's belief that he or she can be, or is being, taught something by the teacher:

Rogers: When I try to teach, as I do sometimes, I am appalled by the results, which seem little more than inconsequential, because sometimes the teaching appears to succeed . . . It seems to cause the individual to distrust his own experience, and to stifle significant learning.[15]

Murray: I mistreated my students and earned a reputation as a good teacher. I behaved as teachers were supposed to behave [in their eyes] and that made me a good one.[16]

However the case may be, the fact remains that once students take responsibility for their own learning teaching sooner or later will come to an end. Prospero must break his staff and drown his book. This final phase of non-teaching I will call the Apophatic Mode—one where teachers "blow out" the flame of their influence. Perhaps it is more accurate to say that the flame now resides in the student (who is no longer a student). This mode, para-doxically, is no mode at all, for there is no teaching in it, only an absence of any extrinsic teaching form. What we have is the presence of the fully inte-grated learner. To look at teaching from the aspect of this final stage lends a very special meaning to the kind of calling a teacher pursues in the course of a career. It requires a gradual renunciation of any power or control a particular teaching form may involve until a point is reached where a total emptying out of the teaching self takes place. One views learners wholly on their own and the teacher is returned to what originally she was—a learner.

Besides the paradox of what I will call fulfillment-emptiness, there is an-other even more dazzling paradox which appears in the fact that the moment the learner fully internalizes the teacher he does not really discover a new presence, but apprehends what has always been there, asleep as it were. When a person finally sees that he is his own teacher he sees that this was always the case. This may be what is meant by the enigmatic Zen saying: "If you meet the Buddha on the road, kill him." The enlightened learner "kills" the teacher outside her because she knows now that this teacher is the false one, the illusion. The fully integrated learner has imbibed (eaten) the teacher and in this act of communion teaching and learning have fused, come to-gether, melted down into one energy. To put this another way: In the last analysis there is no teaching, only learning. And all learning is self-taught.

I believe this paradox can be applied, not only to the more profound aspects of personal realization and growth (to which the Buddha statement is meant to apply), but in regard to the more superficial and behavioral aspects of education. So, for example, a student reaches a point in attaining a competency where he has absolutely no need for a teacher to show, to instruct, motivate, challenge, assist, evaluate, or even be present to witness. He has essential command of his skill (say, woodworking); he has completely internalized the vision of what he does. He doesn't even need the teacher's affirmation of his good work. (This may be pleasing, but it is not necessary.) Such could also apply to advanced cognitive learning in higher education wherein use of concepts and application of principles, evaluation of results can be carried out independently (as in research lab). As Wilkenson puts it: "The final aim of undergraduate education is to make the student independent of the teacher. She or he must ultimately learn to perceive the world, review evidence, form hypotheses and express conclusions unaided."[17] It is when this independence is reached (if indeed it can be in higher education today) that the student finds the teacher within and is fully released into her own learning. Philip Jackson describes the maturely, integrated learner as one who is capable of "self-governance" which means the individual has learned both how and what to learn. The former involves thinking and acting "with ever-increasing power and skill"; the latter" being free to decide what knowledge is worth possessing."[18]

If the learner then decides to shift into another discipline—say from biological sciences to physics, she may again have need of the extrinsic teacher. But the process will be the same, swifter this time. At some point, if she achieves essential competency the need for that teacher will disappear and the flame will be blown out, freeing the student to move completely on her own. To paraphrase Heidegger: The unconcealing of whatever truth is being investigated will take place through the process of teaching, which process itself will flow out into full learning.[19] In short, teaching disappears into the learner.

THE TEACHER AS LEARNER/CO-LEARNER

Teachers, when they see that their task is completed or counterproductive to the student's appropriation of learning, are thrown back to their own unfinished state of being, one where they, too, see clearly and forcefully what has always been true. Carl Rogers said that in the end he realized that he was only interested in being a learner, preferably "learning things that have some significant influence on my own behavior."[20] This is in keeping with the tradition of Socratic Ignorance. Socrates described himself as having the wisdom of one who "knows he doesn't know." His own "teaching" was a way of calling on others to discover their own state of ignorance. He never ceased to see himself as a learner. Such is the state of everyone, but highly developed in committed teachers because they have never stopped being learners, seekers. Since true teachers will have, in Adams words, "highly developed metaself values" they will always be on the hunt, always inquiring. This quality is what so impresses students about the metaself teacher, no matter what the teaching form, and calls to the metaself in them.[21] The teacher seeks to learn and to help others to learn. When this help is no longer needed in specific cases she reverts to her original state as pure learner. Thus, teaching is ephemeral compared to the ongoing process of learning.

One is never sure in the Dialogues which facet of Socrates is more central: The questor who seeks to take others along with him and who is invariably thrown back on himself when his interlocutors lose heart and abandon the journey; or the mentor who seeks to assist others in their quest, who urges them to press on and undertake it with all of their might—who constantly appeals to their highest aspirations. We know that he assures his listeners toward the end that if any futher state of existence is granted him after death he will simply continue to inquire and if in life he were exiled to another city he would go on urging others to do so.[22] This is essential to Socrates: the wondering, the seeking, the questioning, the dialectic stretching to know, even if in the end it turns out only that he knows he does not know.

But the truest view of Socrates may be that he desired to engage in "shared inquiry." Not him alone, nor another with his assistance—but both or all of them together. A number of times in the Dialogues Socrates tells his companions when they have reached a certain juncture that he would like to be their pupil, a learner—to learn from them, from Euthyphro, from Critias, from Protagoras. He may be only indulging in his famous irony, using it as a teaching tool. Still, there are times one feels a genuine longing on the part of Socrates to hear the word of truth from another and then to pursue jointly the topic, to be a co-learner, a collaborator. One hears him saying: "Let us explore this issue together," "let us together learn about what we don't know." Socrates seeks a community of learning, as have all true learners throughout history. Thus, he is both learner and co-learner. Such has been the case through all of his career, but when he is rejected as a teacher or senses the success of his efforts, or more often, their futility, the mantle is removed and he reveals himself as a seeker who would prefer to search in concert.[23]

We have seen that the teacher in higher education—especially in the forms from the Dialogic on—is present to some extent as co-learner. For example, Schon shows us Dani, the design instructor, in a plurality of roles during his encounter with Michal.[24] Donald Murray constantly talks about how much he is learning from his students. With the disappearance of teaching (Apophatic Mode), the teacher moves back to an original state and becomes a full learner. She may pursue or investigate alone. Today we call this keeping up in one's field, doing scholarly research, pursuing an avocation (the math teacher who side lines in astronomy). In cases where these activities are carried on not merely out of institutional necessity and where the motivation is intrinsic, we observe the curious wonder-filled, inexhaustible habit of a "wanting to know" which characterizes the teacher in higher education.

But, true teachers also may long to engage in shared inquiry, to find a community of scholars, to use Paul Goodman's term. They seek to co-learn, to study with. Teachers as learners reveal themselves here in search of that fully human encounter; they seek authentic dialogue, a communion of learning, that great conversation. Ignazio Gotz states: "As human beings we are learners, that is, conversationalists. We are a conversation."[25] And R. S. Peters, investigating the nature of an educational process, describes its most advanced stages as the conversation of the whole person in participatory learning: "The point is to create a common world to which all bring their distinctive contributions. By participating in such a shared experience much is learnt, though no one sets out to teach anyone anything."[26]

The committed teacher who is fundamentally a learner seeks such a concourse—first of all within his own institutional enviroment where, sad to say, he may seldom find it. The reasons for this are many and need not be repeated here. On the other hand, she may be fortunate in having research assistants who are passionately engaged in the same project, colleagues learning as they go, sharing informally the excitement of their quest. She may find it in collusion with former students who have grown to the friends, or even colleagues; or in more radical, open-ended situations where mutual expansion of critical consciousness poses immediate economic and political problems. Here dialogical relations are set up which resolve what Friere calls "the student-teacher contradiction." Technically, one may be a teacher and the others may be students, but as the learning environment takes shape and the issues are pressed the distinction dissolves. All become teachers, all are learners. Friere explains the change that takes place:

Through dialogue, the teacher-of-the-student and the student-of-the-teacher cease to exist and a new term emerges: teacher-student-with-students-teachers. The teacher is no longer merely the one who teaches, but one who is himself taught in dialogue with the students, who in turn while being taught also teach. They become jointly responsible for a process in which all grow.[27]

Discussion groups can occasionally reach this level in higher education. Glassman describes these as Stage 4 or Final Stage where the students' learning and discussion skills are so advanced that the teacher can join the group as an equal.[28] In effect, the teacher has disappeared with the group to become a co-learner. And it represents the fundamental difference between this learning environment and that depicted in the Dialogic teaching form (Glassman, Stage 2, Participatory) where though the teacher and students share equal energies the teacher remains the discussion leader who initiates, directs, clarifies, summarizes, and so on.

PERSONAL EXPERIENCE IN ABJURING TEACHING

I experienced such a conversation of equals within a formal course structure only once in my entire teaching career, yet it was an unforgettable experience, as it apparently was for my co-learners who shared it. I will describe the context in some relief for it represents a first-hand living example of a teacher abjuring his "magic" and becoming a learner again with his students.

We began as a group of nine—myself and eight undergraduates with varying science backgrounds (five different majors), all of whom had been with me before in at least one upper level course. Three of these students had taken four of my previous courses and after their freshman year stayed continually in touch. With one exception, all were intrinsically motivated, used to learning on their own, and unconventional in their approach to higher education.

The course was titled Advanced Philosophy and the catalogue description said we would pick two or three philosophers (or a particular philosophy) and go more into depth with these than in the introductory course seminar. The course was an elective and only ran when a quorum of at least five students expressed enough interest. During the preceding semester I sensed an avid interest on the part of seven former students who were by now quite restless with the usual teacher-centered courses offered as electives at the school. Upon reflection, I began to realize that in the case of the students who had been with me for three years, and probably in the case of three more, any formal teaching presence would be an inhibition to their further learning. When I explained this to them during an informal meeting at the beginning of the semester the reaction was positive. I told them I would not be the teacher for the class and, in fact, would only agree to the course if we all could approach the experience as co-learners. I informed them that I would choose neither the subject or the texts, that I believed we could come to a consensus on a topic and readings of personal interest to us all. Neither would I do any evaluating—though we would have to agree at the end on some grade to submit to the registrar since a pass/fail in our system was not allowed. When I finished my remarks the group unanimously agreed that such a format would be far more appropriate than the traditional ones they were used to. Thus, after serving as facilitator to clarify places and times to meet, I ceased to function as a teacher.

At the end of much discussion and numerous suggestions the group decided on the area of mystical philosophy and came to consensus on the following books for perusal and discussion:

Tao Te Ching by Lao Tzu

What the Buddha Taught by Walpola Rahula

The Way of Zen by Alan Watts

Thus Spoke Zarathustra by Frederick Nietzsche

The Teaching of Don Juan by Carlos Castenada

For the New Intellectual by Ayn Rand[29]

(Ayn Rand is obviously not a mystical philosopher, but one woman was very interested in her approach to living in western capitalist society.) Also, during the course we agreed we would see two films which were easily available: *Being There* and *Koyaanisquatsi: Life Out of Balance.*

Despite their initial enthusiasm for a leaderless discussion it took some time for the students to get used to the reality that no teacher would be leading the group or even serving as facilitator. This should not have been surprising. A number of our sessions in the early going resembled a cold motor coughing and sputtering on a winter morning. Other times, when things did get along, there was a randomness about the comments that didn't lead anywhere. As one young man put it: "Even though I was eager for this new experience I found myself unconsciously looking for a point of reference, someone whose background could validate my points of view." There was also, in the teacher's absence, a subtle competition among a few of the students for leadership of the discussion. But this worked itself out in time.

I, too, at first had all I could do to keep from falling back into the habit of starting the group's motor, of suggesting the sequence or bringing us back to a point at issue when we strayed—all the techniques one uses in previous teaching forms. I had to remind myself that even if I resorted to my old tricks (previous teaching presences) they would learn nothing new and, in fact, to use Carl Roger's words, "harm would be done." The group would be prevented from achieving the kind of learning experience they intuitively so desired. Things became easier when, after a few weeks, as the group gathered confidence, my (former) students began to disregard any statements from me which seemed to them "teacherly." On a few occasions I was ignored in much the same way that a group member is benignly passed over when his comment indicates he is out of sync with where the group is going.

Gradually, a new kind of atmosphere began to emerge in our sessions—one which allowed a gentle anarchy in our meandering, but which at the same time fostered an intuitive sureness that a new kind of learning experience was taking shape, where individuals chartered territory all their own, yet together sought to see what each was thinking. Through it all we talked, discussed, argued as a group. Sustained dialogue began to replace argument or confrontation. We really began to listen, to be sensitive to each individual response to the material we were reading together.[30] We began to see each other in new ways.

We all agreed at the end how much each member of the group had contributed, along with the originality of mind and person that was emerging in each one of us. Slowly, I came to the overwhelming realization that my contributions were neither better or worse than those of any other member of the group's. I had dropped my teacherly pretense to knowledge. I found myself listening to insights and approaches I would have never thought about. (I was fortunate here for I had only read two of the books on the list.) Halfway through the semester I relaxed and settled into being what I really was—a learner. We grew together in the course, and rode through all the ups and downs attendant on such an experience.

I also became used to the silences which often began a session and to other moments when nothing was said. On one occasion I even was able to restrain myself as one of the students began to dominate a session by sprawling his ideas on the board. We would have to deal with this as a group. I remained quiet, remembering how often in the past I had done the same thing—only more smoothly—and no one ever had protested; the students simply took out their pencils and began writing. On the other hand, a high point was reached after we watched the film *Koyannisquatsi* with the spontaneity and depth of the discussion that erupted. I made some small contribution, but was carried by the flow out of myself into new territory along with everyone else.

In lieu of any formal evaluation we jointly decided that each of us would submit a fairly long paper at the end of the course detailing our own approach to the philosophical life as influenced by the dynamics of our experience in the course. Each member of the group would xerox a copy for the others a few days before our final session (a four hour marathon held off campus during which we discussed all the papers). Finally, the group agreed that a grade of B + would be entered for each participant in the course.

At the very end, each of us evaluated the teacherless course we had shared. With one exception all of the students centered on the uniqueness of the unstructured learning experience and how it taught them to rely on their own thinking rather than being directed or even guided by the teacher.[31] Below are the extended comments of two members who reflected on the experience after they left the college:

Advanced Philosophy was truly an experiment in the educational process for professor, students and most certainly for the institution. Responsibility for content and the learning process were put where they should be—in the hands of the students. We all became participants as we saw the classic roles of student-professor fall by the wayside. All of us emerged as learners, working together to expand ourselves while we explored and dealt with this new responsibility for our own education. It seemed a daunting task at the time, but was the most "real" education I had ever experienced during my three years at the college. The rarity of the event that was taking place in our group made it all the more exciting.[32]

In an environment so open as the one we had, room for spontaneous expression as well as mistakes was abundant. In fact, mistakes or misinformation were the greatest source for learning. I was able to take criticism constructively, instead of negatively as happens so often in memorization and grade-oriented learning processes...For the first, and probably only, time I was not afraid to ask questions and expose my problematic areas to a classroom. We were all teaching and learning simultaneously. This course gave me a sense of confidence that in an open environment where positive reinforcements were the norm I was able to understand myself better and confront the subject at hand without fear. Self-reliance was, and still is, the most important lesson I got out of that course.[33]

Both these students also pointed out the problems of getting used to this new mode, problems having to do with the vacuum left by the absence of the teacher which I discussed above.

For my part, I realized that for a brief space of time I had become a learner once again—one who does *not know*. I had initiated the process by refusing to assume a teaching presence, but once we all got used to the equality, it was my former students who made sure I did not climb back on my hobby horse and attempt to employ a teaching form. The flame had truly been blown out. Since that time four of the students have remained in touch and when we see each other we reminisce about that open-ended experience where in an atmosphere of total equality we took part in "a highly active conversation" of the kind R. S. Peters describes, where we shared, listened, agreed to disagree, and most of all came to respect and value each others own personal universe—learners all.[34] One of the students summed it up perfectly in a retrospective, echoing Carl Rogers: "Isn't this the way education should be?" These words reverberated in my head as I returned to more conventional teaching forms the next semester.

I have spent some time detailing my own experiences in returning to the status of learner within the university. Perhaps I was fortunate to have been given the opportunity. I see no reason why this same experience can't be entered into by teachers in other disciplines—even the hard sciences. We have but to await opportunities to find students who can learn no more with us functioning as teachers and are eager (despite unforeseen difficulties) to join with us as co-learners.[35]

Perhaps the most dramatic example in higher education of an ongoing program where the teacher regularly assumes the role of fellow learner in the classroom takes place at the two campuses of St. John's College (Annapolis and Santa Fe). Here the "tutor" or "guardian," as she is called, is asked to hold forth in a subject area outside her specialty. So, for example, the tutor may be versed in classical Greek, but instead is teaching Lobachevski's non-Euclidean geometry in the college's interdisciplinary master's degree program for the first time. Lynda Myers describes the scene:

She is definitely not a fountain of wisdom about modern mathematics, much less about modern physics ... and she has less technical knowledge of mathematics than several of her students: One teaches mathematics at Cairo University, another chairs the mathematics department at a small Texas college. There are also an engineer and an architect in the class. All of the other students have avoided mathematics like the plague since they were last required to take it in high school twenty years ago.[36]

I should point out that in the St. John's program the tutors also use other teaching forms as well with their students—especially those of inquirer, dialogist and facilitator. According to the catalogue " ... the role of the tutors is to question, to listen, and to help ... but first of all the tutors will call on the students to try to help themselves."[37]

CONCLUSION

It is possible to view the last three teaching forms on the continuum as merely degrees in the handing over of the teaching function to the student. Macrorie's "enabling," Murray's "getting out the way," and finally the disappearance of teaching altogether can be seen as part of a sequence. In fact, the whole span from the Dialogic Mode on may simply be one student-centered arc which spreads out over all these forms. Once the work of the Initiatory Mode is effected, the student becomes an active learner, moving on her own power, meeting the teacher as dialogist, guide, witness, and then co-learner. With the student fully activated in a course or learning experience these forms may move in and out of each other. Still, each has its own specific energies and I believe this justifies them being separated as ideal archetypes.

And so extrinsic teaching must end for the learner. When the student has internalized the entire teaching/learning process he or she makes possible the most profound kind of educational revolution, one that focuses on constant open inquiry and takes in the whole of one's being. The result of such endeavor is a process of "unknowing" where one abandons not only previous unsatisfactory knowledge, but as much as possible, prejudice, ideology, and self-deception. This is achieved through a special kind of insight which according to David Bohm:

... without interfering with necessary and useful memories, is able to dissolve the mind's attachments to absurdities that hold it prisoner to its past. When this takes place, a human being is able to act in new ways, not only in abstract thought and in imagination, but also in sense perceptions, in emotional responses, in movement of the body, in relationships between people, and in all other areas of life.[38]

Such is the ultimate purpose of education. Such advanced growth takes place, of course, far beyond the confines of any educational institution and is a life-long, never ending process where the only reliable guide is found within the inmost center of the self—what Thomas Merton calls that "scintilla animae," that apex or spark which is a freedom beyond freedom, an identity beyond essence, a self beyond all ego.[39] Though it may be a rare achievement, there is no reason why the university cannot point to such a goal.

NOTES

1. Peter G. Beidler, "'Students Passionate About Their Learning': The End Products of the Profession," in *New Directions For Teaching and Learning: Distinguished Teachers on Effective Teaching*, ed. Peter G. Beidler (San Francisco: Jossey-Bass Publishers, 1986), p. 44.

2. Morris, *Existentialism in Education*, p. 153.

3. Vandenberg, "Phenomenology and Educational Research," p. 205.

4. DeVito, "Teaching As Relational Development," p. 55.

5. Buber believed that the desire for friendship automatically breaks the teaching relationship. Hendley, however, in his article on Buber, disagrees and cites Socrates' relationships with some of his interlocutors. See Brian Hendley, "Martin Buber on the Teacher/Student Relationship: A Critical Appraisal," *Journal of Philosophy of Education*, 12 (1978), pp. 141–148.

6. Donald M. Murray, *Expecting the Unexpected: Teaching Myself—and Others to Read and Write* (Portsmouth, N.H.: Boynton/Cook Publishers, 1989), p. 129.

7. Georgine Loacker and Austin Doherty, "Self-Directed Undergraduate Study," p. 118.

8. Ibid., p. 119.

9. DeVito, p. 55.

10. Rogers, *Freedom to Learn*, pp. 152–153.

11. Ibid., p. 153. Murray, in a similar vein, seems most bothered by his misuse of power, and even more, his students' easy acceptance of it: "I fought that power and have retired, in part, because of it." *Expecting the Unexpected*, p. 128. Like Rogers, he sees his teaching interfering with the students self-appropriation of learning.

12. Perkinson, *Learning from Our Mistakes*, p. 152.

13. Rogers, p. 152.

14. Ibid., p. 151.

15. Ibid., p. 153.

16. Murray, p. 128.

17. Wilkenson, "The Varieties of Teaching," in *The Art and Craft of Teaching*, p. 8.

18. Jackson, *The Practice of Teaching*, pp. 104–105. This stage in the learner's progress resembles the Autonomous level in Loevinger's stages of ego development. See Jane Loevinger, *Ego Development* (San Francisco: Jossey-Bass Publishers, 1976).

19. See Ignacio L. Gotz, "Heidegger and the Art of Teaching."

20. Rogers, *Freedom to Learn*, p. 153.

21. Adams, *The Experience of Teaching and Learning*, p. 154.

22. Plato, *The Apology* in *The Works of Plato*, ed. Irwin Edman (New York: The Modern Library, 1928), p. 83, 87.

23. Henry Teloh sees Socrates as a pedagogical failure due to the conditions of his time and the newness of his method. See *Socratic Education in the Early Dialogues*, pp. 20–21.

24. Donald A. Schon, *Educating the Reflective Practitioner*, p. 153.

25. Gotz, "Heidegger and the Art of Teaching," p. 8.

26. R. S. Peters, "What is an Educational Process," in *The Concept of Education*, ed. R.S. Peters (New York: The Humanities Press, 1967), p.21.

27. Freire, *Pedagogy of the Oppressed*, p. 67. It should be pointed out that Freire is writing outside the context of institutional learning. He is talking about critical consciousness for political action.

28. Glassman, "The Teacher As Leader," p. 37.

29. All of these books were available in paperback at book stores in the Philadelphia area.

30. The group had agreed that one of us would be a resource person for any of the books we had previously read. I became the resource person for *Thus Spoke Zarathustra*.

31. One of the eight students lost his enthusiasm two or three weeks into the course, and began to miss our meetings. He did submit a paper at the end, but did not attend the marathon session.

32. Deborah Lynn Williams, October, 1990. Deborah is now in graduate studies for Biochemistry at Roswell Park Memorial Institute, in Buffalo.

33. Ramone Martinez. After working for a year as a pharmacist, Ramone returned to the college to study for an advanced degree in Pharmacognosy. In the last year he has switched fields and applied for admission to graduate school in the area of Comparative Literature.

34. Peters, "What is an Educational Process," p. 21.

35. Such learning experiences certainly should be possible on a graduate level. Perhaps I am being naive about the opportunities allowed professors to initiate these kinds of "apophatic" encounters in undergraduate courses. They may be locked into the same course offerings year after year, and even those (usually tenured) teachers who have upper level courses may be required to show more quantitative evidence of their students learning than I was required to. Deborah Lynn Williams gives a sobering appraisal at the end of her written evaluation: "Advanced Philosophy class also made me aware of the incredible deficiencies in the educational process at my college. I felt ripped off. I paid all this money in and felt as though I did not start to really be educated until the end of my third year . . . Although I relish my experience in "Advanced Philosophy" I am extremely pessimistic about the future and quality of education in the United States."

36. Lynda L. Myers, "Teachers as Models of Active Learning," *College Teaching*, 36, no. 2 (Spring 1988), p. 44.

37. Ibid., p. 44.

38. David Bohm, "Insight, Knowledge, Science, and Human Values," in *Toward the Recovery of Wholeness*, p. 21.

39. Thomas Merton, "Learning to Live," in *Love and Living*, ed. Naomi Burton Stone and Brother Patrick Hart (New York: Bantam Books, 1965), p. 8. See also William A. Reinsmith, "The True Meaning of Education: A Radical Suggestion," *The Educational Forum*, 51, no. 3 (Spring 1987).

Conclusion: The Real World
of Teaching

Obviously, no one moves seamlessly along the continuum I have presented in the preceeding chapters. No real institution is an educational utopia. What I have done is to conduct a kind of phenomenological "epoke"—a bracketing out, if you will, of the natural everyday world of teaching in higher education.[1] This for the purpose of seeing more clearly the basic forms that shine through the complexities and entanglements of normal classroom life. Performing such a task, I believe, has value for educators not only because they learn to observe those patterns in teaching which transcend the vicissitudes of moment to moment experience and thus lend to teaching a certain permanence, but also because a crucial aspect of the educational process can be highlighted: those intersubjective relationships called "encounters" that underly the more behavioral aspects of teaching.

In the real world of teaching the forms must often be teased out of the combination of personalities, activities, and circumstances which constitute our pedagogical efforts. In the real world we enter at the nexus where teacher meets students within the emeshment of everyday life. Occasionally, a teacher gets an opportunity to meet the same group of students (usually small) in a number of differing, increasingly student-centered encounters during their graduate or undergraduate career. Roughly sequential encounters can also take place between a teacher and a single student. For example, a graduate research advisor works with a promising student from the time she enters a program until receiving her doctorate. At the start the teacher may be quite directive, but as things progress he becomes less so until at the end the student and advisor cooperate as co-learners.

Now and then a similar sequence takes place on an undergraduate level: A student becomes exposed to a professor in a large lecture class as a freshman. He then takes one of his smaller classes, in which the teacher motivates him to enjoy learning—then catalyzes him to question. There is reciprocity, respect, challange, confusion, and much reflection. The next year he decides on an upper level offering, one where group discussion prevails. He meets the teacher, along with his classmates, in a new light. Discourse takes place; class members know and care for each other while they learn. The student's confidence in his own abilities grows. He begins to commit himself to learning. He now seeks a more independent road, yet at the same time forms ties with new academic companions, those he can talk and learn with. He takes one final course, where the professor sets the tone but allows the students to work independently in small groups almost all the time, offering assistance when needed, gently guiding their progress. The student finds himelf often exhilirated, thinking now about an area of interest which he might pursue in depth. For some time he has been having extended conversations with the professor after class in his office, sharing ideas. He begins work on an independent project. The teacher responds, suggests, and confirms—but as time goes on it seems he talks less and listens more, as if teacher/student share this project together. Eventually, the relationship takes a new turn when the student moves on. They will keep in touch. The professor who was the teacher is slowly replaced by the equal, though older, learning companion who sits across from him during occasional visits. The student is on his own. But he will keep something of that teacher inside and remember him as the one who through so many different encounters let him learn. Is this scenario altogether removed from the real world of teaching? I don't think so. Most teachers who travel the academy long enough will develop a few relationships like this. Usually, however, a teacher picks up students singly or in groups at the level of educational maturity she finds them and initiates a teaching encounter appropiate to that level. Such encounters last for a semester or so. Each form sets up a *relational center* in which teacher and students meet according to the interplay that is possible. Encounters here will not be relegated to a single form. Rather a number of forms may be interchanged—though very likely, if one looks closely enough, one form will be central to a specific course. One has to observe for a while in order to see through the more superficial activities to the basic encounter taking place.

Many teachers find themselves at home with a specific teaching presence, year after year. It becomes their "teaching style." Perhaps, it is a freshman writing class where the teacher will induce her students to see writing in a new light, devising learning activities related to their world; or a Critical Thinking course where learners are presented with an ascending range of questions which initiate them into learning as inquiry. In both these encounters the teacher will remain aware of individual differences, levels of development, and learning habits as she studies her students. Upper level students in an Advanced Psychology class will benefit from a dialogic atmosphere where inquiry can be shared and interpersonal enrichment pursued.

Very large introductory classes, however, will constrain the teacher to a Presentational Mode where information and concepts are delivered with appropiate visual aids as appealingly as possible. Smaller recitations will require didactic drill—though it is still very possible for teachers here to work in an Initiatory Mode, showing strong concern for their students.

USE OF MULTIPLE FORMS DURING ONE COURSE

In some cases, an experienced teacher may work in a complex of forms during a single semester, not only for different courses, but within the same course where no one form predominates. Let me provide a concrete illustration of just such a situation from the real world of teaching. In an extended article from a recent issue of *College Teaching*, Ann Woodhull-McNeal describes an Introductory Science Course for liberal arts students at Hampshire College in Amherst, Massachusetts.[2] McNeal argues that a science course on an introductory level can be far more than just a learning of facts and "cookbook" proceedures which leaves more active inquiry to higher level science courses. For her purposes she concentrates on a rather circumscribed area of study, The Physiology of Human Movement—a course, according to the catalogue, "for dancers, athletes and others who are interested in how their bodies move." (p. 3) Thus, some intrinsic motivation is assured, but those who hoped for a "soft" alternative to the usual hard science offering are often quite surprised. The endpoint of the course is a rather sophisticated independent project which each student must present and discuss with the rest of the class. Some of the skills which are developed during the course are: problem analysis, inductive thinking—i.e. moving from fact to hypothesis—skills in collaborative learning, expository writing, data analysis, oral presentation and discussion, bibliographic search and retrival.

A wide range of teaching forms comes into play during The Physiology of Human Movement. Since the agenda for the first six weeks is to learn to read scientific papers in the field of Kinesiology the teaching mode shifts between the Presentational and Initiatory [my terms]. For example, before handing out the first paper to be read, McNeal explains the structures and functions involved in the stretch reflex. She also gives lectures on energy use in muscles, the circulatory response to exercise, and other background information. In the next class students are given their first research paper to read and interpret. The teacher is quite directive here as to how readings are to be done—she asks them to pick out the words they don't know which she then writes on the board. A short lecture ensues linking all the words together. (Here the students take notes.) They are now asked to re-read the paper for understanding and then next time to come prepared to discuss what is actually taking place in the experiment described.

During these discussions the teacher not only facilitates, but encourages students by identifying with their confusion, making use of examples from their familiar world, praising their progress as well as challenging them to hypothesize from the facts, to ask open-ended questions, while she moves them to share their ideas and resources with each other. Subsequent papers are handled in the same way—but now *students* must look up all familiar words, explain them to each other, and in general grope toward understanding the papers in dialogic fashion. Gradually, the class becomes less teacher-centered as students begin to believe in and share their own resources. The teacher does not supply the answer in their group discussions; students are encouraged to talk to one another.

In reading, interpreting, and discussing these papers students are able, according to McNeal, to understand the hypotheti co-deductive method of science better than any number of passages in a text about "how science is done." McNeal also points out that reading original scientific papers seems to motivate students to a remarkable degree since "they are reading the real thing—and not just a watered-down version." (p. 6)

When the time comes for students to consider their own projects McNeal acts as Facilitator/Guide while individualization increases. (She also works with students in small groups who are working on similar ideas.) The project is meant to be an original piece of research in which things like experimental design, finding specific muscles, deciding on what machine methods to use (students have been learning to use the electromyograph), standardizing the proceedures and so on, are all left to the ingenuity of the individual. The teacher acts as guide in the manner of Dani and Michal in Industrial Design (Schon) except that the teacher tends to be somewhat more directive, especially in working with students' early writing. Proposal drafts are reviewed and the students rewrite as often as necessary—with very weak writers being referred to Writing Center tutors. But when students finally present their project, the teacher is non-invasive and confirmatory rather than critical. The project is in the nature of an experimental inquiry in which there may not be any right answers since most of these experiments have not been reported in the literature. Much peer discussion ensues here. The sense of exploring the unknown while at the same time submitting their work to the scrutiny of their peers proves to be a strong motivator for students to be accurate and conscientious in their lab work. They come to view science, in McNeal's words "as a human enterprise, subject to error, passion and correction" (p. 7)—much the same process as Perkinson describes in regard to students doing science in *Learning From Our Mistakes*.[3]

Finally, it often happens that project findings challenge the teacher's own knowledge and assumptions in the field. (Students are often surprised at this.) McNeal sees herself as a learner in these situations: "This approach demands a certain flexibility and humility on the part of the teacher. We need to handle such challanges intelligently, not defensively, and to say 'I don't know. How could you find out?" (p. 7)

Thus, in the course of thirteen weeks McNeal has created a number of different encounters, shifting into different teaching forms. Overarching these is the teacher's realization that if her students are to grow they must gradually take responsibility for their own learning. As the semester moves on and they gain more confidence she urges and then allows them to break away; her teaching becomes more and more student-centered until at the end she finds them pretty much on their own, at least in this circumscribed area of knowledge.

Obviously, creating and facilitating a course like "Physiology of Human Movement" demands quite a range of teaching experience. The professor's fulfillment comes not from ego-enhancing lecturing or class manipulation, but from allowing students to really learn. As McNeal puts it: "Every bit of this time-consuming process is worthwhile because the students are learning to educate themselves and each other." (p. 5) Here is a teacher who has understood the overall purpose of teaching and has shaped one course accordingly. This is the real world of teaching and it's truly exciting.

Just as we have seen in miniature a portrait of the movement from teacher-centered to student-centered teaching through the course of a semester, so too, an experienced teacher may shift presences within the space of a single class hour—what could be called the inhabiting of micro-forms. Such transitions are common in elementary and secondary teaching. The observer notices, in fact, that forms are emeshed or strewn together as the teacher shifts from presentation and explanation to exhortation, then to dialogue and the facilitation of small groups. In the college classroom during a given class session such shifting is probably less common; it is more likely to happen where the class size is not large. And even here there is probably one underlying encounter supporting the rest.

PROGRESS ALONG CONTINUUM

A number of other intertwined isues concerning the applicability of a Teaching Continuum to the everyday world of teaching need to be addressed in this concluding chapter. One of these has to do with a teacher's conscious, intentional movement to new teaching modes. It is rather easy to see why student-oriented professors will try to adapt their teaching to the type and level of students they encounter. It is also not difficult to understand how poor learning environments are created by teachers who remain constantly in one form regardless of what the situation calls for. But once teachers desire to become more student-centered in their teaching, how is such a progression actually carried out? How does a teacher make the movement in a more or less permanent way to a new teaching form, one he or she has never tried before?

Most often, change of this nature is catalyzed by a dissatisfaction with the current level of encounter and subsequent learning that is taking place. The teacher herself feels cramped, frustrated, distanced from her students. A more personal, intimate connection is sought; the teacher wants to know and work with her students in a new way. She is looking for different results in what her students learn, especially in terms of quality and depth. She wants somehow to move them to take their learning more seriously.

The initiative can also come from the students. Perhaps they sense they are being short-changed. They expected to be interacting with the teacher, yet classtime is consumed with lecturing and the taking of notes. Some of them (older students) hoped to be handling new ideas, learning form each other through small group work; they find, instead, that the teacher dominates the hour rehashing material they have already gone through. Or perhaps they hoped for clear, interesting, enthusiastic lectures and what they get instead is a robotized delivery of information which puts them to sleep. In these situations we are not so much talking about incompetence on the part of the teacher, as a misconstruing the kind of teaching presence called for in a given context.[4]

Whatever the case, the professor must finally see the need for change in the way he is present to the students. Such a change may even be negotiated. But obviously, perception of a problem and desire for change are not enough. A new *vision* of teaching must emerge in the teacher. There is a conversion aspect to changing teaching modes that has to follow upon the dissatisfaction endured. The teacher must see a whole new way of relating to his students, along with a fresh awareness of his students as learners. Flowing out of this creative process will come the more mundane (but equally important) realization that particularized skills must be acquired to forge successfully the change. For those teachers who eventually become craftspersons or artists the full possibilities of a teaching form will be realized.[5]

Of course, opportunities to move into new forms must present themselves. In the case of student dissatisfaction with an encounter, it can be assumed that opportunity exists since the frustration the students are experiencing comes from expectations about a course that were not met. It's up to the teacher to make the adaptation. When the desire comes from within the teacher opportunities for change may not always exist. For example, a teacher who is weary of the Presentational Mode may nevertheless find herself saddled with two-hundred second year students in Introduction to Psychology. She will either have to change her teaching assignment or break down the number into smaller classes (probably necessitating the hiring of more teachers), neither of which may be possible. As I pointed out in previous chapters, institutional constraints often keep one from moving away from teacher-centered forms in the classroom. The equivalent of Dialogic and Elicitive Modes, no matter how frequently discussed in the literature, are far less common than Presentational and Initiatory.[6] But we should not be unduly pessimistic here. For if dissatisfaction and a subsequent new vision of teaching are powerful enough, teachers can create their own opportunities for change, sometimes at great cost. If an institution should commit itself to radical change in its educational philosophy (ex. Alverno) the inhabiting of new teaching forms becomes much easier.

Sequence:

- teacher perceives need to progress
- context exists to allow for change
- teacher attains a vision of new teaching form
- teacher creates new presence
- students respond to new presence—thus creating encounter
- teacher gradually improves skills and attitudes until he/she is working well within new form

To an extent the attitudes and skills required for each new mode will flow naturally out of the new vision of teaching possibility arising in the teacher. They are intrinsic to the new form in the sense that the teacher will understand intuitively what skills must be learned. A new encounter is fundamentally a uniqe perception of students, of a teaching relationship that wasn't there before. With the maturing of that perception the energies required are revealed. However, this doesn't mean that the teacher will be automatically versed in employing them. The skills must be learned through classroom practice—this is the working craft that comes out of the vision. But it is the vision of teaching that will sustain the committed teacher in this trial and error process.

CHANGING FORMS OUT OF SEQUENCE

A related question regarding progress along the continuum has to do with huge change on the part of the teacher—what we might call skipping or leaping across forms. Though I have set out the teaching forms in a certain sequence, it certainly can happen that a teacher in the real world may move, for example, from a Presentational Mode to one where she acts as a facilitator of student learning. A large leap along the continuum may be a relatively easy step for an experienced teacher with a strong proclivity to work with students in small groups, but who has found herself teaching in a large lecture hall. Yet, taking such a large step can often be unsuccessful if either the teacher or students are unprepared. Recently a pharmacology professor at my college took over a teaching block of two hundred students that had traditionally been handled in a lecture format. He decided to involve them in an active learning experiment. After the first day he canceled lectures, broke the students down into small learning groups and asked them to work together to cull the textbook along with his disseminated notes for specific questions which would appear on the final examination. The professor told them he would be available in his office during the usual class time as guide and resource; he also offered voluntary recitations for general discussion of the questions chosen by the students. He shared with them his desire to establish an entirely different teaching relationship, one in which they would be less dependent on him and take more responsibility for their learning.

It soon became clear that most of the students—even though they were in their third year—were completely unprepared for such a shift. A high degree of anxiety prevailed and a definite negative reaction set in to the professor whom (in their evaluations) they viewed as shirking his duty to provide the relevant information through lectures. This leap from Presentational to Elicitive Mode was unsuccessful because the students were not educationally mature enough to handle such a change.[7] Once again we should not underplay how difficult it can be in the real world of teaching to get students to take over authority for their own learning. Kenneth Feldman in his research on the extent to which students and faculty differ in evaluating teaching found that students placed more emphasis on presentational aspects of classroom teaching (though they did want teachers to be available after classes) while faculty stressed intellectual challange, motivating students, and encouraging self-initiated learning—qualities more appropiate to teaching forms further along the continuum.[8]

REGRESS

Regression to previous modes or teaching forms can take place for various reasons, including overwork, student resistance (as we have seen), and changes in physical environment making it impossible to be present as Facilitator or Dialogist. Perhaps the single most important factor affecting shifts in a teaching mode is the prevailing educational climate. It often may appear that teachers remain locked within a teaching form because of student attitudes or institutional restraints, yet both of these may only be symptoms caused by the prevailing mores of the larger society. The most vivid example of a teacher altering teaching presences over a period of time in accordance with societal change is that of Professor Stephen Abbot described by Joseph Axelrod in 1980.[9] It seems that over a period of twenty years (from 1959 to 1979) Abbot went through four teaching modes. For the first five years he taught his subject (literature) in a personal, didactic manner. This coincided with the climate of the time during which the university saw itself in authoritarian terms of rigidity and control. His teaching style changed around 1964 during the time of the free speech movement at Berkeley when his focus shifted from teaching subject matter to teaching students. The emphasis was on the intellect of his students and Abbot tried to develop in them rational, analytic, linguistic modes of perception. Further development took place in Abbot's teaching at the end of the 60s paralleled by the mass student protests, invasion of Cambodia and the Kent State shootings, so that by 1970 he had focused his teaching fully on the students as persons. The atmosphere in his classrooms became intensely personalized and student-centered. More holistic, non-linear modes of learning were stressed while mutual caring among students and the nurturing of community became paramount concerns. Abbot began to view himself as a learner along with his students.

Around 1975 the educational climate in the country began to shift again: Students entered the university who were much less committed to society and more concerned with themselves in materialistic terms. Abbot found it impossible to sustain the student-centered teaching of the five years before. Students began to lose their identity for him. He reverted to his own concerns as a scholar and these concerns became the focus of his teaching. Professor Abbot felt that socially a counter-revolution had taken place quietly replacing the revolution of the previous decade—thus the regression in his own teaching.

While the teaching changes described by Axelrod in Abbot can only serve as a generalized parallel to the forms set out here, perhaps it is not too much to say that ultimately the answer to how a teacher progresses or regresses on a continuum lies in what the educational climate, dictated by social values, allows. I realize that such a viewpoint goes counter to the idea that the university should lead rather than follow, but it may be closer to reality. What are we to say, then, of the 80s? What were the teaching forms most common to univerisities in the decade just past? While descriptions of any decade can be overly simplistic, I don't think it would be an exaggeration to say that the overriding educational concerns were fueled by a highly conservative ideology, one which placed high emphasis on monetary success, marketable skills, vocational concerns—an orientation for achievement rather than deeper personal meaning or altruistic service. Is it any wonder, then, why teacher-centered, instruction-oriented forms are by far the most common in higher education? Alexander Astin has reported that in the late sixties 83% of entering freshmen reported "developing a meaningful philosophy of life" as their most valued goal. Twenty years later that goal had dropped to seventh on the list while "being very well off financially" had increased to 70%.[10]

Thus, teachers may wish to create more intimate encounters in classes yet find themselves blocked by the prevailing climate. They may even find themselves regressing to more instructor-centered modes as did Abbot in 1979. Still, it is interesting that Axelrod notes the period of Professor Abbot's greatest happiness occured during the five years he taught in an extremely student-centered mode.[11] It seems he was most fulfilled in this kind of teaching. This fits with what I have indicated about teacher fullfillment in the teaching forms on the right side of the continuum.

TEACHER'S PERSONALITY AND TEACHING FORM

The whole issue of progress/regress in teaching leads to another problem: that of compatability between a professor's teaching style and a particular form. It seems I am suggesting that college professors should have an infinite plasticity for shaping their personalities into ever new teaching presences. Let me state the problem most baldly in the form of an objection: Don't most good teachers have a certain innate proclivity or "gift" which make them eminently suited for a specific teaching form or style? For example, how can one expect a sterling lecturer who posseses a high degree of skill at moving and informing large audiences to shift into a type of teaching presence (dialogic discussion) that he may be hopelessly unsuited for? Furthermore, why should he? Isn't the university losing a valuable asset in allowing such an artist-lecturer to become at best a passable group discussion leader (with fewer students)? A whole new group of skills and abilities is called for to make such an encounter effective. And it may take quite some time to learn this craft.

Granting that I have stated the issue in its most extreme form, it is nevertheless true that teachers can become rooted in a way of teaching that seems completely natural to them, a convenient, comfortable way of being present to students. On the other hand, it is possible that the question misses the point. The real issue is whether a teacher is maturing in his or her craft. If so, the teacher will see the need to become more student-centered. Most likely this will mean a desire for richer, more relational encounters where students are led to take greater responsibility for their learning. Such a desire, then, will be for a more authentic kind of teaching. The sad truth is that the university possesses an exceedingly narrow view of the range of teaching possibility, as does the public. A striking example of this can be found in the press. In September, 1986, the Philadelphia Inquirer Magazine ran a lead article called "Ten Top Profs" in which the authors stated that their goal was not to find professors who were famous for their research or their publications, but for their teaching.[12] Yet eight of the ten teachers rated as the best were outstanding lecturers obviously used to holding center stage in their interactions with students. In another more recent article in the *Chronicle of Higher Education* a middle aged teacher reflected on the difficulty of becoming a good teacher. Though he speaks fondly of dedicated teachers who keep in touch with their past students nowhere in the article does he ever indicate that college teaching is anything other than preparing and delivering lectures.[13] Even *The Teaching Professor*, an in-house newsletter, heads a recent issue "What Is Good Teaching?" Yet the skills and attitudes enumerated there assume the teacher as a lecturer.[14]

The blunt fact is that most teachers in higher education do not come to their craft with anything other than a rudimentary sense of how teaching should progress. Most of us are thrown into the fray without any compass and teach as we were taught. Joseph Katz puts it well:

The college teacher's teaching experience, if any, is usually acquired through being a teaching assistant while attending graduate school. This work rarely involves systematic and sophisticated attention to teaching. Beginning college teachers learn to cope with students and the classroom through a long and not necessarily satisfying process of trial and error, or they model their teaching style on the style of their own professors, or some combination of these two.[15]

More often than not this means lecturing to (at) students regardless of the context. A few become very adept and have "lively" classes. The large majority perform passibly or below par for most of their teaching career. Even those who develop motivational and inquiry strategies don't see beyond this to the possibility of more student-centered encounters. As Vladimer says in Beckett's *Waiting For Godot*, "Habit is a great deadener."[16]

Yet, teachers can and do change, if circumstances allow, during the course of a career. Even outstanding lecturers have abjured a familiar teaching presence in search of more student-centered forms. The complete teacher is the one who stays open to creative inner growth and eventually learns, often through courageous trial and error, to take in the whole range of teaching, who sees where teaching can lead and tries to follow, even where circumstances are not conducive. Joseph Axelrod holds the position that, at least in the case of the humanities, growth within the stifling, labryinthine structures of the modern university means moving toward "evocative modes" of teaching in which the teachers function as artists in the undergraduate classroom and where they can "probe and learn, inquire and discover" together with their students. Here "the options for structuring the class session . . . will continue to be open enough to allow faculty members significant alternatives if they are serious about becoming artists at teaching."[17]

But this by no means restricts a teacher's individuality. The unique subjectivity of the teacher is as ineradicable as that of the particular student. And as the teacher grows, so does her authenticity shine more brightly. Such authenticity can not be captured on a printed page or in a list of behavioral skills. It can only be witnessed by watching good teachers in action. Artistic teaching is evanescent, fleeting, but exists within the energies of a more permanent teaching form.

Complete teachers should find any form suitable when the context calls for it. This is part of their artistry—the skill to judge (often spontaneously) how they should be present when. But overall, they should be reaching toward "the unknown arts" of evocative or student-centered teaching. For the totally committed professor, teaching is not just a career, it is a kind of destiny, a calling to service in the interests of learning. All authentic teachers realize this truth.

TEACHING FORMS AND PARTICULAR DISCIPLINES

Another, even more trenchant issue, that needs to be addressed is the question of whether some teaching forms are more appropriate for certain disciplines than others. If such is true then one could not apply the continuum I have set out in this book across the board in higher education. Dialogic and Facilitative teaching, for example, may be more appropiate in the humanities than in the sciences where didactic, teacher-centered instruction proves more effective. Tied in with this is not only the issue of whether certain learning activities are more germaine to one discipline than another, but whether certain kinds of student learning styles are more at home in specific subject areas.

Philip Jackson, in his discussion of the mimetic and transformative traditions within the history of Western education, says that the teaching of science in general is more concerned with the transmission of principles and facts—a mimetic mission—while the teacher of humanities is occupied more with transformative concerns. Also, curricular programs in vocational areas with their emphasis on "marketable skills" seem more oriented toward the mimetic than programs in the liberal arts with their underlying emphasis on well-roundedness—thus, transformative. Jackson points out that the correlation is by no means perfect, but it has been sufficient enough to sustain a widespread way of thinking.[18]

Until 1980 not much research had been done on whether subcultures within the university involve certain specific "truth strategies" which in turn call for particularized ways of presenting learning material. From what we did know it could be assumed that professors in the most highly codified or systemetized disciplines (primarily mathematics and natural sciences) tend to adopt a tightly focused and structured teaching style, what Axelrod might call a Principles and Facts Prototype—thus, Presentational. The less codified a field, the more likely professors are to adopt a wide-ranging discoursive teaching style, using improvisational strategies and motivational techniques.

From this it follows that in conducting a course professors will tend to involve their students in fields that are least codified, where a need exists for students to structure the knowledge content for themselves. In the more codified fields there is less opportunity for students to structure course content and thus less student involvement. Thus, teachers in education and the fine and performing arts tend to engage in student-centered teaching modes (open-ended group discussion) while those in mathematics encourage it the least.

More recently, David Kolb, in his research on experiential learning theory, has fleshed out in some detail what kinds of learning styles fit particular disciplines. Noting that the diversity of sub—cultures within a university is staggering (symbolized most aptly by the dramatic differences in the architecture which houses these disciplines on a campus) he postulates that students often switch their major because of "fundamental mismatches" between personal learning styles and the learning demands of different disciplines. Overall results of studies show that the commonly accepted division of academic fields into two camps, scientific and artistic (C. P. Snow, 1963), might be broken down more into catagories where a fourfold typology of disciplines emerges: Abstract/Reflective—natural sciences and mathematics; Abstract/Active—science-based professions or applied sciences; Concrete/Reflective—humanities and social sciences; Concrete/Active—social professions, education, law.[19]

These divisions are connected to Kolb's Learning Style Inventory (LSI) through which he has identified four statistically significant types of learners, a division which has become rather well-known over the last decade. The division is presented in simplified form below:

Convergers—Strength is practical application of ideas. Do best in situations where a single correct answer or solution exists. Unemotional, prefer to deal with things rather than people. Most characteristic of engineers.

Divergers—Opposite of convergers. Strength is reflective observation upon concrete experience. Excel in imagination, in generating ideas, brainstorming. Emotional, interested in people. Usually have broad cultural interests. Characteristic of persons in humanities and some liberal arts—also counselors and personal managers.

Assimilators—Dominant abilities are are abstract conceptualization and reflective observation. Great strength is in creating theoretical models. Less interested in people, more in abstract concepts. Logical soundness and precision. Most characteristic of mathematics and basic sciences.

Accomodators—Opposite of Assimilators. Strengths are in concrete experience and active experimentation. Doers. Adaptation to immediate circumstances. Trial and error—work with people in dynamic way. Most characteristic of those in technical or practical fields such as business.[20]

While Kolb stresses that these types should not become stereotypes, his research findings agree with other studies of representative university and college faculty to show that certain disciplines plainly line up with particular learning styles. Engineering, applied sciences and computer science, for example, are convergent; basic sciences—physics, math, chemistry—are assimilative; humanistic fields—history, English, philosophy—are divergent; business, communications, special and secondary education are accomodative.[21]

Kolb finds the merging in these separate studies (his and others) interesting, but believes a more extensive data base is needed. What seems to follow in terms of the teaching forms set out in this book—at least in undergraduate disciplines as they now exist—is that faculty and students from more codified disciplines where a convergent learning style is common will gravitate toward a more mimetic, instruction-centered, impersonal (lecture-demonstration oriented) teaching form; while those from less systematized disciplines where a divegent learning style predominates will naturally be more open to student centered, relational (dialogic, elicitive) teaching modes. Put another way, faculty will teach and students will respond according to the "truth strategies" appropiate to particular disciplines. Thus, Physics, Mathematics, and Chemistry students may be at ease with teaching presences that are relationally distant and object-oriented. Mathematics, for example, may be taught enthusiastically by a lecturer/dramatist who uses theoretical models and works out problems on the blackboard which students follow and vary on their own.

Given these findings, the idea of a movement along a continuum to more intimate, teacher-centered forms as a sign of teacher growth may not be applicable to fields such as the basic sciences. On the other hand, what are we to say when faced with the example set out in Macrorie's *Twenty Teachers* of Bill Barker's facilitative approach to teaching math on the college level? (Chapter 6) Or Edward Glassman teaching biochemistry by means of setting up independent learning groups and putting them on their own? (Chapter 6) As we have seen in this chapter, Ann Woodhull-McNeal employs a number of teaching forms, moving from small lecture to a more student-centered approach involving group learning activities in order to initiate students into an inquiry based science course. In all three of these examples, as well as other shorter sketches of professors creating teaching encounters we see relational, student centered forms being employed. Perhaps these are exceptions to the norm.[22]

What does seem irrefutable from the studies is that most faculty working in disciplines requiring absorption of a hard data base and dealing mainly in principles and concepts, will tend to use teacher-centered forms and a mimetic teaching mode, at least in the early going. It will probably seem more natural for the professor to see teaching in impersonal terms—subject area—rather than viewing his discipline within a universe of discourse. Students with parallel learning styles will feel at home and do well. Those who are divergent or even accomodative will have difficulties.[23]

However, no real teacher would deny that, regardless of the discipline, the ultimate goal of teaching is to motivate students to take responsibility for their own learning. Perhaps the issue narrows to the question of whether achieving such a goal necessitates a growing educational intimacy between teacher and student. I have said continually that as teachers move toward more student-centered teaching they at the same time move from a completely extrinsic relationship to more direct personal encounters. I have suggested that this is a natural occurence. Yet, we find that certain disciplines—in particular, sciences—with their concomittant learning styles, may not be relation-oriented or need educational intimacy at all. One could argue strongly that the research corroborates this.

At this point, a much larger issue needs to be raised, one having to do with the world view within which the sciences themselves emerged. That issue is whether science (and hence the teaching of science) has for too long been carried out within an overmasculinized, patriarchal (teacher-centered), objective (impersonal) perspective, and whether particular learning styles have evolved in keeping with such a perspective. It is interesting how the

humanities and some social sciences are thought of as "soft" (concrete, reflective, imaginative, emotional) and hold for contexts in which teaching is
more "feminized"—i.e. relational, interactive, student-focused, involving discourse; while most of the sciences are "hard" (abstract, analytical, objective—
thus, free of emotion) and set up in contexts in which teaching is "masculine"—i.e. isolate, atomistic, teacher- or subject-focused. One notes also the
condescension many in the "hard" sciences have for the "softer," "easier"
disciplines where strict knowledge base and long hours in the laboratory are
not required. And perhaps more sadly we have seen how the "soft" sciences
have struggled to become "hard core." Even the humanities have attempted
to adapt quasi-scientific methodologies while in the process losing sight of
what it was that made them unique and so vitally important.

The implication is that the male model of teaching and learning germane
to the sciences is, in fact, the primary way of approaching knowledge since
by its very nature the male mind is more attuned to principles and abstractions
which themselves are in touch with universal laws. But one wonders if science
is an inherently masculine activity. Or whether the scientific endeaver simply
has been appropiated by male (right brain) modes of thought. Connected
with this issue is the extreme polarization of masculine and feminine which
has taken place in Western culture.

Evelyn Fox Keller has addressed these questions most articulately in her
1985 work *Reflections on Gender and Science*. Expanding on T. S. Kuhn who
convincingly pointed out the communitarian aspects of creating new para-
digms in science, Keller, first of all, challenges the view that science is an
autonomous endeavor which approximates ever more closely a description
of "reality as it is." We have failed to take serious notice, she says, "not only
of the fact that science has been produced by a particular subset of the human
race—that is almost entirely by white, middle class men—but also of the fact
that it has evolved under the formative influence of a particular ideal of
masculinity."[24] Such an ideal has been elevated to the power of an absolute
and thought of as unassailable. Keller believes that a radical critique of science
and its ideal of masculinity is in order. Appropos to our discussion here is
her comment that "Just as science is not the purely cognitive endeavor we
once thought it, neither is it as impersonal as we once thought: science is a
deeply personal as well as social activity." (p. 7)

If such is the case (and Keller argues convincingly that it is) then science
is victim of the mythology that has dichotomized the psyche: objectivity,
reason, and mind as male; subjectivity, feelings, and nature as female. In such
a division of emotional and intellectual labor, Keller tells us that women have
been "the guarantors and protectors of the personal, the emotional, the
particular; whereas science—the province par excellence of the impersonal,
the rational and the general—has been the province of men." (pp. 6–7)

This is an enormous subject with equally enormous implications. It is not
my purpose here to expound Keller's full critique, but rather to apply her

basic insight in order to make some connections with teaching. First of all, if science has been overmasculinized, or more likely the victim of an unfortunate and false dichotomy between masculine and feminine, it seems only logical that teaching in the sciences has fallen victim to the same error. Thus, the masculinized, mimetic, principles-and-facts approach to teaching in the sciences may not be something rooted in their nature, but rather rooted in a particular perspective from which the sciences have been viewed.

Secondly, if science is *also* personal, relational, dialogic, communitarian, discursive—which it undoubtedly is—then teaching in the sciences can be carried out in like manner, in fact, made richer by doing so.[25] Thus, the sciences may not be by nature inimical to more relational teaching forms on the continuum, but rather have been traditionally taught and learned as if they were. The examples of teaching in the sciences I have mentioned up above, while admittedly not common in the current world of teaching today, are perhaps signposts of how science can be taught when apprehended from a wider perspective.

Further, if the feminist critique of science is correct, even the research that has been done regarding faculty and student proclivities toward the sciences may have to be seen in a more restricted light. Research opportunities, therefore, should be sought for evaluating the teaching of science in new, unconventional ways. The same holds for "truth strategies" adopted by a particular discipline. Though longstanding, they are by no means etched in stone. As Keller reflects, picking up on Kuhn: " . . . not only different collections of facts, different focal points of scientific attention, but also different organizations of knowledge, different interpretations of the world, are both possible and consistent with what we call science."[26]

As for the condescension from those in the "hard" sciences toward the "softer" disciplines, the ignorance of such a position can easily be exposed. In fact, it may be the learning activites in subjects like the humanities that demand more complex skills on the part of both teachers and students. However, with a more integrated vision, such skills should be also available to the sciences.

Given the critique offered above, I would argue, then, that the sequence of forms on the continuum I have set out represents a growth in maturity for the teacher *regardless of the discipline*, since the teacher can become more student-centered while at the same time moving toward educational intimacy (direct, personal, concrete, dialogic, communal). And the students who assume an increasing responsibility for their education, eventually internalizing the teacher, will not be isolated monads set off to function totally alone, but rather released as fully individualized learners who find themselves (or seek to be) part of a larger learning community. This feminized dimension to learning applys to all disciplines. Perhaps the increasing number of women coming into science will bring this new perspective more and more to the foreground.[27]

Apropos to this discussion are the mimetic and transformative traditions in teaching. While the former may be more common in education today there is little doubt that the latter requires a more profound and multi-leveled educational experience since it can involve deep and permanent change in a student. Thus, the transformative receives more emphasis further along on the continuum (not necessarily excluding the mimetic) just as the encounters there involve more of the whole student. Again, however, as Jackson points out, the bifurcation is too simple. Almost all teaching encounters involve a mixture of both mimetic and transformative, thus avoiding polarization.[28] In fact, many adults, while educationally mature, may often be seeking goals more common to the mimetic tradition in a particular course offering.

STUDENT APPROACHES TO LEARNING

More needs to be said here about how students learn. A learning style doesn't have to do simply with an affinity toward certain disciplines. There are various ways in which a student approaches fundamental tasks which are common to many disciplines. Though it was pointed out in Chapter 6 that, in general, research on student learning is still indeterminate, areas exist where some clear patterns and agreement among researchers can be found. For example, interesting work has been going on (less field-dependent than Kolb's) on how students approach comprehension learning in college. Ference Marton and others have described differences in the way students read argumentative-expository materials. They found that a "deep approach" to learning is taken when students begin with the intention of understanding the meaning of an article or chapter, question the authors' arguments, relate it to their previous knowledge and experiences, try to determine the extent to which the conclusion is justified. Other students seem to rely almost exclusively on a "surface approach" where the intent is to memorize those points of an article which are considered important in view of questions that might be asked (on an exam). Their focus of attention is thus limited to the specific facts or pieces of disconnected information which are rote learned.[29] More recent research has broken down each of these approaches into four categories: deep active, deep passive, surface active, surface passive (from Entwistle, p. 85).

Approach to Learning	Level of Understanding
Deep active	Understands author's meaning and shows how argument is supported by evidence
Deep passive	Mentions the main argument, but does not relate evidence to conclusion

| Surface active | Describes the main points made without integrating them into an argument |
| Surface passive | Mentions a few isolated points or examples |

A related, but anticipated, finding was that students, in order to cope with overwhelming curricula and insufficient time are forced to abandon their ambitions to understand what they read and move toward a surface approach to learning.[30] Also, the type of questions given on a test can induce a surface approach to studying, while factual overburdening of course syllabi and examinations can be responsible for low level of understanding exhibited by students. Fransson found that anxiety-provoking situations induced a surface approach to learning, as well as examinations or syllabi which have little personal relevance. (Entwistle, p. 82)

The implications should be obvious here: The teacher who moves students to become intrinsically motivated to learn, to engage in caring relationships, and who sets up sensible syllabi in terms of volume and time-frames (not all that common in higher education), will involve them in deep rather than surface approaches to learning. The teaching forms in the Initiatory and Dialogic Modes are central to such an endeavor.

Students also have learning strategies that contrast in other ways. For example, students can take a serialist or holistic approach to their work. A holistic strategy (comprehension learning) involves looking at an entire area being learned, taking a broad perspective, seeking interconnection with other topics and making use of personal ideosyncratic analogies. The serialist (operational learning) prefers a narrower focus, concentrating on a step by step process, paying attention to details while neglecting the broader connections with other topics. He is also unlikely to make use of personal experience in studying academic topics. (pp. 89–94) It is also clear that the holist may err by ignoring details and procedures while moving too readily to a conclusion, making use of inappropiate analogies (globetrotting); the serialist falls into the opposite trap of not making for himself any overall map and may not use analogies at all, thus, missing the meaning.

Chapter 6 included a framework based on the research of John Biggs and made some applications to the Facilitator/Guide teaching form. Biggs found that a threefold orientation to learning is possible in college: Reproducing, Achieving, and Personal Meaning. Figure 9.1 is an expansion of Bigg's chart which incorporates motivational factors, as well as student approaches to learning.

I suggest that if the Teaching Continuum I have presented in this book were superimposed upon this chart, we would find that as teaching becomes more student-centered and students assume more responsibility for their own learning they will move more and more toward a personal meaning orientation in their studies. Paralleling this, will be increasing intrinsic motivation along with a deep approach to learning. And the teaching forms

Figure 9.1
A Model of Student Orientations and Outcomes

Orientation and intention	Motivation (Personality type)	Approach or style	Process		Outcome
			Stage I	Stage II	
Personal meaning	Intrinsic	Deep approach/versatile	All four processes below used appropriately to reach understanding		Deep level of understanding
	(Autonomous and syllabus-free)	Comprehension learning	Building overall description of content area	Reorganizing incoming information to relate to previous knowledge or experience and establishing personal meaning	Incomplete understanding attributable to globetrotting
Reproducing	Extrinsic and fear of failure	Operation learning	Detailed attention to evidence and steps in the argument	Relating evidence to conclusion and maintaining a critical, objective stance	Incomplete understanding attributable to improvidence
	(Anxious and syllabus-bound)	Surface approach	Memorization	Overlearning	Surface level of understanding
Achieving high grades	Hope for success	Organized/achievement orientated	Any combination of the six above processes considered appropriate to perceived task requirements and criteria of assessment		High grades with or without understanding
	(stable, selfconfident, and ruthless)				

Source: Noel Entwistle, *Styles of Learning and Teaching*, p. 113.

which assist this movement toward personal meaning would obviously be those further along on the continuum where a greater focus on relational encounters exists.

Paul Ramsden and Noel Entwistle also found some interesting applications to departments in Great Britain. Over two thousand students were queried as to their perceptions of the courses and teaching in sixty-six departments (including engineering, physics, psychology, economics, history, and English). Two different kinds of departments emerged: *student-centered*, characterized by good teaching, faculty open to students and emphasis on students' freedom in learning; *control-centered* departments where teaching was formal, faculty were under heavy pressure to cover content and assess rigorously, with little freedom for students to choose courses or study methods. A positive correlation was established between the two types of departments and approaches to studying mentioned above. Students in departments characterized by good teaching and openness were more likely to take a deep approach to learning with a personal meaning orientation, whereas in control-centered departments students took a surface approach and moved toward strategies of reproducing.[31] Unfortunately, the research results did not indicate whether a pattern existed showing specific departments to be student-centered and others control-centered, but it would not be out of order to suggest that, given the research by Kolb and others described above, the more codified, tightly focused, fact-oriented disciplines may tend to be the ones maintained within control-centered departments.

In any case, the research shows that student approaches to learning are very much affected by their perceptions of particular departments. Those perceived as impersonal which gave tests that are fact oriented leave students in a reproducing orientation while those with faculty who were more inter- active and allow for more divergent questions (creative thinking) on their testing and evaluation move students toward a personal meaning orientation. The following student remarks are in line with this:

I hate to say it, but what you've got to do is have a list of the "facts"; you write down ten important points and memorize those, then you'll do all right in the test...if you can give a bit of factual information—so and so did that, and concluded that—for two sides of writing, then you'll get a good mark.

I find that the courses I do most work in are the courses where I get on with the tutors best and enjoy the seminars, because...a tutor can put you off the subject... some of them don't like students, so they're not interested in what students say...

If the [tutors] have enthusiasm, then they really fire their own students with the subject, and the students really pick it up...I'm really good at and enjoy [one particular course], but that's only because a particular tutor I've had has been so enthusiastic that he's given me an enthusiasm for it.[32]

DEVELOPMENTAL LEVELS AND STUDENT LEARNING

Along with approaches to learning something should also be said about developmental levels in students since they figure prominently in any as- sessment of learning in connection with teaching forms. The well known work of William Perry has been referred to in passing during the course of this book. His research has traced intellectual and ethical development during the college years and broken down that development into a nine position schema which chronicles movement through three world views: Dualism, Relativism, and Committment in Relativism.[33] These world views are revealing in terms of the research already mentioned and the continuum I have set out. For the dualist, education is a process of finding right answers (correct applications of absolutes) with the help of the teacher (Authority). The student Dualist resists exploring academic problems that have no right solutions, and prefers teachers who supply answers and disciplines in which answers can be securely quantified. Note the student is relatively passive, will probably use a surface approach to his studies and reproduce what is given in lectures. The move toward relativism takes place when the notion of absolutes and authoritarian either/or answers crumbles. Some cynicism or at least confusion sets in here. For the student Relativist, education becomes a process of de- vising persuasive answers, since right answers no longer exist. He enjoys exploring problematic questions and prefers disciplines in which they abound. The student also prefers teachers who do not stand on the authority of their office, but relate personally to the student. It is easy to see how the teacher as Persuader and especially as Catalyst can be influential here—as the student begins to question and devise his own strategies for survival. The third view shows the student accepting a world without absolutes in a more positive way. The Committed Relativist makes choices about values derived from various sources in society which impinge on her. She becomes more interested in understanding the reasons for another's way of thinking. Education becomes a process of achieving the knowledge necessary to make committments. She does not seek glib right or wrong answers, but to work productively in a chosen field (learning community) where the teacher is more of a mentor or experienced guide or fellow worker (learner). Here, of course, a student would take a deep approach to learning, be fully activated and work within a personal meaning orientation. Thus, we can see the parallel to student-centered teaching forms from the Dialogic Mode on.[34]

While it has been pointed out that Perry's scheme focuses particularly on liberal arts education—in fact, those of academically successful students at Harvard and Radcliffe—his findings have stood up fairly well and it is not difficult to see the schema applying to large numbers of students in their progress through higher education. It also matches up with the research of June Loevinger on Ego Development. She, too, postulates nine stages, but all the way from birth to adulthood, from pre-social to fully integrated. Three of these stages would seem to apply to students in their college careers: the Conformist-Conscientious, the Individualistic, and the Autonomous stages.[35] A person in the Conformist stage probably parallels many college freshmen (as does the Dualist) who accept what is told to them, see things in terms of polar opposites and have rather superficial—even manipulative social relationships. As the individual moves through the Conscientious toward the Autonomous stages she grows in her ability to accept complexity, tolerate ambiguity while acquiring more sophisticated learning skills which can integrate and compare ideas. Her social relational life deepens; she accepts emotional interdependence and cherishes personal ties. At the same time, she seeks self fullfillment as well as a broader view of life. It is not hard to see parallels here with the Committed Relativist along with teaching forms which allow for increasingly dialogic, relational, communal activities.

Figure 9.2 represents an attempt to bring together a number of the teaching/ learning factors discussed in this final chapter and integrate them into the teaching forms on the continuum. It still remains sketchy, but I believe it suggests that the continuum set out in this book has a definite relevance to the everyday world of teaching in higher education.

THE REMAINING AGENDA

Many other factors are involved in a student's approach to learning including various dimensions of cognitive functioning, the roles of cultural and ethnic background, general life experience, and even (or especially) genetic factors. Most of the research in these areas remains to be done.[36] In fact, it is only recently that attention has begun to be paid to the issues on student

Figure 9.2
Integrated Model of Teaching/Learning Factors

TEACHING MODES	PRESENTATIONAL · INITIATORY ·	DIALOGIC · ELICITIVE · APOPHATIC
	1-2 3-4	5 6-7 8
LEARNING ORIENTATION	REPRODUCER ACHIEVER	⟶ PERSONAL MEANING
APPROACH TO LEARNING	SURFACE PASSIVE ⟶ ACTIVE serialistic	DEEP PASSIVE ⟶ ACTIVE holistic
LEARNING INVENTORY STYLE	CONVERGENT	DIVERGENT
SUBJECT DISCIPLINE	HARD / APPLIED SCIENCES codified - tightly, focused	HUMANISTIC STUDIES less codified - loosely, focused
INTELLECTUAL ethical DEVELOPMENT	DUALIST ⟶ RELATIVIST ⟶	COMMITTED RELATIVIST
EGO DEVELOPMENT	CONFORMIST · CONFORMIST / CONSCIENTIOUS ⟶ INDIVIDUALISTIC / AUTONOMOUS	
FORMAT	LARGE GROUPS · CLASSROOM · SMALL GROUPS · TUTORIAL	
	FORMAL ·	INFORMAL

learning styles and approaches to learning briefly discussed in this chapter, and most of it is in other countries rather than in America. Dunkin and Barnes, in their 1986 summary of Research on Teaching in Higher Education agree that "there has been an almost total neglect of the student academic learning behavior, both in and out of class sessions in this [American] research."[37] Perhaps the situation is best summed up anecdotally in Wayne Booth's recent book, *The Vocation of a Teacher,* when he queries a professor of education as to what is known about teaching. The professor responds: "Not much! I'm just reviewing an eleven-hundred page book summarizing educational research. In my view, the book is pretty discouraging. There is really not a lot of hard knowledge to report."[38]

Dunkin and Barnes also admit that while there has been increasing concern with the nature of teaching behavior as revealed through using observational techniques in naturalistic (everyday) settings, the concepts underlying these observations are highly derivative of concepts used for many years at lower levels of education. Concepts especially applicable in higher education need to be developed and applied. Also the roles played by teachers' beliefs, values, and attitudes in regard to teaching and learning have yet to be explored in any substantial way.[39]

As pointed out in Chapter 6 there also has been little research into the matching up (or mismatching) of teaching and learning styles, though Joseph Katz has taken a step in this direction with his emphasis on making the student the focus of study and engaging the students' collaboration in their own learning as prime conditions for developing the art of teaching.[40] Classroom research by Katz and Mildred Henry suggested that three great obstacles exist to student learning: lack of individualization, lack of collaborativeness in learning, and lack of opportunity for applying ideas to situations in which the student has responsibility. Overarching these is "the passivity that still dominates student learning."[41] If the reader has followed the direction of the teaching forms set out in this book, she will see that movement along the continuum I have proposed constitutes a gradual removal of these obstacles and the transformation of the student into an active learner.

Finally, most of the research that does exist today on any level has been of the mimetic, process-product, behavoristic variety. When it comes to those less measurable aspects of teaching and learning almost nothing exists. Yet it is these that may be the most important and deal with profound inner change in students. M. R. Paffard has pointed out that education has almost exclusively been concerned with the verbal, intellectual, and propositional which eclipses the vividness of perception common to more intuitive kinds of knowing. Such an emphasis cannot comprehend reasons of the heart as well as of the head. This unfortunate situation cuts off and renders nonexistent (at least in the school or college) the most profound aspects of experience. Pafford writes:

One can scarcely blame education for being *verbal*, for helping children to acquire a language in which they can explore and come to terms with their environment... But transcendental experience demands another voice... It craves a language to express the inexpressible, a poetic, religious, extravagant language which is most effective when it is non-prosaic, non-propositional and logically odd.[42]

When looked at from this deeper, wordless perspective I would suggest that despite the ancientness of the craft our understanding of teaching and its possibilities is still in its infancy.

The individual student stands before us in his or her multi-leveled complexity waiting to be fully known. What kinds of teaching encounters can be created to address each and all of these students in all their diversity. This is a question that we cannot adequately answer in our present state of knowledge. It is my hope, however, that the continuum and its forms set out in this book will serve to correct an overemphasis on the more superficial aspects of teaching, as well as provide a broader perspective which can help guide our efforts to understand this most elusive art.

NOTES

1. Edmund Husserl, *Ideas: General Introduction to Pure Phenomenology*, p. 99–100.

2. Ann Woodhull-McNeal, "Teaching Introductory Science as Inquiry," *College Teaching*, 37, No. 1 (Winter, 1989), pp. 3–7.

3. Perkinson, *Learning From Our Mistakes*, pp. 171–185.

4. Dennis Fox describes mismatches between a teacher's and students' theories of teaching. See *Personal Theories of Teachng, Studies in Higher Education*, 8, no. 2 (1983): p. 160.

5. Some research has been done on the process of instructional change. For example, see Ellen Stevens, "Explorations in Faculty Innovation," *The Journal of Staff, Program and Organizational Development* (Winter 1989): 191–200. Also, Robert B. Kozma, "A Grounded Theory of Instructional Innovation in Higher Education," *Journal of Higher Education* (May/June 1985): pp. 300–319.

6. Teaching Centers have arisen on some college campuses over the last few years. However, a perusal of the activities taking place there make it clear that the emphasis is almost entirely on the more obvious empirical skills attached to teacher-centered forms. See Maryellen Weimer, *Improving College Teaching: Strategies For Developing Instructional Effectiveness* (San Francisco: Jossey-Bass Publishers, 1990), pp. 174–200.

7. This experiment has been written up and sent out just recently to the *American Journal of Pharmaceutical Education*. Raymond F. Orzechowski and William A. Reinsmith, "Teaching a Large Pharmacology Class: An Experiment in Active Learning."

8. Kenneth A. Feldman, "Effective College Teaching from the Students' and Faculty's View: Matched or Mismatched Priorities?," *Research in Higher Education*, 28, no. 4 (1988): 291–344. For the difference between what some students think they want and what they are realistically ready for in terms of independent learning, see Wilbert McKeachie, *Teaching Tips*, pp. 60–61.

9. Joseph Axelrod, "From Counterculture to Counterrevolution: A Teaching Career," in *New Directions for Teaching and Learning: Improving Teaching Styles*, pp. 7–20.

10. Alexander W. Astin, *Achieving Educational Excellence* (San Francisco: Jossey-Bass Publishers, 1985), pp. 218–219.

11. Axelrod, "From Counterculture to Counterrevolution," p.15.

12. Michael Schwager and Rathe Miller, "Ten Top Profs," *Philadelphia Inquirer Magazine* (September 21, 1986): pp. 14–18.

13. David Glidden, "A Truly Dedicated Teacher Has Little Time Left Over for Writing, Research, or Himself," *The Chronicle of Higher Education* (April 6, 1988): B1 & B2.

14. "What is Good College Teaching," *The Teaching Professor* 4, no. 1 (January 1990): 1 & 2.

15. Katz and Henry, *Turning Professors into Teachers*, p. 158.

16. Samuel Beckett, *Waiting For Godot: A Tragicomedy in Two Acts*, (New York: Grove Press, 1954), p. 58

17. Axelrod, *The University Teacher as Artist*, p. 225.

18. Jackson, *The Practice of Teaching*, p. 130. This bifurcation seems to go back to a basic division in perception of humanities/arts and science that goes all the way back to early adolescence in our society. Cf. L. Hudson, *Frames of Mind* (London: Methuen Press, 1968), pp. 86 & 87.

19. Kolb's research is based on an Experiential Learning model which conceives of a continuous four stage cycle in learning: Concrete Experience (CE), Observation and Reflection (RO), Formation of Abstract Concepts and Generalizations (AC), Applications of concepts to new situations (AE). See David A. Kolb, "Learning Styles and Disciplinary Differences" in *The American College*, ed. Arthur Chickering, p. 237.

20. Kolb, p. 238.

21. Ibid., p. 239 & 240. Actually the breakdown is more complicated. Some disciplines (for example, physics, foreign languages) fall on the border between two of the four quadrants in the Experiential Learning Model.

22. For two other examples of sciences courses employing more student-centered teaching forms see: David J. Boud and M. T. Prosser, "Sharing Responsibility for Learning in a Science Course—Staff-Student Cooperation," in *Androgogy in Action*, pp. 175–187; Alvin M. White, "Teaching Mathematics as Though Students Mattered," in *New Directions for Teaching and Learning: Teaching as Though Students Mattered*, pp. 39–48.

23. Mihaly Cziksentmihalyi points out that there are also subject matter differences in terms of establishing flow in the classroom. For example, science and math create more difficulty for students at the beginning in presenting too many challanges for their skills, thus not giving them the opportunity to enjoy learning right away. Yet once skills are matched to challenges it becomes easier to sustain flow than in humanities or social sciences in that there is less ambiguity. See "Intrinsic Motivation and Effective Teaching: A Flow Analysis," in *New Directions For Learning: Motivating Professors to Teach Effectively*, pp. 23–24.

24. Evelyn Fox Keller, *Reflections on Gender and Science* p. 7.

25. This second point tallys with the remarks made in Chapter Five concerning the importance of the Dialogic Mode even in high level science seminars.

26. Keller, p. 5. Keller's reference all through this section is to the landmark book

of T. S. Kuhn, *The Structure of Scientific Revolutions* (Chicago: University of Chicago Press, 1962).

27. Unfortunately, women coming into science have more often than not been "co-opted" by the male model. An outstanding exception to this is the geneticist, Barbara McClintock. See the chapter on her in Keller's *Reflections on Gender and Science*, "A World of Difference," pp. 158–176. For a more thorough study of her approach to science and her work see Evelyn Fox Keller, *A Feeling For the Organism: The Life and Work of Barbara McClintock*. (New York: W. H. Freeman and Company, 1983).

28. Jackson, *The Practice of Teaching*, p. 129.

29. Entwistle, *Styles of Learning and Teaching: An Integrated Outline of Educational Psychology for Students, Teachers, and Lecturers*, (London: David Fulton Publishers, 1988), pp. 77 & 78.

30. Ibid., p. 81. The research here (Dahlgren, 1978, Dahlgren and Marton, 1978) was with students in first year economics classes, but certainly could be applied to most subjects. For example, a surface approach is most evident at my college in the applied science courses such as Pharmacotherapeutics which frequently overloads the students to the point where they are forced to memorize and cram for their bi-weekly exams.

31. Paul Ramsden and Noel Entwistle, "Effects of Academic Departments on Student Approaches to Studying," *British Journal of Educational Psychology*, 51, (1981): 368–383.

32. Entwistle, *Styles of Learning and Teaching*, p. 104.

33. Perry, *Forms of Intellectual and Ethical Development in the College Years: A Scheme*.

34. I have switched to the feminine here to include some of the attitudes described by Belenky et al. in *Woman's Ways of Knowing*. Joanne Kurfiss has skillfully integrated the research of both Perry and the authors of *Woman's Ways of Knowing* since as we noted in Chapter 7, Perry's work was done mostly with males. Kurfiss breaks the stages down to four developmental levels which are roughly the same as Perry's original three except that they allow for some differences in the reactions of woman students. See Joanne G. Kurfiss, *Critical thinking: Research, Practice and Possibilities*. ASHE ERIC Higher Education Report No. 2. (Washington, D.C.: Association for the Study of Higher Education, 1988).

35. Loevinger, *Stages of Ego Development*, pp. 23–26.

36. In her chapter on Cognitive Styles, K. Patricia Cross has summed up the findings in regard to field-dependence vs. field independence in students—the one area where research has been more extensive and qualitative. Perhaps the most significant finding is that cognitive styles are largely determined through socialization. Thus, a culture like the United States with its definition of dependence and nurturance for women, and achievement and independence for men (until recently, at least) could well account for the consistent finding that on the average men are more field-independent, more analytical, than women. Implications exist here for teaching in so far as women may seek not only more connected learning, but environments where there is affirmation, cooperative learning and relational teaching encounters. This involves forms further up on the continuum, but the issue remains problematic since those forms must also encompass men who have taken responsibility for their own learning, are field-independent and prefer to go it alone. See K. Patricia Cross, *Accent on Learning*, pp. 114–124.

37. Dunkin and Barnes, "Research on Teaching in Higher Education," p. 774.

38. Booth, *The Vocation of Teaching*, p. 209.

39. Dunkin and Barnes, p. 774.

40. Katz, "Teaching Based on Knowledge of Students," in *New Directions For Teaching and Learning: Teaching as Though Students Mattered*, pp. 3–11.

41. Ibid., p. 6.

42. M. F. Pafford, *Inglorious Wordsworths* (London: Hodder and Stoughton, 1973), pp. 226–227. Quoted in Entwistle, *Styles of Learning and Teaching*, p. 231.

Select Bibliography

Adams, William A.. *The Experience of Teaching and Learning: A Phenomenology of Education*. Seattle: Psychological Press, 1980.

Adler, Mortimer J. *How to Speak, How to Listen*. New York: MacMillan Publishing Co., 1983.

Ashton-Warner, Sylvia. *Teacher*. New York: Simon and Schuster, 1963.

Axelrod, Joseph. *The University Teacher As Artist: Toward an Aesthetics of Teaching with Emphasis on the Humanities*. San Francisco: Jossey-Bass Publishers, 1976.

Belenky, Mary Field, Blythe McVicker Clinchy, Nancy Rule Goldberger, and Jill Mattuck Tarule. *Woman's Ways of Knowing: The Development of Self, Voice, and Mind*. New York: Basic Books, Inc., 1986.

Bernhardt, Elizabeth B. "The Text As Participant in Instruction." *Theory Into Practice* 26 (Winter 1987): 32–37.

Bohm, David. "Insight, Knowledge, Science and Human Values." In *Toward the Recovery of Wholeness: Knowledge, Education, and Human Values*. New York: Teachers College Press, 1981.

Booth, Wayne. *The Vocation of a Teacher: Rhetorical Occasions 1967–1988*. Chicago: University of Chicago Press, 1988.

Brody, Maurice. "The Conduct of Seminars." In *Teaching Thinking By Discussion*, edited by Donald Bligh. Great Britain: The Society for Research into Higher Education and NFER-NELSON, 1986.

Bruffee, Kenneth A. "Collaborative Learning and the 'Conversation of Mankind.'" *College English* 46 (November 1984): 635–652.

Buber, Martin. "Elements of the Interhuman." *The Knowledge of Man*, edited by Maurice Freedman. London: George Allen & Unwin LTD, 1965.

———. *I and Thou*. New York: Charles Scribner's Sons, 1958.

Bullmer, Kenneth. *The Art of Empathy: A Manual For Improving Accuracy of Interpersonal Perception*. New York: Human Sciences Press, 1975.

Cashin, William E. *Idea Paper No. 14: Improving Lectures*. Manhattan, Kansas: Kansas State University, 1986.

————, and Philip C. McKnight. *Idea Paper No. 15: Improving Discussions*.

Civikly, Jean M. "Humor and the Enjoyment of College Teaching." In *New Directions For Teaching and Learning: Communicating in College Classrooms*, edited by Jean M. Civikly. San Francisco: Jossey-Bass Publishers, 1986.

Cross, K. Patricia. *Accent on Learning*. San Francisco: Jossey-Bass Publishers, 1976.

————. "A Proposal to Improve Teaching or What 'Taking Teaching Seriously' Should Mean." *AAHE Bulletin* 39 (September 1986): 4–17.

Crow, Mary Lynn. "Teaching As An Interactive Process." *New Directions for Teaching and Learning: Improving Teaching Styles*, edited by J.L. Bess. San Francisco: Jossey-Bass Publishers, 1980.

Czikszentmihalyi, Mihaly. "Intrinsic Motivation and Effective Teaching: A Flow Analysis." In *New Directions for Teaching and Learning: Motivating Professors to Teach Effectively*, edited by J. L. Bess. San Francisco: Jossey-Bass Publishers, 1982.

Denton, David. "That Mode of Being Called Teaching." In *Existentialism and Phenomenology in Education: Collected Essays*, edited by David Denton. New York: Teachers College Press, 1974.

DeVito, Joseph A. "Teaching As Relational Development." In *New Directions For Teaching and Learning: Communicating in College Classrooms. See* Civikly.

Douvan, Elizabeth. "Interpersonal Relationships: Some Questions and Observations." In *Close Relationships: Perceptions on the Meaning of Intimacy*, edited by George Levinger and Harold L. Raush. Amherst: University of Massachusetts Press, 1977.

Dunkin, Michael J., and Jennifer Barnes. "Research on Teaching in Higher Education." *Handbook of Research on Thinking*, edited by Merlin C. Wittrock. 3rd Edition. New York: Macmillan Publishing Co., 1986.

Eble, Kenneth E. *The Aims of College Teaching*. San Francisco: Jossey-Bass Publishers, 1983.

————. *The Craft of Teaching*. San Francisco: Jossey-Bass Publishers, 1976.

Elbow, Peter, *Embracing Contraries: Explorations in Learning and Teaching*. New York: Oxford University Press, 1986.

Enwistle, Noel. *Styles of Learning and Teaching: An Integrated Outline of Educational Psychology For Students, Teachers, and Lecturers*. London: David Fulton Publishers, 1988.

Frederick, Peter J. "The Dreaded Discussion: Ten Ways to Start." *Improving College and University Teaching* 29 (Summer 1981): 109–114.

————. "The Lively Lecture—8 Variations" *College Teaching* 34 (Spring 1986): 43–50.

Glassman, Edward. "Teaching Biochemistry in Cooperative Learning Groups" *Biochemical Education* 6 (April 1978): 35.

————. "The Teacher As Leader." In *New Directions For Teaching and Learning: Improving Teaching Styles. See* Crow.

Gotz, Ignacio L. "Heidegger and the Art of Teaching." *Educational Theory* 33 (Winter 1983): 1–13.

Green, Thomas, F. "A Topology of the Teaching Concept." In *Concepts of Teaching: Philosophical Essays*, edited by C. J. B. MacMillan and T. W. Nelson. Chicago: Rand McNally, 1968.

Gullette, Margaret Morganroth, ed. *The Art and Craft of Teaching*. Cambridge, Mass.: Harvard University, 1982.

Hendley, Brian. "Martin Buber on the Teacher/Student Relationship: A Critical Appraisal." *Journal of Philosophy of Education* 12 (1978): 141–148.

Hornung, Alice. "Teaching As Performance." *The Journal of General Education* 31 (Fall 1979): 185–194.

Husserl, Edmund. *Ideas: General Introduction to Pure Phenomenology*. New York: Collier Books, 1962.

Jackson, Philip W. *The Practice of Teaching*. New York: Teachers College Press, 1986.

Katz, Joseph. "Teaching Based on Knowledge of Students." In *New Directions For Teaching and Learning: Teaching as Though Students Mattered*, edited by Joseph Katz. San Francisco: Jossey-Bass Publishers, 1985.

————, and Mildred Henry. *Turning Professors Into Teachers: A New Approach to Faculty Development and Student Learning*. New York: MacMillan Publishing Co., 1988.

Keller, Evelyn Fox. *Reflections on Gender and Science*. Yale University Press, 1985.

Knowles, Malcolm S., ed. *Androgogy in Action: Applying Modern Principles of Adult Learning*. San Francisco: Jossey-Bass Publishers, 1984.

————. *Using Learning Contracts: Practical Approaches to Individualizing and Structuring Learning*. San Francisco: Jossey-Bass Publishers, 1986.

Kolb, David A. "Learning Styles and Disciplinary Differences." In *The Modern American College: Responding to the New Realities of Diverse Students and a Changing Society*, edited by Arthur W. Chickering. San Francisco: Jossey-Bass Publishers, 1981.

Krishnamurti, J. *Education and the Significance of Life*. San Francisco: Harper and Row, 1981.

————. *Things of the Mind: Dialogues with J. Krishnamurti*, composed and arranged by Brij B. Khare. New York: Philosophical Library, 1985.

Loacker, Georgine, and Austin Doherty. "Self-Directed Undergraduate Study." *Androgogy in Action: Applying Modern Principles of Adult Learning. See* Knowles, 1984.

McCown, Joe. *Availability: Gabriel Marcel and the Phenomenology of Human Openness*. Missoula, Montana: Scholars Press, 1978.

McKeachie, Wilbert J. *Teaching Tips: A Guidebook for the Beginning College Teacher*. Lexington, Mass.: D.C. Heath & Company, 1978.

McLeish, John. *The Lecture Method. Cambridge Monographs on Teaching Methods. No. 1*. Cambridge, England: Cambridge Institute of Education, 1968.

MacMurray, John. *Persons In Relation*. London: Faber and Faber Limited, 1961.

Macrorie, Ken. *Twenty Teachers*. New York: Oxford University Press, 1984.

Milton, Ohmer. *On College Teaching: A Guide to Contemporary Practices*. San Francisco: Jossey-Bass Publishers, 1978.

Morris, Van Cleve. *Existentialism in Education: What It Means*. New York: Harper and Row, 1966.

Murray, Donald W. "The Listening Eye: Reflections on the Writing Conference." In *Learning By Teaching: Selected Articles on Writing and Teaching*. Portsmouth, N.H.: Boynton Cook Publishers, Inc., 1982.

Noddings, Nell. *Caring: A Feminine Approach to Ethics and Moral Education*. Berkeley: University of California Press, 1984.

————. "Fidelity in Teaching." *Harvard Educational Review* 56 (November 1986): 486–510.

Passmore, John. *The Philosophy of Teaching*. London: Gerald Duckworth & Co., Ltd., 1980.

Perkinson, Henry J. *Learning From Our Mistakes: A Reinterpretation of Tweintieth Century Educational Thinking*. Westport, Conn.: Greenwood Press, 1986.

Perry, William G., Jr. *Forms of Intellectual and Ethical Development in the College Years: A Scheme*. New York: Holt, Rinehart, and Winston, 1968.

Peters, R. S. "Education As Initiation." In *Philosophical Analysis and Education*. London: Routledge and Kegan Paul, 1965.

Reinsmith, William A. "Educating For Change: A Teacher Has Second Thoughts." *College Teaching* 35 (Summer 1987): 83–88.

————. "Humanistic Education in a Professional-Technical School: An Advanced Humanities Course." D.A. diss., Carnegie-Mellon University, 1982.

Rogers, Carl R. *Freedom To Learn*. Columbus, Ohio: Charles E. Merrill Publishing Company, 1969.

Schwab, Joseph. "Eros and Education: A Discussion of One Aspect of Discussion." In *Science, Curriculum and Liberal Education*, edited by Jan Westbury and Neil J. Wilkof. Chicago: University of Chicago Press, 1978.

Seeskin, Kenneth. *Dialogue and Discovery: A Study in Socratic Method*. Albany: State University of New York Press, 1987.

Sheridan, Jean, Anne C. Byrne, Kathryn Quina. "Collaborative Learning: Notes From the Field." *College Teaching* 37 (Spring 1989): 49–53.

Smith, B. Othanel. "A Concept of Teaching." In *Concepts of a Teaching: Philosophical Essays*, edited by C. J. B. MacMillan and T. W. Nelson. *See* Nelson, Green.

Taylor, Robert, ed. *The Computer in the School: Tutor, Tool, Tutee*. New York: Teachers College Press, 1980.

Teloh, Henry. *Socratic Education in Plato's Early Dialogues*. Notre Dame, Indiana: University of Notre Dame Press, 1986.

Theunissen, Michael. *The Other: Studies in the Social Ontology of Husserl, Heidegger, Sartre and Buber*. Cambridge, Mass.: MIT Press, 1984.

Tiberius, Richard G. "Metaphors Underlying the Improvement of Teaching and Learning." *British Journal of Educational Technology* 17 (May 1986): 144–156.

Toppings, Anne Davis. "Teaching Students to Teach Themselves." *College Teaching* 35 (Summer 1987): 95–99.

Vlastos, Gregory. "The Paradox of Socrates." In *The Philosophy of Socrates: A Collection of Critical Essays*, edited by Gregory Vlastos. New York: Anchor Books, Doubleday & Company, Inc. 1971.

Wiener, Harvey, S. "Collaborative Learning in the Classroom: A Guide to Evaluation." *College English* 48 (January 1986): 52–61.

Index

ABOUT THE AUTHOR

WILLIAM A. REINSMITH is Professor of English at the Philadelphia College of Pharmacy and Science. His articles on education have appeared in *College Teaching* and *The Educational Forum*.